I Was Playing Their Song

I Was Playing Their Song

Foreword by Michael Feinstein

Larry Blank

Cover and Interior Design: Creative Publishing Book Design

ISBN Paperback: 979-8-218-12142-6
ISBN Hardcover: 979-8-9875419-0-6
ISBN eBook: 979-8-9875419-1-3

Foreword

My friend Larry Blank is an original. An original thinker, an original story teller, an original musician and an original innovator of Broadway musicals. He is part of a long tradition of MD's on Broadway (my favorite kind of MD) and learned from the best of them. He has also learned from the worst and everything in between, for he was born with the ability to understand certain complexities of the human condition that give him a fresh perspective in his work, life and art, all which have contributed to his formative education. There are very few who have an innate musicianship on the level that Larry has, especially in relation to theatre music, singers and the art of telling a story on stage. He understands everything it takes to bring a piece of music to life in confluence with a singer and orchestra so it has the maximum effect on an audience. Larry is facile and brings order and calm to any rehearsal situation because he always seems to know exactly what to do to make something work, or how make something better. He's a problem solver and his confidence is borne from experience coupled with his observant assimilation of life.

He started young, with a passion that has remained undiminished through the years. As a kid Larry saw musicals that most people don't even know existed and it always astounds me when he recalls in detail a show that you can't even find on the internet. Like "The Genius Farm" by Hal Borne and Norman Retchin. Larry saw it and can tell you the plot, describe the scenery and analyze what worked and what didn't. I have learned not to doubt his memory.

Composers and songwriters love him because they trust him. Through the years he has become the preferred conductor and arranger for everyone from Jerry Herman to Marvin Hamlisch to Stephen Sondheim and has the anecdotes to prove it. It is hard to impart the intimacy of that kind of relationship between creator, arranger and conductor, for in some ways they have to channel the intent of the composer and amplify it, bringing to life their seeds of dreams in confluence with performers, directors, producers, all of whom have an opinion on how it should be done.

Larry started as a conductor/pianist and while at the height of that hard earned but considerable success set his sights on orchestrating. It's funny, because at one time he was thought of as the 'go to' guy to conduct a new musical on Broadway and then his ability as an arranger eclipsed or obscured his original baton waving talent, so much so that some did not even know he could conduct. His years in Hollywood gave him ample opportunity to write music for films and arrange for others on a larger scale. With a deadline he can be very quick in whipping up an arrangement when he needs to, but it never sounds that way. The music 'plays down' down easily because his knowledge of instruments and orchestral color is second nature and organic. He has also "ghosted" many arrangements (for theatre in particular) for which he received no credit, and that ghost work has sometimes garnered the arranger on record a Tony award. And Larry got 'bupkas'. There's No Business Like Show Business.......

Our work together has afforded many rich rewards. Friendship is number one. He is faithful and will always be there when he says he will. Learning from him is a close second. When I started conducting, with tremendous trepidation, he became my primary teacher and cheering section. You'd think that after so many years as a singer, performing with dozens of Symphony orchestras that I might have paid more attention to what the person with the stick was doing behind me, but no, I was too self-involved. When I learned what really was required to accompany a singer with an orchestra, it was a humbling to see how easy he always made it seem. It's not. One has to conduct ahead of the beat to stay in synch with singer and orchestra and it takes a different kind of counter intuitive pulse to be able to do it successfully. Larry has shown me so many of his hard earned short cuts in conducting that they have made playing certain perilous passages a piece of cake. He makes it look easy because for him, it is.

He has also become kinder and gentler through the years and has a genuine desire to help others in this business when he recognizes talent or feels that he might contribute something that might benefit them. So much of what he knows is unique, and to pass it along means that he is sharing the combined knowledge of his mentors whom I sometimes feel, all standing behind him nodding in approval.

Possessing a razor wit, he frankly scared some of the people he worked with in earlier times and paid the price for a quick quip that cost him a job here and there. While observations in acid can be accurate, they don't always cement relationships with collaborators. Damn funny, yes, but not always good for business. That part is intact but is now tempered by a gentleness borne from success, life lessons, therapy, and most of all a deep desire to become the best person he can be and help others be the same. Not many people evolve much in life. Larry's is a constant evolution and an inspiration.

With the world evolving away from some traditional forms of music, while passing fancies steal the spotlight and sully the reputation of Broadway, it makes Larry's mentoring all the more important. When he works on a show, he not only provides the best orchestrations and musical direction one can hope for, but brings the savvy and history of the tradition with him. He knows that the next great enduring talent is just around the corner and will appear. If they're lucky, they'll have the good fortune to know Larry and work with someone who gets the bigger picture and keeps the continuum safely flowing, for what is life without learning from what came before and expressing it in the current style?

With Larry's book, some of his multi-hyphenate adventures are saved for savoring but I guarantee he has a thousand more that could have been added, yet it's the next best thing to hanging out and enjoying him in person. There are new stories waiting to be told as he continues doing what he loves and happily enriches our own lives along the way. Simply put, he's a keeper.

Michael Feinstein

Chapter One

"PLEASE WELCOME TO THE STAGE YOUR RESIDENT POPS CONDUCTOR, LARRY BLANK"

It's July 23, 2022, one week after my big birthday. I'm about to lead the Pasadena Symphony in an Aretha Franklin tribute concert. There is an audience of 5000 + at the Arboretum in Arcadia, California. I'm facing an orchestra of my peers and some people I've known for forty years. I have been married for thirty-five years, with three grown children. I am booked with work, making music, through the summer of 2023 with no end in sight. I'm in good health, of good humor and in general have a happy disposition. How did I get here?

My ambitions were set pretty early in my life, before I was ten years old.

I was born July 15, 1952 at Crown Heights Hospital in Brooklyn, New York. I am the third child of my parents, Milton, and Dorothy Blank. My sister Phyllis was ten years older than me and claims that when I was born, she said, "He's mine," and we have remained close to this day. My brother Howard was seven years older than me. I have little recollection of him from the early days of my life and that continues to this day. Despite the age differences with my siblings, I was told that I was a planned child at the end of the Korean War. I remember watching TV, seeing episodes of *I Love Lucy* and *Superman*. (I was so obsessed and there are photos of me proudly wearing my Superman outfit around the house.)

My father was co-owner with his brother and father of Trio Chemical Works in Brooklyn, New York. He was well-educated and played the mandolin on occasion.

My mother was a housewife, raised my sister, brother, and me, and played the piano very well. I clearly remember the sheet music for *South Pacific* on the piano. She also played a few classical pieces she enjoyed. Apparently, as a young girl she had studied seriously and won an actual piano in a contest. But by my time that piano was long gone, probably to help support her family in Brooklyn. My father bought her a Chickering upright piano. I grew up practicing on that piano, which now resides in the home of my cousin Judith, in Wisconsin.

I didn't find out until I was a young adult that my mother had been born in Russia, actually the Ukraine, somewhere near Kiev in 1915 and had escaped to America in 1920 with most of her cousins; her parents, Harry and Minnie; her brother Bernie; and her older sister Rose, who died en route and was buried in Belgium. My mother carried that horrible family tragedy with her to the end of her life.

They had departed for the US from Antwerp, Belgium. The only passport that my mother kept included the whole family and was issued in Bucharest, Romania, circa 1920. In 2014, shortly after my mother's ninety-eighth birthday and several months before she passed, she told me that she still missed her sister.

My mother explained to me that she had been told by her parents not to disclose that she was an immigrant, or she would be designated as a "greenhorn," which was not a compliment. Over the years I have done some research and found the family's US arrival papers in the Ellis Island archives. My mother's memory (like mine) was always very accurate.

My father and his younger brother Harry were born in Brooklyn, my father in 1913. Their parents, Nathan and Minnie, were also from Eastern Europe. I found out from papers that my Aunt Shirley (Uncle Harry's wife) kept, that Nathan had emigrated through Canada. I saw some postcards, dated 1907, written from Centre-ville, (part of Toronto) that said, "Dear Cousin."

I have clear and fond memories of my grandparents and of my Uncle Bernie. Uncle Bernie took me for an excursion to Coney Island and to his card club in Brooklyn. I couldn't have been more than six years old. I vaguely remember eating some coconut candy from Chinatown and being introduced to his friends at a pinochle game. I also remember that when we returned to my grandparents' home, Uncle Bernie caught a lot of heat. The only phones were pay phones in those days, and we had been gone many hours and he'd neglected to phone.

When I was a bit older Uncle Bernie taught me to ride a bicycle in front of our house in Queens. From the time of my birth, my father had been ill with early-onset Parkinson's disease. While he continued to work for a few years, he was pretty much incapacitated by the time I was ten years old. Uncle Bernie was trying to fill the gap.

My Grandfather Nathan died when I was very young, perhaps four years old. My Grandfather Harry died when I was about seven.

The year 1962 was very bad for the Blank family. My mother's mother, Minnie, died of heart issues en route to the hospital with my brother in the ambulance with her. My Uncle Bernie couldn't be found and when he was located about a week later, he was diagnosed with a brain tumor and died suddenly right after that.

My mother was orphaned, and it took a toll on her. Shortly thereafter, my father's Parkinson's had become pretty bad, and he decided to have the then-experimental brain surgery to prevent the tremors (which he never had). Basically, it was cryosurgery, freezing a portion of the brain, and it resulted in improvement for many patients at the time. Much later, when my father was one of the guinea pigs on L-dopamine, they decided that the previous surgery had really hindered more than helped his treatment. While the surgery and treatment for Parkinson's is far improved now, there is still no cure, just management and palliative care. Michael J. Fox is the poster boy for the most current treatments.

The movie *Awakenings* with Robert Di Niro and Robin Williams was about the discovery and use of L-dopa for various forms of Parkinson's, and it had quite an impact on me. I had grown up hearing, "Poor Larry, his father is ill and poor Dorothy has to take care of him." Truth is, I didn't know anything different, so I was not aware that I was missing anything.

While under treatment with the L-dopa, my father apologized for not being there for me and not being able to play ball with me. I said, "I didn't know you were supposed to." My parents were as loving and caring as they could be and did their best. All that was just part of my daily life. I still went to the park across the street almost every day after school, played baseball with my friends, and rode on my bicycle almost everywhere. Because my mother was preoccupied with my father, I had a lot of freedom and became very independent and self-sufficient. My sister Phyllis always described me as a rough-and- tumble kid. As early as age three or four, I would leave the house and walk around the corner to my friend Michael's home. Phyllis would have to search the neighborhood for me. But I have always had a very strong memory and I remember locations, so I knew where I was going even if no one else did.

In the summers, my parents sent us to Camp Oakdale in Connecticut, somewhere near New London. In later years I located the campgrounds, and it was fun to relive that time. In camp they would do musicals. At first, they did *South Pacific,* and *My Fair Lady.* I was too young for those. But then they did *Fiorello,* where I played Mr. Lopez and then *West Side Story,* where I played Action. The pianist for *West Side Story* was Steve Margoshes, who many years later was my replacement as conductor for *They're Playing Our Song* on Broadway. I recall that *Fiorello* was in 1961, because after the summer, in October 1961, just before the show closed, my brother and I were provided tickets for a Saturday matinee at the Broadway Theatre in New York City. I really took an interest in *Fiorello* and listened to the cast recording to the point of distraction for my family.

We did *West Side Story* in 1962 and as my interest in theatre continued, my parents found ways to get me to see shows. I was taken to see Robert Morse in *How to Succeed in Business Without Really Trying* and *I Can Get it for You Wholesale* with Barbra Streisand and Elliot Gould. I saw the play *Dear Me, the Sky is Falling* starring my mother's beloved Gertrude Berg, who played Molly Goldberg on radio and TV.

My sister and her then-husband Ken took me to see a matinee of *No Strings* at the Broadhurst Theatre on January 1, 1963. For dinner, we went to Scandia in the Hotel Piccadilly where I had my first lobster. It was a smorgasbord, and you truly could eat as much as you wanted. There were lobsters hanging on a metal rack and at the time, it seemed like Fantasy Island.

During *No Strings,* the entire band was brought on stage to play the exit music. There was no orchestra pit for the show and the piano/conductor was center stage. Many years later I recognized him to be Peter Howard, who recommended me for jobs when I first started out. I mentioned this to Peter, who said, yes indeed, he was associate conductor and presided at all the matinees.

My visual memory was quite a plus for me in my early days. Seeing all these shows whetted my appetite. I started following The *New York Times* ABCs of shows and keeping track of the upcoming musicals. In late 1962, my parents also took me to the Martin Beck Theatre to see *Milk and Honey* just before it closed. I saw Mary Martin in *Jennie* at the Majestic while sitting in the first row able to look into the orchestra pit. There were a few faces of people I would meet later in my career. I was more interested in the orchestra than I was in the stage.

In early 1964, when I was all of eleven years old, I announced that I was going to take the subway into New York City from Bayside, Queens (where we lived) to Manhattan to see a matinee of *Foxy* with Bert Lahr. I put on a jacket and tie, did just that, and that was the start of my theatre-going career. Beginning in February 1964, I would trek into Manhattan and get tickets at $3.25 for standing room and see *everything*. Sometimes my parents would splurge and allow me to get a better seat. They were preoccupied with my father's health and were happy that I kept myself so busy. I was very good in that I'd go to the theatre, get something to eat, and come home promptly.

Sometimes my parents would splurge and allow me to get a better seat. It was $6.25 for an orchestra seat at a matinee for *What Makes*

Sammy Run, Funny Girl, Anyone can Whistle, High Spirits, 110 in the Shade, A Funny Thing Happened on the Way to the Forum, Café Crown, Bajour, Golden Boy, Ben Franklin in Paris, Half a Sixpence and everything else there was to see. These were all on my schedule along with shows at Westbury Music Fair and Mineola Playhouse. It was a formidable list of shows, where I would see and remember many of the people, several of whom I later met and became acquainted with.

I felt tremendous comfort in Broadway musicals. It was an escape from the inherent grief in my household. While I wasn't aware of it consciously, there was a constant tension because of my father's illness. My mother was constantly under duress from the daily care. Getting away from the house and submerging myself in the world of "musical comedy" was my escape. It gave me purpose and something to look forward to during the daily stress of life at home. Saturdays in Manhattan were a weekly gift. I enjoyed the weekly trip on the bus and train and immersed myself in reading books about the subject. Remembering names, places, and dates came in handy when I later did meet many of the people I was seeing on the stage. I knew their backgrounds and was able to impress them because of my knowledge of their careers.

I began to become clearly focused on becoming part of this community. I was going to be an actor. My mother insisted I study the piano. I insisted that it be guitar and so guitar was my first instrument. But in short order, I realized my mother was right and I switched to piano.

My parents enrolled me in a Saturday morning class at AMDA, the American Musical and Dramatic Academy, for singing/acting/dancing classes for young performers. I now had more reasons to be in Manhattan on Saturday mornings. I would have my classes and then go to a matinee.

My teacher was Margot Moser (in 1962, she was the last Eliza Doolittle on Broadway). The pianist was Sandy Campbell. AMDA was on 23rd and First Avenue. I'd trek crosstown and take the uptown subway. I don't remember much about the other students. I had a nice singing voice, but as my voice changed a short time later, I became embarrassed and that was the end of my singing career.

My main interest in theatre, though, was in the musicals, and I often was able to get seats in the first row, which nobody wanted because they were too close. They were almost always available.

It seemed that everything had lined up just right. From my early days, I was observing the pit up close and I reveled in seeing the orchestra and in being able to hear the orchestrations and watch the conductor close up. At this point, my interest was in acting and performing because of my days in summer camp. However, I had a deep interest in the music, remembered all the conductors' names, along with the names of other members of the music department, and noted who was doing the orchestrations.

As I went to more shows, I noticed that the same names appeared in the music department show after show, especially on the piano and at the podium. I noticed the sounds, improvements, and the freshness that was happening on Broadway at the time. It was a harbinger of things to come to whet my future interest. As I started to become one of the habitués of the theatre, I ran into the same people over and over. I became familiar with the denizens and regulars on the Broadway scene, at the least the part of the scene that was familiar to me.

There was a notorious autograph hunter named Dave, who hung out at stage doors and outside restaurants. He was notorious because as people came out of the stage door he would ask, "Are you anyone?"

Dave was a Good Humor ice-cream man. Good Humor was a brand of ice cream delivered on trucks driving through neighborhoods. He would ring his bell and come out of the truck and all the kids would gather around and buy the different ice cream bars on a stick. This was very popular in the '50s and '60s, at least to me in Brooklyn and Queens. I knew him as a kid when I would hang out at stage doors and I'd see him again, not much later. when I was coming out of the stage doors.

There is a photo of Dave outside a stage door at the entrance of Joe Allen's restaurant in New York City. He was an icon to those of us in the theatre community. Though I'd known him since I was a kid, he still asked me if I was anybody when I came out of stage doors as an adult. Apparently, I hadn't made much of an impression on Dave, but Dave was hard to forget.

There was also Larry, who was a fixture in front of the Brill Building at 1619 Broadway. The Brill Building is where most of the music publishers were based. Larry would have Band-Aids and bruises on his face and occasionally a cast on his arm. He stood in front of the building in a long pea coat, shouting obscenities at all the tourists. Since I was one of the denizens of Broadway in those days, he would smile at me and anyone else he recognized as being a regular. All the rest were greeted with "Fuck you" and "You son of a bitch," which caused many of the bruises, bandages, arm slings, and casts he sported over the years. Larry was around through all the years in the '60s that I was around and perhaps beyond. One day he just wasn't there anymore.

The same goes for Moondog. Moondog was a guy who dressed as a Viking. He had recorded some poems/songs, I think.

And then there was the other guy, Gene Palma, with slicked back hair and makeup, who carried two drumsticks and played the sidewalk.

Walking up and down Broadway in the theatre district in those days of the '60s and beyond was much like being in the theatre district in London. There was the Covent Garden-like area, which was full of mom-and-pop shops and places like Colony Records, Tad's Steak House, and a penny arcade on 52nd St. and Seventh Ave. There was also the automat, Howard Johnson's. Jack Dempsey's and Lindy's. The Hotel Astor was still on the corner of 45th and Broadway or was it 44th? Hotel Manhattan spanned 44th to 45th on Eighth Avenue. There were coffee shops galore and places to hang out and have a meal too. It was a haven for youngsters spending the day in Manhattan without their parents. It was a different world than today and quite safe, at least for someone who knew their way around—a New York kid.

I attended a matinee of *Anya* at the same Ziegfeld Theatre where I saw *Foxy* on my first venture into New York City on my own. *Anya* was a musical based on the play *Anastasia*. George Abbott directed. After the matinee, I went backstage to get autographs, and no one stopped me. I wandered to the edge of the stage where I witnessed George Abbott restaging a scene with Michael Kermoyan and Constance Towers (whom I worked with much later). A very old man walked past. It turned out to be Guy Bolton, the playwright who had written

10

many shows and scripts with Abbott and Cole Porter and plenty of others in his day. This would've been November 1965. Bolton and Abbott were part of the old guard of Broadway. These men were giants to those of us who knew musical theatre history. *Anya* was quite long and dull. But to be in the old Ziegfeld watching a musical put together by these legends was very heady stuff for a 13-year-old wannabe.

When I saw *Jennie*, I went backstage to get Mary Martin's autograph. Her dresser was going to bring me into her dressing room. That wouldn't happen today, but I was an eleven-year-old who had just seen a matinee. The dresser returned and said Mary couldn't see me because she had an important guest waiting but handed me an autographed picture addressed to Larry and signed, Mary Martin. It was a photo of her as Peter Pan. As it happened, the very important guest, standing next to me at the stage door of the Majestic, was Vinton Freedley. He was the "vin" part of the Al-vin theatre on 52nd Street. He had produced many musicals, including Mary Martin's *Leave it to Me* in 1938.

This was November 1963. To the eyes of an eleven-year-old, Freedley was seemingly ancient at the time. Although I suspect he was younger than I am right now writing these memories. What strikes me in retrospect is that no one stopped me from walking backstage or from standing in the wrong place at the right time. Apparently, I was supposed to be there and there was something inevitable to every move I made to find my way. It seemed to be part of my destiny to be in these places at that time.

One year later, I was at the stage door of the Mark Hellinger Theatre trying to get an autograph from Carol Burnett before she entered for a performance of *Fade Out Fade In*. I recognized Jack Cassidy as he was coming to the theatre, and I asked for his autograph. We struck up a conversation and he asked where I was from. I said Bayside, and he said, "Come with me." He invited me to his dressing room, which was just in a bit from the stage door, and he chatted with me at length before doing a matinee.

Jack was from Richmond, AKA Queens Village, so he was another boy from Long Island. He talked about various chorus girls (by name) and about singing on Broadway. He told me that his favorite theatre to work in was the Eugene O'Neill (where *She Loves Me* had played). He was genuinely warm and paternal. He told me to feel free to say hello anytime, and I wandered off (probably to see *Bajour* or *Golden Boy*) with happy memories of being befriended by Jack Cassidy.

Some two years later when I was a student at the High School of Performing Arts, I was standing on Broadway with a few friends from school (all theater aficionados). Jack walked by on the way to something, and he waved and said, "Hi Larry, great to see you again. Hope your career is coming along," or something like that.

My friend's jaws all dropped. They asked, "How do you know Jack Cassidy?"

Years later, I had the pleasure of telling this story to Jack's sons, David and Patrick. Jack was a much-beloved performer on Broadway and TV. I was very saddened when I heard he had died in a fire in Hollywood. He was good friends with my mentor Don Pippin, along with Robert Goulet and John Kander. He was also a favorite in summer stock and knew *everyone*.

The entire theatre community was a special place and truly everyone knew everyone else. They had all come up in the business together doing stock—Lambertville Music Circus in New Jersey and various other venues around the country. The New York theatre world that I was indoctrinated in, first as an attendee and later on as a musician/pianist, was a very special community. While it was very competitive, there was so much work to be gotten. Between summer/winter stock, small theaters, and the many venues around New York along with the night clubs, and Off-Broadway, there was just so much to do. If you didn't get a Broadway show, you got an Off-Broadway show, or a theatre outside of New York. Summer stock was very popular and was just around the corner. There were a lot of ways to make some money, including waiting tables, which was just a pastime between jobs. But that wasn't part of my life as a young wannabe-actor who played the piano.

Shubert Alley, the little alley that runs between 44th and 45th Streets was always a quick shortcut for everyone to get to their various theatres, especially after having a meal at Sardi's or nearby. The stage doors for both the Shubert and Booth Theaters are in Shubert Alley.

Before a matinee of *Bajour*, Chita Rivera was standing talking to two men. One was Sammy Davis Jr, who was starring in *Golden Boy* around the corner. As I walked around to see, I realized the other man was Bobby Kennedy (Robert F. Kennedy), the Attorney General of the United States. There were no apparent Secret Service. The world was just a different place at that time with no one bothering them. As a matter of fact, people were just walking by, as I was. Chita, of course, had known Sammy for many years from *Mr. Wonderful* in 1956 and Bobby Kennedy was a pal of Sammy's. No one really noticed the three of them, except me, being the stage-struck kid from Queens. Although, it was difficult to miss Chita Rivera, Sammy Davis Jr., and Bobby Kennedy chatting away in Shubert Alley.

I recognized faces and names and just easily remembered who everyone was. On that occasion, I did stop and get Chita's autograph as well as Nancy Dussault's, Chita's co-star in *Bajour*. This was a very heady time for an eleven-year-old growing up in New York City. Much later, I worked with Chita and Nancy many times.

Between 1964–1966, I was in junior high school, playing baseball and attending theater as much as I could on Saturdays. All of this was a continuing diversion from my ailing father. My older siblings were not much of an issue at this time. With the age difference between me and my brother and sister, I was virtually an only child by age ten. My sister was married, and my brother was out and about, so I saw him infrequently. Since I was the "baby," I was treated as the favorite, and it just seemed natural to my way of life. I was preoccupied with playing baseball, which I still love to do, and with listening to theatre music and going to the theatre on Saturdays.

In November 1965, my friend Don Oliver and I decided to write a note to Don Pippin, who was a major music director on Broadway. Don agreed to meet us both and invited us to his apartment in New York. He played some music for us, and we talked. He said to keep in touch. We were both about thirteen years old.

I was accepted as a drama student to the High School of Performing Arts (known as PA) and started commuting regularly from Bayside to Manhattan. I was in Manhattan virtually six days a week. I was starting a new adventure.

There were some perks at PA; two friends were Jane Actman, later married to my friend Gene Castle, and Melissa Manchester, who was a year ahead of me. I have a few friends from school that I am still in touch with today. My very best friend was Clifford May. Many years later I became good friends with his first cousin, James May, who assisted me on Broadway and has conducted many shows on Broadway in his own right. But that's a separate story. Cliff lived with his parents at 16 W. 16th Street, and I had a home away from home if/when I needed it.

In the spring of 1966, I went to see *Mame* at the Winter Garden Theatre, went to the stage door, and re-introduced myself to Don Pippin the musical director for the show. I pointed out that I was president of his fan club. He asked how many members there were, and I said "One." We have been friends ever since. Ultimately Don became responsible for my career on Broadway and beyond. He recommended me first, as a music director and later, as an orchestrator. As he said many times, "It's good to know who to blame."

From that time, I decided I wanted to be a music director (MD) and not an actor. I was attending PA as a drama student but the glamour and the sound of the orchestra at the beginning of the overture, seemed so much more interesting to me. I was drawn by the music and theatricality of it all. It wasn't a desire to be a leader or the seeming power of fronting the orchestra. It was the sheer drama and impact of the music.

Chapter Two

Somehow, in the summer of 1968 I was engaged to be the music director for *Oliver* at the Gateway Playhouse in Bellport, Long Island. The director of the musical, who also played Fagin, was Anthony Doren. The leading lady was Beth Austin, whom I later worked with on Broadway in *Onward Victoria.* My friend Jon Eisen, a neighbor from Bayside and two years ahead of me at PA, was playing Bill Sykes, and he had a car. That would explain my ability to get to Bellport, which was quite far from Bayside. Come to think of it, Jon recommended me to be musical director because I played the piano. I suspect too, that my price was right.

My career at Gateway was short lived. At that time, we were all cigarette smokers. It was very cool in those days to smoke. I shared a cigarette with one of the girls in the show, which contained some other substance than tobacco, and I wasn't asked back when she showed up "out of sorts" at the housing facility.

In the fall, Tony Doren was engaged to be director for a theatre in New Jersey called Club Béné. It was owned by Joe Beninato and was near Perth Amboy, NJ. It became a popular dinner theatre for upcoming talent to work. Tony asked for me to music direct *Sweet*

Charity. The cast was a mixture of wannabes and never-to-be's. The guy playing Herman was character actor Jim Brochu, who is still a friend and very popular in theatrical circles. His one-man show, *Zero's Hour* was brilliant and well received. The girl playing Charity was typecast and never to be seen again, although quite popular in Times Square. We called Club Béné, "Club Bidet" simply because it sounded right.

The owner, Joe Beninato, was a nice man. It was a good place to cut your teeth, and not very far from New York City. They were doing a lot of musicals and it was good work for everyone. It was non-union (meaning non-Equity). A lot of upcoming talent worked there, either non-union or by using a nom de plume. It was good employment with an Italian buffet which was a feast for low-paid actors and musicians. We were all treated quite well.

Now that I had a couple of solid pro credits as an MD, back at PA I tried to change to the music department. It was not permitted to switch departments, so I left PA and did my last year of high school at Bayside High School, directly across the street from my parents' home. I was working on the side and managed to finish high school without much ado and went onward. My parents were disappointed I didn't want to go to university and become a doctor or something useful, but my career seemed to be in motion.

Out of the blue, I received a call from another pianist around town named Barry. Barry said he had heard about me and was doing an act for the "mountains." The "mountains" was a euphemism for the Catskill Mountains in upstate New York, also known as: the *Hebrew Himalayas*, and the *Borscht Belt*. These were the hotels in upstate New York that were occupied by a large part of the New York Jewish population enjoying holidays with a pool, too much food, and entertainment. Many great comedians like Woody Allen, Robert Klein, Henny Youngman, Rodney Dangerfield, and Mel Brooks worked the mountains. The act Barry recommended me for was called, *Adam and Ira*. Adam was Adam Paul (I'm sure his real surname had a lot of vowels). Ira was Ira Robbins, who was a Jewish comedian.

They were two very nice fellows very much in the mold of then-popular teams like Sandler and Young and Martin and Rossi. One was a comedian, the other a singer. Sandler and Young were two pretty good singers, but they all followed in the tradition of Dean Martin and Jerry Lewis. I asked Barry why he couldn't do the act and he told me that he had a job in a bath house with a chick singer in a bath house named Bette Midler.

Barry was BarryManilow, another young pianist from Brooklyn. Many years later I enjoyed relating this story to him when he hired me to orchestrate for one of his recordings. Adam and Ira never made it to the Catskills, but I was paid for a few rehearsals.

One of the girls I knew at Bayside High School, Honey Waldman, introduced me to her aunt, a major force in New York theatres AKA Honey Waldman, who owned the Bouwerie Lane Theatre in lower Manhattan. They were doing a musical called *The Happy Hypocrite*, directed by Tony Tanner. The MD was Richard Leonard. Sometime later, Dick was the original MD for Angela Lansbury's *Gypsy* in London. The other two musicians were Ian Finkel, son of Fyvush Finkel, and brother to Eliot Finkel (one of my classmates at PA), and Joel Kaye, who ended up as one of the reed players in the pit of the first Broadway musical I conducted. I somehow got the job as assistant stage manager. In those days they needed anyone, and I was anyone. I was happy to do what was asked, became friendly with cast members, and got my first taste of working up close with pro musicians.

Dick, Ian, and Joel were great musicians. It was really a thrill to hang backstage and listen to them play. Hearing them fed the fire that was burning in my belly to make myself succeed as a theatrical musician. Dick was a superb pianist, and he can be heard on the cast recordings of *Minnie's Boys* and *What Makes Sammy Run*.

Along the way I was asked to be substitute prop man for *The Memorandum* at the Public Theatre for Joe Papp. Olympia Dukakis was a member of that cast. Through one of the actors, Bob Ronan, I was asked to play through a few songs with Penny Fuller, a cast member from another show at the Public. I played a discarded Sondheim song called *I Do Like You* from *Forum*. Years later, I related this incident to Penny, who naturally had no recollection whatsoever. However, to an impressionable and ambitious sixteen-year-old it meant a lot.

I got myself involved with Equity Library Theatre (ELT) on 103rd St. in Manhattan. A lot of actors started there doing mini revivals of shows for no money but for recognition. As with many other venues, agents scouted these places, and a lot of talent was discovered. I worked as a stagehand on *Under The Gaslight,* which led to my becoming a rehearsal pianist for *Redhead*.

I ended up doing several other shows at ELT. One of them was an opera called *Sacco Vanzetti*. One of the girls in the ensemble befriended me and was very kind to me. She was a dark-haired beauty with a very thick New England accent and a glorious voice. Her name was Susan Waldman. A bit later, I did a production of *Man Of La Mancha* with Allan Jones and Susan was Aldonza. She later became Suzyn Waldman – note the new spelling) and still is the voice of the New York Yankees along with broadcaster John Sterling.

Because of my being a stagehand Off-Broadway and at ELT, I wangled my way into being a rehearsal pianist. I was friendly, played a little, and was probably the least expensive pianist in all of New York City. Coincidentally, while I was a stagehand at ELT, there was an unemployed actor working as the fire marshal. His name was Peter Riegert. Later, he dated Bette Midler and became a very successful actor.

Slowly building a reputation as a reliable (and inexpensive) pianist, I was hired by comedian Will Jordan to play piano for an industrial for Ruffino Wine. It was a one-off. Will was a great impersonator and was well known for his impression of TV host Ed Sullivan. Will's intro for me was, "Ladies and gentlemen, I have the most wonderful pianist in the world; he can play anything and everything, unfortunately, he wasn't available, so I got Larry." I was being indoctrinated into the ways of show business very quickly. Will only used me once, so he was clearly telling the truth.

Through one of the actors on *Happy Hypocrite,* I was engaged to play rehearsals for a musical revue called *Graffiti* at one of the old musician bars on 52nd Street. The actor was called John Aman. John was in several Broadway musicals and was a songwriter as well. He wrote a very nice song and they hired me to play rehearsals because I could play his song. The choreographer/director of the revue was Karin Baker, who along with Randy Skinner was later Gower Champion's associate on *42nd Street* and Gillian Gregory's associate on *Me and My Girl.* Our paths would cross again much later.

There were many dinner theatres around the US, creating more job opportunities for actors and musicians. I got a job as music director/pianist on *The Fantasticks* for the Barn Dinner Theatre Circuit. Next stop, Jackson, Mississippi. *The Fantasticks* was a finger-buster piano job for all young pianists wanting to play shows. The music by Harvey Schmidt and lyrics by Tom Jones are iconic, and in 1969, the show had already been running Off-Broadway for nine years. Every pianist on Broadway cut their teeth playing through the score and learning the overture, which was a marvelous show-off piece on the piano. Being a poorly trained but enthusiastic pianist, I somehow blustered my way through it. The Barn dinner theatres in Jackson, Mississippi; Lexington, Kentucky; and Nashville, Tennessee were littered with my wrong notes. However, I made some good connections for the future.

The tour of *The Fantasticks* was a great learning period for me: having to play the piano on a regular basis, dealing with the cast, and meeting people in places that were extremely alien to a nice Jewish boy from New York. To be in the Deep South (Madison, MS. outside of Jackson) at the same time as the film *Easy Rider* was a new experience. There was a scene in that movie where one of the characters hitches a ride in a pickup truck. This was exactly my experience. I hitched a ride on a rural road and was picked up by a guy in a pickup truck with a gun rack behind the seat. Not exactly the same as getting a taxi in Manhattan.

I also became accustomed to eating mysterious foods like fried oysters, greens, and grits. I was introduced to these delicacies at an iconic restaurant in Jackson called The Mayflower. It is still very much in existence and has been featured in some films. I also browsed Cagle's Music Store on the main street, which had tons of Broadway sheet music. I was able to purchase lots of obscure sheets from flop Broadway musicals at very reduced prices. Obviously, Cagle had stocked up and no one was interested until I came along. I found out much later that Jackson was the childhood home of legendary Broadway music director Lehman Engel. It was interesting to me that there were Jewish people in the Deep South. Let alone Jews that would be interested in musical theatre.

Next door to the Barn Dinner Theatre in Madison, MS was a small airport that had a sign: FLYING LESSONS $10. Having nowhere to go and being as far away from Bayside, Long Island as one could be, I took to the skies. I was at the barn theatre for one month and I spent my days taking lessons from an old "salt" named Carmen Curcio. Carmen was from Pittsburgh and was somewhere in his fifties, which was ancient to me. Since he was an Italian from points east, he took a liking to me. I enjoyed the flying lessons, and he brought me to be able to solo the Cessna 150 before I left Mississippi. I wasn't old enough to obtain a pilot's license. For ten dollars an hour it seemed insane not to be able to learn to fly. That was including fuel. I have never been able to resist a bargain even in a life and death situation. I told my mother that I was taking flying lessons and she started to cry over the phone. She was sure that between flying and my being Jewish that I'd never make it out of Mississippi.

I believe my interest in flying was the same as my interest in music or in playing the piano and conducting. I wanted to learn how to do things and do them well—to accumulate skills. It was a desire to horde abilities. I had no desire to horde things, but I wanted to accomplish things. This was a drive I had then, and I have now. With time I have found that once I accomplish things, I lose interest and move on. Not so with music, which to me is a never-ending quest for more knowledge. I believe that flying and music are mathematical, and I feel the same way about medicine, which was an interest as well.

In 1985–86, while working on *My One and Only* in New Orleans, I rented a plane and flew to Madison, MS to say hello to Carmen. After arriving, I found out that he had died only a month or so before. Many at the airport remembered me and it was a nice visit. By that time, I had actually become a licensed flight instructor. It was something I wanted to do and so I did it. Carmen would've been proud.

The Fantasticks continued through Nashville and Lexington, and I had many new and interesting experiences. The girl playing The Mute was a very fine singer named Rhoda Butler, and we become romantically involved. Rhoda was from Maine. Even with a name like Rhoda, she wasn't Jewish. However, I did find out that her father's accountant in Sanford, Maine was the only Jew in town.

Back to New York and home to Bayside. After a very short period, I moved in with Rhoda and was living in Manhattan. It was a good set-up for both of us. I had a steady girlfriend who had an apartment in Manhattan—Rhoda gained a live-in accompanist.

We found some work together doing a dinner theater tour of *Little Mary Sunshine*. She was Mary and I was the piano player. It lasted a short while down in South Carolina where I realized that was not what I wanted to do. My ambitions were pretty strong and touring the south on solo piano wasn't to my liking. Truth is that I was not comfortable playing the piano. I spent a lot of time practicing and it just wasn't as natural to me as conducting and, ultimately, writing music was. I practiced and practiced, and I got complimented, but never really believed any of the compliments. I still don't. As hard as I've practiced, I always felt that everyone played better than me. I am not fishing for compliments. It just wasn't where I thrived.

Before these tours, I had worked at ELT on *Of Thee I Sing*, the first major revival of the Gershwin musical in many years. The music director was named Leslie Harnley. He was a lovely man with a history of doing summer tours of musicals with two pianos and had been conductor for Katherine Dunham's dance company.

I persuaded Les to give me the piano lessons I desperately needed. He became a very good friend and mentor, gave me some indoctrination into piano so that I could play a lot better than I was playing, and brought my piano playing to an acceptable level. Acceptable at least for theatre music. I was able to maneuver to the point that he eventually asked me to play second piano on one of his tours.

Les taught me a great deal about music and other musical literature aside from musical theatre. He had gone out with the show *Love Match* as pianist and was friends with and sometime-accompanist for Laurence Guittard. Larry was a very well-respected, and admired leading man on Broadway, having had great success as Curly in the revival of *Oklahoma* as well as the Count in *A Little Night Music*. In subsequent years, I was able to give Larry the piano music from Les's collection from *Love Match*.

Les lived to see my success as conductor for *They're Playing our Song*. I had met him in 1968 and *Song* rehearsed in the fall of 1978. He had developed some stomach issues, was diagnosed with pancreatic/liver cancer, and passed in November 1980. His passing left a hole in my life. His influence over my musical judgement was monumental.

After the tour of *Little Mary Sunshine*, I managed to get hired at the Tibbet's Opera House to be assistant to music director, Wendell Kindberg. Wendell's partner was Jeffrey K. Neill who was a director/choreographer doing small shows around New York City. I did *Pirates of Penzance* and *How to Succeed*, playing second piano. It was a good and necessary skill to learn how to do shows with two pianos. In some of the smaller theatres, it was the norm, and there was an art to dividing up the piano parts. It was also a good way to learn orchestration, picking out all the little counter lines that were indicated in the scores. Jeffrey would always count off all dance numbers at rehearsals as "One, two, three, go," regardless of the tempo. He thought it was funny! We all knew he had no sense of rhythm.

Rhoda and I decided to marry. At the time, I was in the state of Michigan and eighteen years old. I didn't need parental consent to marry, so we did. It really didn't make much difference to our relationship, but it mollified our parents and seemed the right thing to do. Rhoda was a few years older than me and was poised to have a good career. She was a fine singer, and we were both making money and enjoying our lives.

I managed to get more jobs as a pianist and was hired as music director for the tour of a small rock musical that was playing on Broadway called *The Me Nobody Knows*. The musical featured a diverse cast with me, a white Jewish boy, playing the piano. It toured for a very short while with me, a bass player, Jeff Berlin, who is a very successful bass teacher these days, and a drummer, Freddy. We picked up some horns in a town or two and we chipped in to pay them. It was an interesting tour for me—all new music and traveling with a diverse group of people different from what I was accustomed to. I was no longer surrounded by white Jews, who sang musical comedy songs and ate bagels. It was a wonderful and happy experience. The show was directed by Eddie Roll, who had been Action in the original *West Side Story*. Eddie was a good director and a nice man, and we would cross paths again later on. I was learning to play better and better, but never good enough for me.

After the tour, Rhoda and I were hired for the Twin Coaches Dinner Theatre in Uniontown, PA. We did *You're a Good Man Charlie Brown*, *I Do I Do,* and *Mame*. I was getting lots of experience with various musicals from the catalog and learning my craft. Living in the coal-mining region of Pennsylvania was a change of pace and working with musicians in different parts of the country was very important to my musical growth. I was getting more experience with different groups and in how to run a rehearsal. I don't recall that the shows were very good or well attended, but they were certainly fun to do. I think I had piano, drums, and saxophone. I was getting closer to working with orchestras!

Back at home, I made some money playing piano for children's shows around New York City, which was big business in those days. One of the people I worked for was Pixie Judy, now known as ubiquitous Broadway producer Judy Abrams. There were two other production companies doing children's theatre: Maximillion Productions and John Ahearn. These people were quite innovative. Children's theatre included original musicals with some very interesting actors. I worked with Eric Conklin, who was one of the founders of experimental theatre in NY.

He was the original director of *Torch Song Trilogy* with Harvey Fierstein. Eric was giving the performance of his career in *Gabriel Ghost*. At least, I thought so.

Children's theatre sounds rather low on the totem pole of musical experience but as a matter of fact, it was major employment for a lot of out-of-work Broadway actors and musicians. I was building repertoire and so much experience.

The musicals were originals written by major talents like Michael Valenti, who went on to write several Broadway musicals. Rhoda and I were working young people in New York. I think the apartment, 256 W. 21st, was about $175 a month. We had no other real expenses. If we made $1000 per month, we were living high. I knew that while working in children's theatre might not be Broadway, it was a steppingstone to the things I wanted to do—a step closer to my ambitions.

Rhoda was hired for the ensemble of the Lerner/Barry musical *Lolita, My Love*. This was a very big deal. A new musical written by successful composer John Barry with book and lyrics by Alan Jay Lerner—half of Lerner and Loewe. I traveled to Philly and Boston with her during the tryout and was allowed, or at least not stopped, from observing orchestra rehearsals with the very skillful conductor, Herb Grossman, and orchestrator, Eddie Sauter. I was learning the traditions of trying out a Broadway musical. *Lolita* was one of the first shows that had a MOOG synthesizer in the pit. This was very new.

I found out that the very good overture had been ghosted (orchestrated without credit) by Larry Wilcox. Herb Grossman knew him from the failed musical, *Walking Happy*, and had recommended him. Larry became a good friend and major influence later on in my life. Grossman also made a strong impression on me. He had trained in the classics and opera, applying his conducting/coaching skills to musical theatre. It was an early lesson to me that musical theatre and its music were not insignificant fluff. Music is music and should be treated with respect, regardless of its use. John Neville and Leonard Frey were very good in the show. I attended many run-throughs and rehearsals.

The understudy for both leading men was Larry Guittard. Dorothy Loudon had a show-stopping song called, "*Sur La Quais de Ramsdale, Vermont.*" I was to cross paths with Larry and Dorothy later on.

Lolita, My Love was a hopeless show with no improvements being made and a lot of bad choices. They sacked the very good Lolita, Annette Ferra, and replaced her with the talented but far too young, Denise Nickerson. The show, which had bordered on being a bit lascivious, was now soft-core porn. It was a perennial closer, having closed out of town in both Philadelphia and Boston. Although it was Rhoda's show, it was a big learning experience for me.

On the recommendation of Broadway music director Peter Howard, whom I had met as a music gopher on another project, I was hired as pianist/assistant conductor for *The Most Happy Fella* and *The Great Waltz* for the Kenley Players. Peter's recommendation carried a lot of weight.

John Kenley was news to me. Apparently in the winter, he was Joan Kenley, and in the summer, he was John. John/Joan had been a hoofer for the Shubert's in the '20s and then switched to management. He was a savvy producer, creating one of the most successful summer stock theatres of all time. It featured first class musicals with big names, large orchestras, and affordable prices. His theatres in Ohio and Pennsylvania were very popular for several decades.

The conductor, Gordon Munford, assigned me to train the chorus for both shows, and I knew just enough to make it sound good. Howard Keel, Karen Morrow, and Dean Dittman were in the cast of *Happy Fella*. Earl Wrightson/Lois Hunt, and Sally Ann Howes were in *The Great Waltz*. These were first-class performers and really knew their craft. It was a pleasure to be around them and to experience their talent and professionalism. I had to work very hard to bring my pianistics up to snuff. I was playing with an orchestra and learning rapidly what *not* to do. I had to listen to the rest of the orchestra, and to play in such a way to support it and blend in at the same time. It was good to learn how to play rehearsals and then change your technique to play with the orchestra.

At the end of the summer, I heard that Papermill Playhouse was planning *Man of La Mancha*. Papermill Playhouse was in New Jersey, close to New York City. It included the closing cast from Broadway with the leads played by opera singer Jerome Hines and young upcoming singer, Jana Robbins.

The supporting cast were all Broadway regulars: Jack Dabdoub, John Aristides, Shev Rodgers, Renato Cibelli, and on and on. Rehearsals were going to be intimidating. I wrote a note to the music director Rudi Bennett, who hired me sight unseen, because I had done an earlier production in Newburgh, NY. This group from *La Mancha* were a rather salty bunch of old timers and had been with the show from the beginning. John Aristides had been a Jack Cole and Bob Fosse dancer. Cibelli had been Judd Fry in countless *Oklahoma's*. Shev and Jack had been in numerous Broadway musicals for a very long time. The talented Eddie Roll was the director/choreographer. He had been the assistant to Jack Cole from the beginning of La Mancha's tryouts. He was also the director of *The Me Nobody Knows* that I had toured with.

Rudi heard me play and promptly took the New York phone directory and placed it under the pedals of the piano. He taught me to play rehearsals without using the pedals for sustaining and showed me how easy it was to transpose the score. He had me put the chord changes in and showed me that *La Mancha* was basically very simple, if you understood the multiple meters. I was young, and this kind of music was becoming part of the basic skill set for young pianists and conductors.

Rudi recognized my abilities, took me under his wing, and became an important mentor, who taught me to conduct. Over the years we became close He was very paternal to me and regaled me with many stories about the shows he worked on and the rehearsals he'd played. When I went through rocky parts of my marriage to Rhoda, I always had a place to sleep under the piano in his West 57th Street apartment. Always very down to earth, he was one of those unrecognized people who had participated in the makings of many musicals, and he gave me exactly the kind of information I needed to progress.

Rudi conducted most of the Broadway run of *Man of La Mancha,* taking over from the original music director, Neil Warner. He could easily play piano or the violin as required. Rudi played violin in the pits of all of my shows, leaving hit shows to join me, to show his loyalty to me. He taught me serious conducting techniques and was relentless in making sure I really got the message. As I climbed the stairs of my career, his extensive knowledge was very helpful to me, and we stayed close until his death in 2003.

Between Les Harnley, Rudi Bennett, and much support from Don Pippin as time went on, I really had my career on a roll. I realized that I now had to put a lot of effort into music study since I had never been properly trained.

I paid for piano lessons with Les, who was always showing me tons and tons of opera literature and music I should know. Rudi gave me tremendous technical and practical advice as a conductor and pianist. Don taught me show business, along with a lot of practical ways to get things done.

He had significant arranging skills and showed me a lot of great tricks in vocal arranging for theatre. I was moving rapidly into more work.

While I was never a great technician at the piano, my sense of rhythm was good, and I would put in the time to learn the music I had to play. I was hired to play rehearsal piano for the bus and truck tour of *Applause* with Patrice Munsel. Pia Zadora sang the title song. Don Pippin was the MD for the Broadway production, but had little to do with this production, though he was pleased to hear that I had been engaged. He showed me some of the music and was interested in my progression professionally. A music director needed as much help as he could get.

I learned to play the show within an inch of its life, and the cast and director, Ron Field, came to rely on me to pull through rehearsals. Ron took a liking to me, and I could do no wrong at the piano. The drummer on the show was Michael Keller, who came along with me on later projects and eventually became Marvin Hamlisch's orchestra contractor.

The affectionate name for all of the Broadway singers and dancers was "the gypsies," and in those days, before a show went on the road, there would be an invited "gypsy" run-through. These run-throughs, along with Actor's Fund performances, were the only time that the working gypsies could see other shows. Our *Applause* run-through was at the Ansonia Hotel on West 72nd street. I was playing piano by myself with the conductor flapping his arms needlessly. Everyone who was everyone in the NY theatre community attended. *Applause* was the big deal show of that time, and Ron Field was a big name. Realizing that this was a golden opportunity, I worked my butt off trying to play well. I felt well prepared.

One little gaff occurred during the run-through. Pat Munsel was singing "Hurry Back," not a typical Strouse/Adams composition. Pat was a legit singer and was having difficulty with the quasi-jazz aspects.

I had managed to accompany her in rehearsals, giving her lots and lots of room, but the conductor was flapping and making faces at me to follow him, so I did. Pat stopped cold, glaring at me, like it was my fault, which it was, because I followed the conductor. Ron Field came over to the piano and said quietly to me, "Today of all days you choose to follow him?" We quickly got it back on track and got through the run-through. I realized then, as I do now, that it was deliberate on my part, and I chose at the time never again to draw attention to myself in that way.

Eventually it paid off. I found it's much better to let others let you know if you are doing a good job or not, no need to grandstand. In any event, at the end of the run-through, I was surrounded at the piano by highly-regarded conductors Stan Lebowsky, Bill Cox, Rene Wiegert, Don Jennings, and Jack Lee. These people were very important to my future.

After the run-through, they wanted to know who this "wunder-kind" at the piano was. Little did they know I could play the hell out of Strouse/Adams, but even the most basic Bach was a mystery to me. This gypsy run-through did wonders for my career and for getting me known around town.

I went on the tour for a short while. Orchestrator Phil Lang was present for the orchestra rehearsals and befriended me. The assistant to the producers was Charlotte Wilcox, who later became one of the great general managers on Broadway. After a short while on the road, the MD realized I was not an asset to his longevity with the show, so he had me fired. It was a very good thing for me, and I realized early on that the amusing definition of an assistant conductor, "a mouse in training to be a rat" applied to me. I was far too ambitious to be an assistant conductor, or for that matter, anyone's assistant. I always worked hard to be a good assistant when it was called for but tried to get myself elevated ASAP. Don Pippin called me "the Eve Harrington of the pit." Eve Harrington was the "evil" opportunist character in *All About Eve,* which was the basis for the musical *Applause.* I took it as a compliment, but perhaps he was just telling the truth.

I was very ambitious, but I was not eager to see others fail so much as I wanted to do a good job. Don continued to support me to the end of his life, so I can only assume I wasn't really as scary as Eve Harrington.

I continued to get jobs as a music director and ended up doing several *La Mancha's* with Allan Jones and Suzyn Waldman. I was twenty years old. Around town in New York City, I did a lot of auditions and eked out a living. Rhoda was getting singing jobs here and there and was constantly working too.

I received a call from Bob Brandzel, who was MD for a Kung Fu musical called *Ride the Winds,* booked for the little Bijou Theatre next door to the Morosco. Later, it was torn down along with the Morosco and Helen Hayes Theatres, to make room for the Marquis Hotel and theatre.

The choreographer was Jay Norman, who played the very scary looking Puerto Rican dancer in the film of *West Side Story.* He befriended me and I was his ally as rehearsal pianist. The show was written by actor John Driver. Chip Zien (talented, non-Asian actor—the original baker in *Into the Woods*) was one of the leads. The plot was a bit silly and was about a Japanese man learning to be a samurai. The part was played by Irving Lee … a very talented Black man. The first song was called *Run Musashi Run*. The band consisted of me, Bob Brandzel waving his arms with flute or clarinet in his mouth, and Joe DeLuca (just back from Vietnam) playing drums and percussion. The great Dave Moore played electric bass, but the brunt of the show fell on my keyboards.

The reviews were terrible, and we closed after the Saturday matinee, having opened Friday night. I seemed to be in the middle of some very strange musical events happening around Broadway, *Ride the Winds* being among them.

I became friendly with the music director Jack Lee, who lived down the street from me on 45th Street. Jack invited me to sit in the pit of *Irene* to look at the piano book. The piano was being played by the brilliant Bob Colston, who did all the flashy stuff on *No, No, Nanette*. As I sat next to Bob, he said, "I'm going to reach down between your legs and put on the tack piano attachment for the next number. Please stare at Jack on the podium and smile." Jack was hysterical, Bob was very pleased, and we all bonded. Jack became one of my dearest friends and indeed another mentor till the end of his life.

Out of nowhere came a call from Bill Cox. He offered me and Rhoda, a job on *Promises, Promises* for Music Fairs. I would be his assistant and Rhoda would be one of the "pit voices" for a summer tour on the Music Fairs circuit. This was a plum job in stock. *Promises* was a hot show, very contemporary for the time. It was going to star Frank Gorshin, who was a very popular actor/impressionist. Though Frank was popular, he may not have been the nicest guy in the world.

Bill knew how ambitious I was, but Bill was extremely intelligent and disarmed me by giving me opportunities like conducting matinees. He knew who he was and that his career with music fairs was solid, and he just wasn't threatened by me. Because of that, he had the greatest ally in me, and we are friends to this day. Beyond *Promises,* he hired me for *No, No, Nanette* with Ruby Keeler and Cyril Ritchard, and then Don Ameche, and for *Annie Get Your Gun* with Barbara Eden. Even when all of the big guns from New York came to see *Nanette* at Westbury Music Fair, he insisted that I still conduct the matinee because my parents were present. If he made a mistake on the podium, he would say to me in jest, "Don't do that."

Bill taught me one of the greatest tricks in conducting. I couldn't get a proper start on a trumpet solo to end an act of *Promises.* No matter what I did with the stick—*nothing*. He said, "Watch me at the next performance." That night, he looked at the trumpet player and without moving the stick said out loud, "One!!!."

The trumpet player came in on beat two. It works every time, even with the New York Philharmonic. Bill is a very great musician and a wonderful man. He is still teaching at AMDA in New York City.

The Music Fairs jobs kept me and Rhoda employed for a quite a while with the income rolling in. I treasure the memories of my time in stock and working in the "tents."

All the Music Fairs, Westbury, Shady Grove, Camden, Valley Forge, and Painters Mill were in tents or rather semi-permanent structures. There was also Cleveland Musicarnival, Storrowton, and many others. This was solid training ground for several generations of Broadway performers, writers, directors, choreographers, and conductors.

I saw *The Rothschilds* with Jan Peerce at Camden County Music Fair. During the opening-night performance, the MD fell asleep and

Jan Peerce was downstage tapping his cane to wake him up. That was so shocking to me.

One night, I was sitting in the bar at Cohasset, Mass, where I was pianist for *No, No, Nanette* with Ruby Keeler and Don Ameche. I was invited for a drink by Betty Kean (who played the maid). Betty was part of the famous Kean sisters. She was met by Jerry Lester, a much-loved TV comic from Chicago, and they started drinking. I don't remember much else that night. I might have been twenty or twenty-one. It seemed I was learning to drink with pros.

In some of these tents, when it rained, the noise was so loud on the canvas that nothing could be heard. One time at Camden County Music Fair, I was assisting Bill Cox on *Promises* with Frank Gorshin. Bill had me conducting the matinee and it was raining very hard. Frank wondered why I was waving in front of the orchestra and it was because you couldn't hear a note. He might have even stopped the show, but it didn't matter, because we couldn't hear him either.

The culmination of all of the Music Fair shows was playing West-bury Music Fair. It was just short of playing Broadway. The musicians were all the Broadway guys who didn't have a show currently, and the contractor was Mel Rodnan. Mel was a very good woodwind player, who had done many shows in New York. He ended up as orchestra contractor for Andrew Lloyd Webber and Cameron Mackintosh up until his death. He was also friendly with my friend and supporter Don Pippin. The feedback was getting back to Don that the young kid whom he'd met at age thirteen was now an up-and-coming conductor at age twenty-one.

My studies with Rudi Bennett and Les Harnley continued, and I was observant of all the conductors on Broadway. I was listening to much legit music and observing first-class conductors. I would ask lots of questions and studied the scores endlessly. I wanted to know what made it all tick.

I soon realized that musicians were befriending me in case I became successful. They wanted to get on the bandwagon and keep working. It's the nature of the business. There were a few old timers, though, who just wanted to be supportive. One was Ray Shanfeld, who was playing baritone sax on *Promises*. He was a regular with Elliot Lawrence and had played several of his shows. I would sit next to him when I played piano when Bill was conducting. After a matinee I conducted, he said, "Listen kid, when you get on the podium, you have the orchestra on the edge of their seats wanting to play. It's a gift and you will do really well." I really took his words to heart and continued to study. It was guys like Ray who spread the positive word and enhanced my blossoming reputation. When musicians like Ray and Harvey Estrin and others complimented me, it meant a great deal. These guys were my heroes. They were *big* names to those of us invested in the musical theatre. These were the regular rank and file players who played one show after the other and were part of the legacy.

Rudi was forever working with me on how to use the baton. He would say things like "Why are you goosing butterflies?" By goosing butterflies, he meant waving one's hands around for no purpose or direction other than looking pretty. "Bring the stick down and make them play."

Rudi came to hear me play a solo piano performance of the show *The Apple Tree* at the Bert Wheeler Theatre in New York. I was so intimidated and nervous about my piano playing. He said, "You have no chops at all, and yet when you play, you have great tone on the piano and your intention is fully realized and you sound great."

I realized I was never going to have endless facility at the piano, but I could get my point across.

I decided, however, to get as much facility as I could as a conductor. I wanted to have unlimited technique with the stick, worked hard to realize that, and tried to apply that to my writing later on, as well as to everything I attempted. It was so heartening to have the encouraging words from Rudi. In a way, he had encouraged me to really pursue a course of excellence.

As nice as it was to have the compliments about my piano playing. I knew I played well enough to get by. Les Harnley and Rudi Bennett pushed me and pushed me, instilling a desire in me to work on my strong points. I was a constant student. Perhaps that's why I did things like taking flying lessons and becoming a flight instructor. I was not satisfied with just getting the pilot's license; I wanted to be *really* good at it. Not to show off, but for my own satisfaction. I just wanted to be facile at what I did—not restricted by limitations of technique. I had a level of stick-to-itiveness that also persisted in my musical endeavors.

I was twenty-one years old, conducting shows at Westbury Music Fair with Broadway musicians. Not only was I extremely ambitious, but also very eager to get recognition for being good at it. I wasn't driven by money, but by wanting acknowledgement. I realized that in getting married as young as I did, I could totally focus on my career and work, which is exactly what I wanted.

I really didn't know where I was going, but I knew I was getting there. After assisting Bill at the Music Fairs, I picked up a few more conducting jobs at various theatres around the country doing some more musicals.

Glen Clugston asked me to play piano, and then take over as conductor for a production of *Nanette* in Florida. This one was with

Helen Gallagher, Russell Nype, Barbara Britton, and Jerry Antes. I was playing the 2nd piano and the local pianist hired to play the other piano was Ted Saidenberg.

Ted had been the music director of several Broadway musicals and had been Jasha Heifetz' accompanist. Jerry Herman told me much later that it was Ted who had notated Jerry's score for *Hello Dolly*. Jerry played by ear and needed someone to transcribe his playing.

Ted befriended me in a paternal manner and took me to Hialeah Racetrack to play the horses. The band was well past its prime when I took over as conductor. One night, I gave a downbeat to a very old (and tired) clarinet player, who didn't respond. Going into panic mode, I gave the downbeat about three times with no result. Ted said out loud, "Don't break your arm, kid," and played the solo on the piano. I've never forgotten him for that.

Some years later, Ted was conducting the revival of *My Fair Lady* at the St. James with my mentor Rudi Bennett as his assistant, and I was able to say hello again. Ted died in 1986. I was so fortunate to meet people like him. He was a formidable talent and I picked up little tidbits of knowledge that added to my bag of conducting tricks. This bag of tricks ultimately became a big bundle of usable musical knowledge.

In retrospect, it's astounding to me that I was accepted as a MD/conductor without really having that much experience with orchestras. In a very short amount of time, I had managed to accumulate a lot of experience. This was 1974 and I was facing my twenty-second birthday!

Chapter Three

Don Pippin had written a show for Off-Broadway with Anthony Stimac called *Fashion,* and he asked if I would play rehearsal piano for some of it. In addition, I even helped paint the scenery with a bunch of singers/dancers, including Tom Reed and Dennis Birchall, with whom I'd later work on *A Chorus Line.* When one of the girls backed out, Rhoda was hired to sing one of the parts. Don was trusting me a bit more. Jerry Herman, Don's patron saint, who'd been hiring him to conduct many of his shows, came to a performance and I was introduced. Jerry was a giant, and so very well-respected and loved because of *Hello Dolly, Mame,* and *Milk and Honey.* It was a big step up for me to have Don hiring me.

Things were starting to pop for me at this time. Along with some others of my generation, I was getting a reputation for being facile/ ambitious/talented/young. Colleagues coming up were Bob Billig, David Friedman, Danny Troob, Larry Hochman, and Glen Roven. The scene on Broadway was changing with some younger faces popping up. Steve Margoshes (pianist from summer camp) and Bill Brohn were other names being mentioned for shows as orchestrators. Michael Gibson and Jim Tyler were working all the time. Paul

Gemignani was coming up as a force since the death of Hal Hastings in 1973. Jonathan Tunick was becoming the top orchestrator for Sondheim and others. This was all happening very rapidly. Michael Bennett and Pat Birch were choreographing and directing shows. Hal Prince was directing new ones all the time.

I assisted Arthur B. Rubinstein on a revival of *Juno* at Williamstown, Mass. Richard Maltby, Jr. was on board for new lyrics, and we became friendly, as well. Arthur was a very talented composer. He was writing a lot of TV music and ultimately scored some important movies as well as being a sometime Broadway musical director. Arthur was also a very spiky character. He had tremendous musical skill but was one of those guys who shot himself in the foot.

He had been the original MD for *Promises, Promises.*

His brittle personality had caused a run-in with composer Burt Bacharach, so he was replaced before it came to Broadway. However, his initial involvement was very important in making that show sound the way it did. I learned a great deal working with him, and he ultimately caused me to get my first Broadway musical as conductor. He ended up writing a few really brilliant film scores: one for *Wargames,* and another for *Blue Thunder.* He taught me a great deal about orchestration.

I enjoyed working with Geraldine Fitzgerald and Milo O'Shea on *Juno*. It had a brilliant score by Marc Blitzstein, but it remained a failed musical even in this production. But, I did have fun hanging out at the local bar with actors Raul Julia and Jobeth Williams.

Jonathan Tunick was a friend of Arthur's who came up to see the show, and we met for the first time in Williamstown. Arthur had also imported much of the band from New York, and I became friendly with woodwind player, Bob Steen, who was a very busy guy on Broadway at the time. Knowing people like Bob was very helpful in my ascent to the podium. Bob played several of the shows I conducted in New York City. We had an accordion in the pit played by Val Dennis, who was one of the more accomplished players, and I learned a lot about the accordion. Arthur had me do some of the minor orchestration, as well. All of this was leading to the inevitability of me wanting to be a writer (composer/orchestrator).

I was hired to be music director for a dinner theatre production of *Guys and Dolls* with Julie Newmar as Adelaide. The director/choreographer was Marvin Gordon. Marvin was a very solid dancer, who'd established a strong career regionally and in stock as a choreographer. I had done *Promises* and *Annie Get Your Gun* with him as rehearsal pianist for the Music Fairs, and he had recommended me for the job. It was two pianos and drums. I hired Rudi Bennett to be my second piano, and Michael Keller on drums.

Marvin and Rudi taught me so much. Now and then on a new show, there were dance arrangers or rehearsal pianists who would either compose, arrange, or select dance music that we as orchestrators would have to make work with our various orchestras. Irv Kostal would often speak of dance arrangers who would write huge chords for the brass. He would point out that there were three trumpets and two bones, so pick out your favorite five notes, because the woodwinds are busy. However, I was the music director for *Guys and Dolls*. The opening number is called "Runyanland." It is a composed piece of music. Marvin pointed out that the music didn't fit his choreography, and he wasn't going to match the music, because of his smaller cast. He staged the number like so: Eight bars of couple dancing; sixteen bars of zoot suit; eight bars of purse snatcher; twelve bars of couple fighting; eight parts of Apache; sixteen bars of chase; and so on. He would say, "Let's run it with just counts." We'd do the counts and he'd say, "Great, pick your best music for each section, cut it and paste it together, and if you need to write a transition, write it."

Voila! Dance music that ultimately fit his choreography to a "T" with really a minimum of effort, as compared to writing/orchestrating/copying in a hurry with limited budget and crew. This was a lesson well-learned in creating dance music in a hurry for a new production. Maybe it wasn't *Rite of Spring*, but it sure was a great version of "Runyanland" that hit all the high points. When there were a lot of local productions with various re-stagings, it was always easy to piece something together in a hurry that was very effective.

Marvin had choreographed the Duke Ellington fiasco called *Pousse Café* in the '60s. He died some years ago. I remember him so fondly because of his kindness and his practical knowledge. It has stuck with me through many situations.

Working with choreographers is challenging for all of us as orchestrators in theatre. There are never enough instruments (especially brass and percussion) to cover requirements. Fosse very cleverly liked to use various colors of percussion, not just piatti (hand cymbals), but triangle, claves, washboard, and sandpaper blocks. Fosse's orchestrators: Ginzler, Kostal, Ralph Burns, and his disciple Besterman, had a field day. Most of the other choreographers required a lot of piatti. A cymbal crash seems to cover a multitude of sins. I was learning these tricks along the way.

Rhoda was hired as swing on the Broadway revival of *Candide*. Swing is the understudy for all/many roles in the ensemble. She was sharing a dressing room with Carolann Page, who became Mrs. Paul Gemignani and the mother of future actor/director Alex Gemignani. Because of Rhoda's friendship with the future Mrs. Gemignani, Paul took notice of me. Paul, now the MD for Hal Prince's productions, had become a powerful force and was able to create employment for people like me.

Danny Troob was leaving the national tour of *A Little Night Music* as assistant conductor to do the dance music for a new musical called *Goodtime Charley* with Joel Grey and upcoming dance star (and Bob Fosse girlfriend) Ann Reinking. Paul Gemignani asked if I'd like to take over as assistant conductor. Right after my twenty-second birthday, I shipped off to Chicago and became the assistant conductor for a Hal Prince/Stephen Sondheim blockbuster. I was a little frightened, because the show had been out for many months, and they were a family. I didn't know anyone, except Marcia Brushingham, who had been a singer in *No, No, Nanette* in Florida the year before. Marcia was a lovely woman and was like a big sister. When I ran into her in the lobby of the hotel, I was so grateful to see someone I knew. Sadly (several years later), she was murdered by her brother in a grisly crime. Rhoda was subletting Marcia's apartment at that time (we were separated) and had to identify the body.

I quickly fit in with the company and enjoyed doing the job. The piano part for *ALNM* is very simple but exposed and is mostly an assistant conductor position. The conductor for the show was Dick Parrinello, who was very capable and not particularly friendly to me. I was an up-and-coming young guy and very aggressive and ambitious. Of course, I was not his choice. I was Paul Gemignani's "plant" for checking up on Dick, etc. ... at least it was perceived that way. But Danny Troob was and is extremely talented and showed me the show before he left.

I stayed with the show till the end of the tour a few months later. We played Chicago, Philly, Wilmington (Delaware), and finally closed in Boston. Dick was not very nice about having me conduct the show, but I successfully conducted most of the first act during the Chicago run. Actually, very successfully and that was about it until I conducted the second act on closing night in Boston, when Dick had to leave prematurely to rehearse the show somewhere else. However, my connection with the show did not escape the notice of Hal Prince and Steve Sondheim, or any of the management for Prince's office. My work on the tour paid off a few years later.

Jean Simmons was Desiree in *ALNM*, and a nicer person there never was. She invited a bunch of the cast (and me) to see Michel Legrand perform with an orchestra at Mister Kelly's in Chicago. I was flattered to be asked, and it's a great memory. Legrand was very impressive, and it was a real treat.

Margaret Hamilton was the costar and very nice as well, and Hermione Gingold came in for a few performances here and there. George Lee Andrews was Frederick and very good in the show. He and his wife Marti Morris, who played Fredrika, were so kind to me when I was alone at Christmas. Rhoda was doing *Candide* in New York City and here was this Jewish boy with no place to go. So, they invited me over to string cranberries and stuff which was a very nice thing to do. I became friends with Ed Evanko, who played the count, and worked with him a lot later on down the road. Karen Gibson, who was one of the Liebeslieder girls, worked with me later on, and we are still friends. Marshall Borden, who was the understudy for the male leads, married Lee Meriwether. Marshall and Lee were neighbors of ours until very recently when they went into retirement facilities. The harpist on the tour was Henry Fanelli, who has played the entire run of *Phantom of the Opera* and is still there.

The cellist Dean Kelso went on with me for several shows. Sadly, he was an early victim of AIDS.

I later caused Dick Parrinello to be hired as replacement MD on *They're Playing Our Song*. He unfortunately didn't get along with the new leading man and his time was short lived.

Dick was a very good conductor and that was an unfortunate event.

The *ALNM* tour was as good time for me. I became friendly with musicians around the country, some of whom I had known from earlier shows with the Music Fairs. In the meantime, Rhoda left *Candide* and was hired to play a secondary role in *Goodtime Charley*. I was very pleased for her.

When I came back to New York, things were a bit of a mess work-wise, and my marriage to Rhoda was unraveling. All the time apart was putting a strain on the marriage. Arthur Rubinstein was conducting *Goodtime Charley* and was planning to leave the show. He told me that he was going to make me the replacement conductor. There was no real associate conductor on the show. It had received mediocre reviews and was hanging on at the Palace Theatre. It was announced that I was going to take over and so I did. I walked into a performance in May of 1975, prior to my twenty-third birthday in July, and conducted my first Broadway show. Joel Grey was a very big name at the time, having won an Academy Award for *Cabaret*. *Goodtime Charley* was running on his steam, which wasn't enough to keep it open, but it lasted long enough. I used to hang out in the alley behind the Palace with one of the male dancers, sharing a cigarette or two (it was still cool to smoke in those days). His name was Patrick Swayze. The orchestra was full of great players. The best that Broadway had to offer.

Jonathan Tunick was the orchestrator, and so he became aware of my abilities. Not only that, but composer Larry Grossman and lyricist Hal Hackady also became strong supporters. In the pit was Felix Giglio playing violin. Felix was David Merrick's orchestra contractor, and that paid off for me when Eddie Strauss was conducting *Very Good Eddie* at the Booth and had to take a week or two off. Felix told him about me and *voila*, I was conducting my second Broadway show exactly one year later.

My memory worked well for me when taking over shows in a hurry. I learned to imitate whomever I was replacing. Imitation, being the best form of flattery, worked in my favor. When I got up on the podium without much muss or fuss, it went a long way in creating a firm reputation.

Goodtime Charley was a major push in my career. I had come from nowhere, in the scheme of things to conducting a major Broadway musical at the ripe old age of twenty-two. Now, in retrospect, it seems unfathomable that anyone would entrust a musical to a twenty-two-year-old kid. But at the time it seemed oh-so natural to me. I was totally prepared in terms of knowing the music, the cues, and the way the show worked, and I had spent the last few years totally immersed in this world of musical theatre. It seemed so inevitable to me. I had been doing lots of conducting of smaller musicals and had cut my teeth on the Music Fairs circuit, conducting several big musicals with various celebrities. No one seemed to be the slightest bit at odds with my doing it.

I got along easily with Joel Grey and Annie Reinking, and the various other old-timers in the show like Jay Garner, Louis Zorich, and Chuck Rule (who had been in countless musicals). The singers/dancers were mostly closer to my age, and it all just seemed so natural. In fact, … a very short while after … Joel Grey engaged me to conduct for him on a number of occasions. Much later I was engaged to orchestrate the Yiddish production of *Fiddler* and Joel was the director. When I say much later, we are talking forty years later.

My motivation was to be acknowledged and to be recognized as being good at what I did. I studied my scores all hours of the night till I knew them backwards and forwards. I didn't know it at the time, but I know it now in reflection, I had so much determination in order to justify my escape from Bayside and my troubled home. My focus on work and the continual study of music gave me validation. I was continually reading and discussing music with whomever was willing to talk to me, especially my colleagues and my mentors like Les Harnley, Rudi Bennett, and Bill Cox. They were accessible to me and freely gave me advice and encouragement.

After *Goodtime Charley*, Joel engaged me to be his music director. I did one gig with him in Nashville, Tennessee with the Cincinnati Pops. Erich Kunzel was their MD, so Erich did the first half and I did Joel's show. Erich became a very important conductor in the symphonic pops world until his passing.

At a rehearsal with the Cincinnati Pops, I was conducting when Joel clapped his hands to stop and said very sharply, "Larry, *why* is the tempo so slow?"

I stood there for a minute and said very sharply back to him, "How many guesses do I get?" The entire orchestra fell out laughing and that set the tone for my relationship with Joel till the end of time. Later on, Joel was engaged to be the opening act for Liza Minnelli at the Chateau de Ville in Framingham, Mass. Liza's conductor, Jack French, had just left to do something else, perhaps Shirley MacLaine. They had decided to have Liza's drummer Bill LaVorgna become her conductor from the drums. Bill had played for Judy Garland, most notably at Carnegie Hall, but he didn't have a clue. I was asked to conduct the rehearsal by him and John Kander, who was supervising, so I conducted the rehearsals with the band for Liza and Joel.

John Kander was very kind to me. When the choreographer Walter Painter got a little salty with me verbally, I chose not to respond to his tirade. When I got off the podium, John handed me a tumbler of scotch and said, "Here you deserve this." Walter and I later became friends, but at the time it was not great. I was working my butt off and was put off by the attitudes that people took to secure their positions. I was in my late twenties by then, had Broadway credits as a music director, and was much in demand. I thought it was inappropriate to be yelled at. I had difficulty in accepting criticism, especially gratuitous criticism.

I was disappointed that Joel didn't take any action on my behalf or defend me and I told him to find another conductor. Joel and I have since become friends again and remain so. When he directed *Fiddler on the Roof* in Yiddish, forty years later, I was the orchestrator. He was my greatest supporter.

In the middle of all these things, I had written an Off-Broadway musical called *Christy*, (which is a whole other story chronicled in a memoir by the author of the book and producer of the show). I was working anywhere and everywhere I was asked to be, hungry to do everything.

Prior to my short stint at *Very Good Eddie,* I took over as music director for a little Off-Broadway show from Miami called *Becoming.* Pia Lindstrom, the then-critic for NBC television, said in her review: "I never stayed for the second act to see what *Becoming became.*" It was a nice little show done by some nice people from Miami U.

Before *Becoming,* I took quite a break from my ramblings around Manhattan and at the request of Larry Grossman and Hal Hackady became the music director for their original musical *Snoopy.* This premiered at the Little Fox Theatre in San Francisco, the same theatre where the original *You're a Good Man, Charlie Brown* had premiered. The theatre was owned by Francis Ford Coppola and held his offices for his film company. We shared the green room with Francis and his staff. It was a cute little show, and I was asked to do the orchestrations for a small group, which were later used everywhere.

Somewhere along the way, the show evolved differently, and Larry Grossman had my name removed from the piano conductor scores. I never quite understood this, but it involved some financial disagreement about the cast recording. In any event, the show went on to be licensed forever and ever with my scorings and some additional materials added to it from various productions in New York and in London.

There is a cast recording from San Francisco with much of the original cast, including the wonderful Pam Myers, and it is representative of what the show was originally. I never had any problem with Hal Hackady, the lyricist, who remained a friend for the rest of his life. It's a great show and I think it's still in the repertoire of nice small musicals to do. It had a very under-rated score by Grossman and Hackady. Their scores for *Minnie Boys and Goodtime Charley* are pretty great too.

Larry was one of the greatest of coaches and arrangers and was responsible for a lot of stuff that was done on *The Muppet Show*. Larry wrote the scores for two unsuccessful Hal Prince musicals, *A Doll's Life* and *Grind*. He was helpful to me when I wrote the score for the Off-Broadway musical *Christy*. He came over to my apartment, went over some spots with me, and really helped me to improve the composition. I never understood his animus towards me regarding *Snoopy*. Much later I brought him as a guest to a meeting/luncheon for the American Society of Music Arrangers and Composers (ASMAC). I was the president and honored him at a luncheon.

For *Snoopy*, I lived in San Francisco for six months or so, with Rhoda as the understudy for the female roles. My second pianist, Jon Olson, became a lifetime friend. He was a wonderful associate and was loved by many. I took him on the road as my assistant on the tour of *Sugar Babies* some years later. Unfortunately, his life ended prematurely with a heart attack.

After *Snoopy*, I was asked by Dick Lewine and John Fearnley at the Rodgers and Hammerstein organization to MD and orchestrate a rehash of their *Rodgers and Hart Celebration.* The show had recently opened and quickly closed on Broadway with a stellar cast including Laurence Guittard and others. We had Constance Towers, her husband John Gavin, Tony Tanner, Toni Kaye, Lee Roy Reams, and Dorothy Loudon. This was for a dinner theatre in Des Plaines, Illinois outside of Chicago.

One day at rehearsals as I was pounding at the piano playing "Jupiter Forbid" from *By Jupiter,* the door swung open and Mr. Richard Rodgers came in the room. He had recently had a laryngectomy and he walked with a cane. He sat down and as I finished the song, he beckoned with a come-hither finger. I came across the room and very politely said, as I offered my hand, "Mr. Rodgers."

Looking me straight in the eye and with a very guttural voice using esophageal speech, he said, "Dick." It took me a second to realize that it was *his* name and not mine. "Dick" gave me an awkward smile and said very carefully and slowly with a gulp in front of each syllable, "Too ... fuck ... ing ... fast." After that, he was very nice and said a few nice things to the cast and left.

The show continued in rehearsals, with Connie Towers and Jack Gavin calling the shots... mostly Connie. Finally, she insisted that Dorothy Loudon had to go or she would.

Dorothy was released and replaced with Beth Fowler. Peter Lawrence (the stage manager) and I comforted Dorothy and told her that it was ridiculous. She was a pro and left. Connie felt that Dorothy was too much competition for her, except she didn't quite say it that way. It forever tainted my opinion of Connie Towers, which wasn't so good to begin with.

A couple of years later, Dorothy had a huge success as Mrs. Hannigan in *Annie,* and became the Broadway star that she deserved to be. She later did *Ballroom* and succeeded Angela Lansbury in *Sweeney Todd.* I had known her slightly when I was around *Lolita, My Love.* She was a very lovely woman and a tremendous talent.

Peter Lawrence became the number-one stage manager and production supervisor on so many shows. We ended up doing another show a few years later, *Copperfield,* with me as MD and Peter as production supervisor/stage manager.

As *Rodgers and Hart* ran its course, I was doing the orchestrations for the very small band.

I was very surprised to find out that the bassist would double on Harp. I have never known a bassist that played harp or a harpist that played bass. Most peculiar!

I would orchestrate *Rodgers and Hart* at Associated Music, which was run by Bob and Judy Haring. It was an old music copying office that had a crew working on many shows and recordings. Bob was Robert Russell Bennett's copyist and supplied music paper and writing supplies to many in the industry. When they were actively copying music, there would be a long table with many copyists scribing away.

I was given a seat at the table to knock out some orchestrations. I really wasn't equipped or ready to take this on. Nevertheless, I had been hired. I was sitting there along with an older character named

Brick Fleagle. He was an arranger/guitarist who worked regularly as a copyist for Luther Henderson, Jr. At the other end of the table was a much older gentlemen named Hans. He commented on a few of my arrangements and said, with a very heavy Viennese accent, "Veddy interesting harp parts." He pointed out a few things to me and said, "Y'know, I orchestrated the originals."

He was Hans Spialek, who was Rodger's orchestrator for many of his early Broadway musicals. Later in life, he was relegated to being a copyist. A few years later, John Mauceri brought him back to recognition with the orchestrations for *On Your Toes*. I would run into Hans on the street when I lived on West 86th street. He was a very nice man and told me a few stories as we walked. One day, he casually said, "Russ Bennett and I went up to Boston to help George finish up *Porgy and Bess*." It has always been assumed that Gershwin orchestrated it himself. Well, maybe not. I don't think Hans was fibbing. It was so common, and a matter of fact that it took an army to orchestrate a show. I found out later from personal experience that there are always many hands working on the orchestrations of a Broadway musical, credited or not. Rodgers referred to Spialek as "the bouncing Czech."

I came back to New York City unemployed and picked up odd jobs as I could, playing rehearsals here and there and doing whatever I could find. I seemed to do ok but nothing was forthcoming. Then Bob Colston, the excellent pianist from so many Julius Monk revues and one of the dazzling pianists on *No, No, Nanette* and *Irene* phoned me.

Bob knew I had conducted a lot, and he had not and wanted my advice. He had been hired to conduct *Fiddler*, with famed opera tenor, Jan Peerce. It was a bad fit and he knew it. He didn't want to conduct but had taken the job and he appreciated my advice. So I played rehearsals.

54

One day, Jan Peerce came to me at the piano and said, "You a Jew???"

I answered "... ish."

He said, "Come with me." He grabbed a few other obvious examples, including character actor, Fyvush Finkel, went into the hallway, and shoved the door open to the adjacent studio where the original *Annie* was rehearsing. Then he shouted, "Any Jews in here?"

A couple of chorus boys in hot pants came out saying, "We're Jews, we're Jews", along with Charles Strouse and Peter Howard and a few others."

Jan hustled us all into a vacant room. He needed a minion of ten Jewish men to say the prayer for the dead for his brother-in-law, Richard Tucker. Years later, I told this story to Charles Fox, who shared this story with his best friend Larry Peerce (Jan's son). Larry's response, "That's funny, Dad hated Richard and the feelings were mutual."

I had fun playing *Fiddler* and working with Jan, who was a lovely man. Sometime later, his manager Phil Schapiro phoned me and said, "Jan is doing a summer tour of opera and Yiddish songs and would like you to play piano and be music director." I was very flattered, but felt I was not well-versed in opera, and really wasn't up to the job. I could deal with the other stuff, but I really felt ill-equipped for all of the legit stuff. I told Phil that and he said, "I'm really sorry to hear that, and I know Jan will be disappointed, as well. Maybe next time?" Then he added, "Please give my regards to Dorothy," and hung up.

My mom's name was Dorothy, and her maiden name was Shapiro. I picked up the phone, told my mom the story, and asked if Phil was related. My mom's words, "Larry darling, remember my best friend Ruth who lives in Bayside, and you used to have play dates with her daughter Maxine?" I said, yes, of course, and she said, "Phil Schapiro was their next-door neighbor, no relation." This is called Jewish Geography. Everyone is related or knows the person you are working with or their parents. Put two Jews (especially in show business) in a room and you will find out that they are cousins once removed. Lightning was about to strike.

The biggest show in New York at that time was a little gem called *A Chorus Line.* It had opened at the same time as *Goodtime Charley* and was already show-biz history. Michael Bennett was now the greatest director/choreographer in history and the show was already legendary in its own time. It had spawned a national tour based in LA and a company in London with an American cast. The UK company was coming back to the States and was going to tour as the International Company. Don Pippin had been mentoring me quietly over the years and he had now heard enough feedback to know that I might know what I was doing. My good friends Harvey Estrin and Don's usual assistant, Skip Redwine, had both seen me conduct, along with Westbury music contractor, Mel Rodnan. They told Don I was worth pushing along.

Don recommended me to Michael Bennett as the obvious choice to conduct the international company. As the show was already rehearsed, it really meant just stepping onto the podium and opening the show in Baltimore. I was all of twenty-four years old. I put on my best suit and went up to Michael Bennett's posh office, which I think was on Fifth or Park Avenue. He greeted me officially, also in a suit, along with Bob Avian and his associate, Sue McNair.

It was so out of character for a choreographer/director to be meeting me in an office in a suit. Michael didn't keep that image for too long. We hit it off, but he didn't offer me the job straight away and I was scared that it would go away. Don told me not to worry and I put it in the back of my mind. Finally, one day, the phone rang, and I was officially offered the job. It was the job of a lifetime, thanks to Don Pippin's faith in me.

Literally ten minutes after being offered this job, my phone rang and it was Peter Howard, who was still in rehearsal for *Annie.* He had seen me recently as part of Jan Peerce's minion. He said that the assistant/pianist he had chosen for *Annie* was not working out, and asked would I like to be the pianist for *Annie,* opening very shortly at the Alvin Theatre? I told Peter about the offer I'd just had, and he said, "I'm very happy for them and you, but I'm very unhappy for me." I quickly recommended my friend Bob Billig, a very good conductor/pianist, who was unfortunately at liberty. Bob really didn't want to be a pianist or assistant any longer, but work is work. He took the job, and it was a great springboard for him.

A Chorus Line on the road was a life changer for me, especially working with such high-caliber dancers as Pamela Sousa, Jane Summerhays, Eivind Harum, and working with Michael Bennett's associates Baayork Lee and Bob Avian, for starters. Everyone was just top of the line.

I was going to join the company in Baltimore. This was a company that had played together in London for one year and were totally bonded together. Pam was new, as was I, but she was a gypsy, so fit right in. I was just a young conductor, younger than most of the cast or about the same age. I really hadn't even gotten to know anyone before I had to conduct the sitzprobe (the first rehearsal for the singers with the new city's orchestra). I had studied the score scrupulously and told Don Pippin that I was going to conduct it beat for beat as he did. I had watched him do it many nights in the pit at the Shubert in New York. There was one bar of music just before it transitioned into the song "Nothing", which was a 3/2 bar. That's the musical meter meaning there are three beats in the bar and a half note gets one beat. I told Don that I felt more comfortable doing it in six, and Don said, "sure, go ahead." Later, after doing the tour for about a year, I switched to doing it in three. When I went to see Don backstage in New York, he had switched to doing it in six. We had a good laugh about that.

Don and I had a very symbiotic relationship, and he really was responsible for many of the successes and opportunities I had going forward. I knew how lucky I was to have gotten this *A Chorus Line* job, and I was ready for it, but it was thanks to Don Pippin recommending and promoting me that it happened for me. Considering he thought I was the "Eve Harrington of the pit," it showed his great trust in me and my skills. I was forever grateful to him then, as I am now.

I got through the first sitzprobe in Baltimore. Michael Bennett was happy with me, the cast was happy with me, and the only note or comment Don had for me was, "Good boy!" Then, he bought me dinner. There were no notes from Michael or Don. Much later, in San Francisco, Michael did give me one note, pointing out that if I accelerated at a certain point, the audience would applaud. He said, "Try it both ways," and he was absolutely right. He knew his stuff.

The tour was mostly a lot of fun and was a good training ground for the future. We played long stops in wonderful cities with very good orchestras: Baltimore, Detroit, Miami, San Francisco, Washington, DC, Philadelphia, and Boston, where I left the tour in February 1978. This, as well as the numerous cast changes kept me on my toes, plus I got to work with all the best dancers in the business. However, I was in a covered pit. Unless I was friendly with them outside of the pit, I was just the guy who kept the orchestra together.

I established and maintained a lot of good friendships, and I'm still in touch with Jane Summerhays, who played Sheila, and sometimes with Pam Sousa, who played Cassie, and who I introduced to my friend Michael Keller. They have been married since 1977. I was their best man. Later, Michael was my original drummer on *Playing Our Song*, and established a relationship with Marvin Hamlisch that led to him contracting the orchestra for Barbra Streisand, and ultimately for many, many musicals on Broadway and beyond.

During the run of *A Chorus Line*, Michael Bennett married his long-time muse, Donna McKechnie. Everyone thought it a little bizarre, as Michael was known to be bi-sexual at best. Everyone accepted it as a bit of show-biz normality. They really were best friends in any event. The marriage quickly went awry, and Michael decided to hang out in San Francisco with his "favorite" company. Well, of course they were. The dancers were very young and enthusiastic, and all were fit as a fiddle and gorgeous.

One day, Michael decided to work with Pam Sousa and make her even better than she already was. Pam was a gorgeous dancer, who possessed limitless technique She was a wonderful Cassie. Michael asked if I'd join them in a studio to rehearse. My associate was the wonderful pianist, Eddie Strauss, so I said, "Why don't you ask Eddie?" Michael said, "I'm asking you." And we did just that.

I was never secure in my piano playing but people continued to hire me. Perhaps now, in hindsight, I realize it didn't come as easy to me as conducting or writing music did. It was something I had to work at. Well in any case, I could play the "crap" out of "Music and the Mirror", so why not? We worked in a room, and finally Michael said to Pam, "Let me dance it and you just watch." I dug in at the piano, and Michael danced his heart out as if he were Cassie. I played my fingers off. The final spot on the run up to the final denouement was absolutely thrilling. It was just like in the movies. Michael's dancing was so thrilling, you wanted to jump up and cheer.

Michael turned to me and said, "Y'know on the run up, you left out a beat and made it a measure of 3/4 rather than 4/4." I was terrified that I was going to get fired for my error. But he said, "I really liked it, maybe we should put that in the show." After toying with that idea for twenty minutes, and then realizing that he'd have to institute it in all the music and all the companies, he said, "Forget it." I still think it's a great idea, even though I probably just did it to avoid another difficult run under my fingers.

San Francisco was a great town and a very enjoyable time for all. Between Japantown, Chinatown, and the Italian neighborhood, what's not to like? I learned to love sushi there. I also had my history of living there during *Snoopy,* a few years before. I loved the musicians at the Curran Theatre and vice versa. It was my home away from home.

After San Francisco, the tour moved on back to the east coast. Pam injured herself, as dancers do, and had to take time off. Various "Cassies" came in for short periods: Lynne Taylor Corbett, Gail Mae Ferguson, Sandahl Bergman, and finally, when Pam left the show, Debbie Henry.

Debbie was a gorgeous dancer from Tennessee and had a glorious voice. She probably sang the number as well as Donna McKechnie did. Debbie always introduced me as "my conductor, Larry." Unfortunately, she died very young from ovarian cancer, during the run of *Cats.*

There were many Sheila's, as well, but my favorite was Jane Summerhays. Jane was/is a beautiful dancer trained in Salt Lake City. She was very kind to me during the run and would ask me to play piano and work on songs with her. Many years later when I was brought into *Sugar Babies,* she convinced Ann Miller and the rest of the cast that I was ok. She made my transition into that show a walk in the park. She has had a great career and was nominated for a Tony for her role in *Me and My Girl.* Jane, and later, Rita O'Connor were my favorite "Sheila's" to work with in *A Chorus Line.* Because of our mutual friendships with Jack Lee, Wally Harper, Barbara Cook, and Mary Rodgers, Jane and I have stayed in touch over the years. Rita, unfortunately, passed away a few years ago from cancer. She was also a favorite of Michael Bennett.

The dancers that Michael used repeatedly were the best of the best and have been my friends over the years: Larry Fuller, Sandy Roveta, Donna McKechnie, Jane, Rita, Kate Wright (another great Sheila, whom I didn't work with), Carole (Kelly) Bishop, Eivind Harum, Buddy Vest, Tony Teague, Debbie Henry — Michael knew talent and good people.

While in Washington, DC, I had an unfortunate incident with Michael Bennett. There was a lovely dancer/singer in the show named Gina Paglia, who was playing Morales. Gina was a great gal, who had danced for Michael in one of his earlier shows, *Henry Sweet Henry.* I loved her, but really had little interaction with her, except to see her and say hello. She was great on the songs *"Nothing"* and *"What I Did for Love."* Occasionally, I would give her a note and she might balk a little, but really nothing negative happened. One day, though, Michael said to me in passing, "How's Gina?"

I said, "Gina's great. Why do you ask?"

He intimated that she was bad about taking notes and I capitulated, "Well occasionally she's a little petulant, but not a big deal."

At the note session after the show, Michael started to pick a fight with Gina (apparently this was very old news between them), and she became very defensive. Michael then said to Gina, *in front of the whole company,* "You are very difficult. Isn't that right, Larry?" I hemmed and hawed, and he said again in a louder voice, *"Isn't that right, Larry?"*

Out of fear, I hesitatingly said, "I guess so." With that, he fired her from the show on the spot, saying that tonight was her last performance. She left the room humiliated.

I went to her and said I didn't know what to say. She brushed it off and said it had been coming for a long time between her and Michael. I can say here and now, and I said it then and there, that it was a horrible moment and unfair to both of us. Apparently, this was the 'bad" side of Michael Bennett. Gina was and is a great performer and didn't deserve that fate. It almost seemed that Michael had come to DC to dismiss her. Her replacements, who were always solid, were never as great as she was in the role. This certainly made me very fearful and mistrustful of Michael.

I was very ambitious, had been with the show about nine or ten months, and really wanted to move on. After our next two stops of Philly and Boston, the tour was going to become a real tour, playing a lot of smaller cities with constant moves. I had to rehearse the new orchestra in each town, so it was always starting from scratch and very difficult and frustrating till the orchestras got the hang of it. The DC orchestra had been particularly trying. There were some very good players, but some difficult personalities in the percussion section dealing with some alcohol issues.

I told Michael that I wanted a Broadway show. He said, "Stick with me and I'll give you one."

I said, "When?"

He said, "Hang around."

Sue McNair (his right-hand businessperson) added, "We really need you to rehearse the orchestras; you are so good at it and so good for the show."

I said, "I'm so physically tired of that." That was pretty arrogant coming from a very lucky twenty-five-year-old. "How about giving me the Chicago company," which was a sit-down, Chicago-based *A Chorus Line.* It was the company that had played LA and then moved to Chicago forever. The conductor was Tom Hancock, who really had few credentials and had lucked out. He was the assistant and had moved up. I said, "Why don't you switch Tom and me, and give me Chicago as a gift, and let him train all the orchestras?"

Michael re-iterated, "Stick with me and I will give you a Broadway show."

I thought about it, and I knew Michael was telling the truth; however, I was very impatient. I made the decision to leave the tour after the Philly and Boston runs. Michael offered me a lot of money to stay, but young arrogant/ambitious fellow that I was, I said, "Nah."

After I left the show in February of '78, right after the giant snowstorm in Boston that practically shut down both *A Chorus Line* and *On the Twentieth Century*, which was trying out at the Colonial … Michael asked me to step into the international company for a few performances, when my replacement Sherman Frank had to rehearse the band in the next town. Then, he asked me to fill in for Tom Hancock with the Chicago company. I hit it off with Tony Teague and Wanda Richert, who were doing Zach/Cassie, and was asked back a few months later to fill in again. At this time, I was asked by Sue McNair if I would stay on, and they would move Tom somewhere else. This was too little and too late for me, so I said I really wanted to get a Broadway show and wanted to try my luck hunting for work in New York.

While it was arrogant and perhaps a little stupid on my part, there were a lot of shows and I was an established and known conductor with some real credits behind me. I was now twenty-six years old, and as far as I was concerned, there was nowhere to go but up. I think Michael thought I was an arrogant little shit, but he was ambitious too and had some respect for me. It didn't necessarily translate into more work, but I did have respect.

During the course of the *A Chorus Line* tour, a musical called *Shine it On,* later called *The Act,* tried out in San Francisco at the same time. Mathilde Pincus, the copyist, rang me up and asked if I had any experience copying music. I had a little from earlier times doing shows in stock, but not really. They were shorthanded and asked if I would help out. They handed me a pen and some scores, and I copied the woodwind parts for a song called *"City Lights."* Ralph Burns was the orchestrator and Stan Lebowsky, the conductor. Stan remembered me from my debut playing the piano at the gypsy rehearsal of *Applause.* Ralph took notice of me. Both were very kind to me, and it all came back to me in good will later on.

Back to New York. I was fishing around for employment, and I stopped by to see Don Pippin at the Shubert. Don said, "Don't worry, something will come along." My old friend, music contractor Mel Rodnan rang me up and said, "Gene Wolsk and Manny Azenberg are producing a show called *Let's Dance,* or rather doing a little workshop, based on Gene Kelly's and Cole Porter's *Les Girls.* It will be Michael Davis (the tenor from "Springtime for Hitler"), Janie Sell, Trish Garland, and Carolyn Kirsch." I was thrilled at the chance to work with all of them.

The director really was clueless and inexperienced. He kept giving me Steve and Eydie medleys from recordings, that he wanted to recreate for the show. I argued that they were Steve and Eydie medleys, and we should do our own versions of the Porter tunes. I suggested that if he wanted to do those medleys, he didn't need our cast or me, and should just play the recordings. Mel Rodnan, Gene, and Manny came to a run-through and agreed that the work I had done with the group was excellent. They also agreed that the director's ideas weren't so hot, and that was the end of *Let's Dance*. But they immediately hired me to do a workshop of *Sarava*, a new musical by Mitch Leigh and N. Richard Nash. Mitch was the composer of *Man of La Mancha* plus a few bad flops. N. Richard Nash (the N was for Nathan) was the playwright for *The Rainmaker*, among others, including *110 in the Shade* and *Wildcat*. He had also written the lyrics for *Sarava*, which weren't bad.

Mitch hired Lonette McKee and PJ Benjamin to do the leads, and some very good supporting people and excellent singers and dancers. I hired Larry Hochman as my associate, and Michael Keller to play drums. We brought in Montego Joe to play congas and other Latin stuff during the run-throughs. One day, Mitch came in with one of those little single stave music pads you get when you are studying music as a child. On it were written about twelve notes. He handed the pad and a lyric sheet to me and Hochman and said, "Set this."

Larry Hochman. who was a little younger than I asked, "What does he mean by 'set this'?"

I said, "Larry, he means we are to write it."

While Larry and I were writing a song called "Muito Bom," Mitch fired Lonette McKee and hired Donna Cyrus. They were both very talented girls, the only difference being Donna was a bit more full-figured than Lonette. Both sang the songs very well, and it was a sideways move in any case. They were both great and lovely people. When we two Larry's presented Mitch's song, he said, "That's not what I wrote." He changed two eighth notes and said, "There."

Whoever had really written the themes for *Sarava,* some of it wasn't too bad. There were a few catchy tunes. However, I want to say here and now that the ending of *Sarava,* with the singer shouting "Sarava!", which was played on endless TV commercials and became a joke in New York theatre, was my creation. Maybe Larry and I did it together.

One day, Mitch said to me, "Please wear a jacket tomorrow, I want to take you to lunch."

Next day, I came to rehearsals at the studios above Phil Gluckstern's deli on 48th Street in a jacket and tie. At lunchtime, we strolled past Sardi's and Mitch said, "That's crap." We went past Barrymore's (a favorite hangout), and he said, "Ersatz 21."

I said, "How about Joe Allen's?"

He said, "Crap."

We ended up at 49th and Eighth. He took me to Mr. Custard, and I had a black and white. That was my lunch with Mitch Leigh. He'd also told me he was going to take me to the south of France. When I finally did make it to the south of France, many years later … there wasn't one soft ice cream place to be found.

Later, Mitch did hire me and Larry Hochman to do a film that he was producing, called *Once in Paris.* It starred Wayne Rogers and Gayle Hunnicutt, and was written by Frank D Gilroy, who had written *The Subject was Roses.* Mitch gave me and Larry the main theme from his flop musical *Home Sweet Homer,* to use as the main title, which sounded like variations on "Here's that Rainy Day." He said to orchestrate it for harmonica, saxophone, and two keyboards (one a piano and the other a harpsichord), and to use an Alberti bass. Alberti bass is a broken arpeggio based on the chords to form a repeated bass line.

We two Larry's played our two keyboards using Alberti bass figures and generally hamming it up, while Michael Chimes played harmonica and Leon Cohen played saxophone. We played this mashup-theme in many keys and many different ways … while Mitch conducted in a jumpsuit, pausing to inhale on his baton/Cuban cigar on the upbeats. It reminded me of Reginald Van Gleason … "And away we go." I found a copy of the video of *Once in Paris,* and there is not much to say about it.

When we finished the workshop of *Sarava,* there were rumors of it going to Broadway. The director would be Rick Atwell, who was very talented and should have had a bigger career. Mitch offered me the conductor's job on the Broadway *Sarava,* which was going into rehearsals shortly. He told me there was no negotiation—that I would be paid minimum wage for conductors on Broadway and indicated that I should be grateful to have a Broadway show composed by his own special self. The thought of spending any more time with him was something I was hoping to avoid. Then, the fickle finger of fate stepped in!

During this period, I had kept in touch with my benefactor, Don Pippin, while continuing my conducting studies with Rudi Bennett, as well as piano with Les Harnley. These gents were still very much in my life. Don was doing the vocals for *The Grand Tour* and for *A Broadway Musical* by Charles Strouse, both at the same time. He needed a little help and had me "ghost" three vocal arrangements on *The Grand Tour.* I was happy to do it. *The Grand Tour* was a Jerry Herman musical.

I did the vocals and sent them in with Don's name on them. It amused me at the time, how canny Don was. The numbers he had me "ghost" were the numbers that ended up cut from the show. One of them did turn up later in Jerry Herman's *Miss Spectacular,* which allowed me a second shot at it.

One night I stopped by the Shubert to see Don, who was still conducting *A Chorus Line.* At the end of the show he said, "Marvin Hamlisch has written a new show with Neil Simon and Carole Bayer Sager and has asked me to do it. I don't want to leave a hit show like *A Chorus Line* for anything as flimsy as this, would you like to do it?"

I said, "Sure."

He picked up the phone in his dressing room, called Marvin and said, "Marvin, remember the kid who conducted the international company of *A Chorus Line?* I think he'd be the perfect conductor for *They're Playing Our Song.*"

"Ok, ok!" Don said, as he hung up the phone. "Go to Marvin's apartment at 970 Park Avenue tomorrow at noon."

The next day, I headed over to Park Avenue and announced myself to the doorman. Marvin Hamlisch was a giant and sudden superstar, having won two Oscars for *The Way We Were* and *The Sting,* all the awards for *A Chorus Line,* and being on TV on every talk show all the time. He was quite the celebrity and, although we had spoken once briefly on the phone, we had never met. He opened the door in his robe and said, "If Don says you are good, you got the job." He handed me the demo and a cup of tea, and then sent me on my way.

I picked up the pay phone on the corner of Park and 84th, called my mother and said, "I'm conducting a new Broadway musical written by Neil Simon and Marvin Hamlisch." I had gone from a kid conducting summer stock and getting a few lucky breaks to having a new Broadway musical written by giant names. I was one happy camper.

When I got home, I put on the "cassette," which contained the songs "*Fallin',*" "*If He Really Knew Me,*" "*They're Playing Our Song,*" and one other song called "*One Foot Blues,*" which didn't make it and became "*Fill in the Words.*" Rhoda and I listened to the demo, and after I heard the title song, I knew I had a hit Broadway show on my hands, and they'd have to work really hard to screw this one up.

I had the distinct pleasure of telling Mitch Leigh that I wasn't available for his show *Sarava*. In fact, I had my agent at the time, Yvette Schumer, make the call. Don Pippin had given me a tremendous gift.

Bob Moore was the director. He was a big star as Broadway directors go, with *Promises, Promises* on his plate. He was a lovely man with his partner and assistant. George Rondo. Pat Birch was the choreographer and loved having talented men around her. She was great fun and both affectionate and supportive at the same time. She was a big supporter of orchestrator Michael Gibson and of me too. It was so nice to have her as an ally. Fran Liebergall, Marvin Hamlisch's right arm, was my assistant. We were a month apart in age and were friends from *A Chorus Line*,

Franny was the music guru for all companies. I hired my pal Michael Keller as the drummer and he advised me to find some local musicians in LA. Ralph Burns was hired as lead orchestrator for Marvin, along with Dick Hazard and Gene Page to do the disco writing. Buster Davis, the great vocal arranger, was hired to advise and do any additional vocals. He was Marvin's mentor and was around to advise and help. He was mostly retired. But it was good to get to know him. Neil Simon was totally in charge, both financially and artistically. Manny Azenberg was the producer. He was Neil's business partner and his muscle. Nothing would happen without Neil's approval.

Rehearsal began straightaway. Lucie Arnaz and I got along as our birthdays were two days apart and a year. Robert Klein was funny and charming and always very warm and agreeable. The alter egos (chorus) were nice kids and happy to be there. They had been chosen by Pat Birch. One of the boys, Wayne Mattson, was a friend from an earlier tour of *Promises,* and I was happy to see him. Ralph Burns was very happy to see me from our earlier meeting on *Shine it On,* and allied himself with me as the MD of the production. I knew I had good mentoring between him and Pat Birch. They were my allies and guardians. Bob Moore took no shit from anyone, and I was happy following his guidance. Marvin Hamlisch and Carole Bayer Sager treated me with the deference they had bestowed on me.

It was clearly Marvin and Carole on one side, with Neil Simon on the other. I was going to learn very quickly not to be on the firing line between the factions. And there were definitely two separate factions. However, Neil held all the cards.

Marvin was at that time, the fair-haired boy of stage and screen. With his Academy Awards, Tonys, and Pulitzer Prize, he was a popular and known guy. Carole was an up-and-coming songwriter on the scene. They were both a few years older than me and treated me like a gifted younger brother. Neil, of course, was the uber successful playwright of the Western world with enormous success from his comedies and film scripts. He was known to all.

Marvin had a terrible habit of saluting Neil, as if he were the leader of the Third Reich, and it was a bit ugly. There was no apparent reason for any of this, except that Neil being the script writer, as well as the de facto producer with Manny Azenberg, decided that made him the king. In fact, he really wanted this show to be a straight play without music and I feared that we were in real danger of that happening. Pat Birch warned me that there were actual discussions to that effect. She was working very hard to come up with ideas for production numbers so that it was clearly a musical.

The first thirty-five minutes of the show were pretty golden except for some long-winded (but very funny) scenes. The show opened with the song "Fallin'" after a short scene of explanation. Then came the very good production number, "Workin' It Out", followed by and then Marvin and Carole's song, "If He/She Really Knew Me," which was autobiographical. Once we got through the title song of the show in a discotheque, referring to the real-life situation of Marvin (and Carole) sitting in a restaurant or on an airplane where the Muzak would be playing one of their songs, they would happily acknowledge, "I wrote that" with the very funny and catchy "*Oh Ho, They're Playing My Song*".

Neil's very funny script was a huge plus along with Robert Klein's perfect timing. Lucie was no slouch either, having grown up with Lucy and Desi. The show was a very entertaining audience pleaser. The only real problem was after the "Playing Our Song" numbers, the show just was treading water with the up and downs of a loosely based version of Marvin and Carole's relationship with the audience knowing full well that it would work out at the end.

Neil had lost his beloved wife, Joan a few years before and was now married to actress Marsha Mason. Neil's work at the time (at least from my perception) was about the struggles of relationship and this was reflected in *Song* and his play *Chapter Two*. He was a nice man and unfortunately, he made the audience suffer along with him, albeit with a lot of very funny jokes and perceptions along the way. His plays and movies at the time were similar in this feel. The only real issues we had on *Song* were Marvin and Carole coming up with a decent song to end Act One, when the two characters are having their first planned tryst in Quogue out on Long Island.

The plot was clearly the lonely composer looking for a lasting relationship and the sexy young lyricist (Lucie) trying to break up a long-term bad relationship and begin this relationship with lonely composer. It wasn't hard to miss the resemblance to a neurotic but talented composer and a hippy/dippy neurotic lyricist, and not too much tension in the plot.

In the second act they break up because they are both clearly neurotic, and then come back together surrounded by a hilarious script. There were six alter egos, three for each of them and that was our chorus/ensemble. Pat Birch was looking for ways to amuse and ultimately, Marvin came up with the idea of a toy piano. When the leading man (Robert Klein) ends up hospitalized with a broken leg after having been hit by a car, leading lady Lucie comes to visit him, with the alter egos playing the toy pianos. Marvin and Carole came up with a delightful ditty called "Fill In The Words." The words never said in the song are, of course, "I love you."

The kids played the toy pianos along with Robert Klein. It was written in a pop quasi-baroque style. Marvin, being the excellent composer and dance arranger, came up with the fills and if my memory serves virtually staged the number himself for Pat, who just cleaned it up. I might be exaggerating a bit, but only a bit. It was a very successful moment in the second act and it helped get us to the end of the show and not a moment too soon.

There was a song and scene in the recording studio, which Neil refused to trim. All of his angst was in the scene and when the song finally came, called, "I Still Believe in Love," it was a huge relief.

In my presence much later, John (Johnny) Green, the famed songwriter and MD from MGM's glory days, sat with me and Marvin and said, "Marvin ... why couldn't you write a decent hit song for that spot in the studio?" Marvin and Carole tried and tried. There were several versions of "I Still Believe In Love," or "I Still Believe In Lovin'," or "Break It To Me Gently" with different lyrics and every night for a week we changed the song.

One night they put in half of one and half of the other. Lucie looked at me in the pit for help with a lyric. She (so very diligent and a real pro) couldn't remember which one we were singing. When I finally threw the lyric to her from the pit verbally, she was still confused because we couldn't remember which version. She still finished with huge applause. We finally went back to the original.

At great expense to the show, Marvin was calling orchestra rehearsals for the slightest musical changes. They were things I could change with a fifteen-minute talk down in the band room before the show with the orchestra. Two bar fixes and he would call a half hour orchestra call, which cost a lot of dough. So, one day, Manny approached me and said, "Please cancel tonight's orchestra rehearsal." I agreed because it was just a few bars.

When I showed up dressed for that evening's performance, Manny grabbed me by the lapels and started shaking me violently. As I was being jostled, I said, "Manny, Manny what did I do?"

He said, "I told you to cancel the rehearsal!"

"I did, Manny, I did!"

"I know you did."

"Why are you shaking me?"

"Marvin rescheduled it and he's not here!" He had let his frustration out on me, and we both had a huge laugh.

"*Fill In The Words*," the new song for the hospital scene in Act Two, had to be presented to the powers-that-be, to see if it was worthy of inclusion. I went over to Marvin and Carole's rented home in Stone Canyon in Beverly Hills/Hollywood. Marvin sang the song for me, to my enthusiastic approval. He told me that I was to present it to Neil, Manny, Bob Moore, and Pat Birch, because at that time, he wasn't speaking to "Herr" Simon, as he put it. I begged him to appear, and he said, "*No,* it's your gig, babe."

I showed up at the Ahmanson and was taken to a small dressing room where an electric keyboard was set up. (This was 1978, so an electric keyboard was a big mutha, and likely a Fender Rhodes). I sat down and dutifully sang and played "Fill In The Words." Not being a song writer , nor much of a singer, it was a pitiful performance, on reflection. Everyone was stone-faced except Bob and Pat, who were hoping for some enthusiasm from Neil, so we could get to work. Neil, absolutely stone-faced, turned to me and said, "Is it any good? I don't know the difference from one song from another."

I said, "I think it's great."

Neil shrugged and said, "Put it in the show."

Clearly Don Pippin's remark about my career was in full force. "It's good to know who to blame." In this case, my career rested on the success of "Fill In The Words" in the show. Fortunately, it ended up being one of the highlights.

The Ahmanson Theatre was part of the Music Center complex. There was the Dorothy Chandler where the Academy Awards were presented and the Ahmanson where new shows would try out. In the middle was the Mark Taper Forum where smaller plays would try out. The orchestra contractor for the complex was a holdover from

Ed Lester's great days running the Los Angeles Civic Light Opera. His name was Louis Adrian.

Louis Adrian had been the conductor of the original Broadway productions of *Peter Pan* and *Kismet* and many other shows in LA. He had also done the Mary Martin/John Raitt *Annie Get Your Gun*. He was a known name and had started out in Vaudeville in Chicago. At this point he was around ninety and was an autocratic leader of the personnel at the Music Center. Manny insisted that Louis play in the band. He was a violinist. He did play and assembled an orchestra that was full of his buddies. I had Fran Liebergall on piano and my pal, Michael Keller on drums. Ralph Burns suggested some reed players and we had a very great sounding bunch of blowers, a strong concertmaster and rhythm section and the rest of the string section from the original production of *Desert Song* from 1926. I'm exaggerating. but only a little.

Lou Adrian was, of course, very experienced, and aside from being too loud vocally when it was time for a break, was very supportive. He gave me one piece of advice about a spot I was having a little trouble with. He said, "Forget about the music, just look at the band, lift your hands and say, "Boys, play," and bring your hands down.

He was right and it solved the problem. I've never forgotten that. Considering he had conducted most of the Broadway run of *Kismet,* with Alfred Drake, he knew what he was talking about, and I appreciate his advice to this day. I had learned early on when someone as experienced as a Louis Adrian speaks, it's best to take it on board. The experience of gents like Lou, Rudi, Les, Don Pippin, Ralph Burns was never wasted on me.

We made the cast recording in LA, at Marvin and Carole's insistence using a film contractor and different players. I insisted on Keller, Fran, and the rest of the players I had personally chosen. Not using the pit players caused me great grief with the band at the Ahmanson. That ultimately subsided when they realized it wasn't my doing. It caused a lot of grief with Michael Keller because Carole wanted a recording drummer. Michael was "our" drummer. We split the difference with Michael playing the production numbers and Carole's drummer playing the ballads. It was not a pleasant solution. I took the heat.

I was twenty-six years old and very happy with my place in the scheme of things. Things had progressed as I had really planned. I felt very confident in my skills and had worked very hard to get there. In my spare time, I studied music constantly. I continued to listen to all sorts of music, was conducting an orchestra daily and was surrounded by the best people in the business. I felt very fortunate. I was never over-confident, but I did feel that I had earned my place. I had a lot of confidence in front of the orchestra and enjoyed working with all of the various personalities. I don't know if I behaved in the best way, but I was learning as I went.

I was fortunate that enough people cared about me and would guide me along. Choreographer Pat Birch was always free with advice and advised me to sit tight around people like Neil Simon and Manny Azenberg. She reminded me that they were friends, but they were also, ultimately, employers. These were important life lessons. I was learning to keep my mouth shut, at least, sometimes.

At one performance before the recording happened, I was standing in the pit, waiting for the lights to dim to begin the show when Marvin came running down to the pit. Marvin was six-foot two and very recognizable. He said, "Hey Babe, [he called everyone Babe] give me your score." He grabbed my entire score and ran up the aisle as the lights dimmed, and the spotlight hit me for the overture. Fran Liebergall looked up at me from the piano totally bewildered. Truthfully, I wasn't too shaken, because I could visualize the pages as the music happened and I could call out measure numbers if necessary. While that might sound boastful, I actually didn't know I had that ability until that moment. The score for *Song* was not all that complicated.

At the intermission, Marvin brought back the score with a "Sorry Babe," clearly not even realizing the implications of having taken the score. Apparently, he'd needed it for a meeting with the record producer during the first act. Marvin and Carole were both heavily ensconced in the recording scene in LA.

The orchestra tracks were recorded, and the vocals were done on a separate day, tracking the recording. That's very common now, but back then cast recordings were usually done simultaneously. I was asked to be at the tracking sessions. One day, Eydie Gorme came in with her two little boys. There were a few high notes at the end of "When You're In My Arms". Marvin had asked Eydie to pop the notes in on Lucie's behalf, literally at the end of the reprise. We had also forgotten to record the cast playing the toy keyboards on the bows, so I sat on the floor with a keyboard under each hand and played the notes. Yes, that's me on the cast recording, plunkin' it out. Eydie and her kids had a big laugh out of that.

I was never thrilled with the cast recording because the tempi were all slowed down. The show was quite short. I didn't have either the pit band from LA or my very wonderful pit band in New York. As much as I loved Richard Hurwitz on lead trumpet, Dick Perry was my lead trumpet in New York. Dick was the famed lead trumpet from the shows *Gypsy* and *Funny Girl* and many others. He had a distinctive style and sound and was hired at Marvin's insistence. I was happy to have him. The orchestra contractor in New York was a man named Earl Shendell. Earl had been a barely adequate woodwind player who'd ended up at the union. He got in some trouble at the union but became the producers' favorite orchestra contractor, because he knew where all the bodies were buried. There were a lot of questionable practices going on—stuff that I really didn't want to know about, though I found out more than I bargained for. This was a part of Broadway and the New York theatre that I didn't need to know.

Unfortunately, Earl argued about orchestra personnel, preferring to use his favorites and not necessarily the players I wanted to use. Because I was young, his argument was that I didn't know who the good players were, while in fact, I had been researching this all my young life. It wasn't that I wanted my young buddies. I wanted the old timers, just not the same old timers he had in mind. Manny Azenberg acted as Solomon, and we got a half and half band. I got several of my choices and Earl got some of his.

This kind of stuff ultimately led to my decision to move west to Los Angeles. It wasn't much different, but it was sunny and warm. Los Angeles had a much bigger market outside of the theatres. Films and TV were a much larger pie. On *Playing Our Song*, I argued bitterly to use Red Press on my first reed chair, but Red was in direct competition with Earl, so it didn't happen.

Red passed recently at the age of 98. He was working as a full-time contractor for Broadway orchestras to the end. I ended up with Hank Freeman on the first reed chair. Hank was one of the great players from the big-band days and had been Hal Hastings' first call for so many shows including *Company* and all of his earlier shows. However, Hank was extremely problematic personality-wise. Ultimately Earl had to move him to another show or risk his being brought up on charges at the union for assaulting one of the other reed players during the show. This was all part of the job of being an MD on Broadway. It was an unruly group at times, but there were great characters and players in the New York pits.

Playing Our Song was a huge hit. I was now conducting Broadway's newest success. Richard Rodgers, the very same "Dick" who had told me that my tempi were *too fucking fast,* was sitting directly behind me at the opening night in New York. At the end of the show when I took my bow, he tapped the rail with his cane, looked up at me, and said "Good boy." I was very flattered and years later when I passed on both of the stories to his daughter Mary, she said, "That's my daddy."

Opening night, I attended the party with Rhoda and double-dated with Lucie Arnaz and her date for the evening, Michael Bennett. Michael toasted me and Lucie since he had started us both off, me with *A Chorus Line* and Lucie with the tour of *Seesaw.*

The show received three Tony nominations: Bob Moore (Director), Robert Klein (Lead Actor), and Best Musical. We did the "Playing Our Song" number on the Tonys. It's all pre-recorded but I had to get in the pit and mime conducting while the number was on stage. We had pre-recorded it a few days before with Elliot Lawrence's wonderful Tony orchestra, but I had to get in the pit and mime conducting while the number was on stage. Most of the band was sitting in their chairs reading The *New York Times.* The number was very well done and had an enthusiastic response. However, we all knew we'd lose the Tony Award to *Sweeney Todd.*

After I conducted the number, I come out of the pit and Jack Lemmon was standing there smoking a cigar. (He was starring in a play that season.) We had a nice friendly chat, about what I don't remember. I walked into one of the chorus rooms in the basement of the Shubert, which is the green room where everyone was waiting. I was watching the TV monitor where the host, Henry Fonda, was introducing the next bit of business. I was standing there in my tuxedo, relieved that my work was done. A women slid up, wrapped her arm around my back, and put her head on my shoulder. I didn't look, thinking it was probably Lucie or one of the other women from the show. As we were watching the monitor, she said, "Dad really looks great, doesn't he?" I realized I had Jane Fonda on my arm and shoulder. She smiled at me and moved on. Show biz is a very collegial business.

Playing Our Song put me on the map professionally and I was the hot new guy. Everyone came to see me and say hello and other composers would talk to me as if we had been friends for years. I went to a party at Marvin's and sat at the piano with Jule Styne. Carly Simon was sitting on the sofa. I attended recording sessions for Johnny Mathis TV specials with Marvin.

Marvin rang me in New York and said, "Tell Fran she's conducting, get on the very next plane to LA, and bring a tuxedo. Tell me what flight, there'll be a car waiting."

I showed up in LA and a driver approached me and took me to the Dorothy Chandler Pavillion at the Music Center. I was on the stage with a huge orchestra. Marvin said, "Put your bag down and conduct."

I got on the stand and the first horn stood up and said, "Hey Larry." It was Bill Lane, who had been my first horn in Buffalo, New York doing *Man Of La Mancha* five years earlier. He had become first horn with the LA Phil. I now knew the orchestra was the LA Phil.

There was *no music* on the stand, and I said, "Marvin????"

He said, "It's in four."

So, not knowing what I was about to conduct, nor having a clue as to any part of it, I brought my hands down and it was "Nobody Does it Better." It was a rehearsal for a TV special featuring Marvin. Though I had *no* idea what I was going to conduct, at least it would be familiar Marvin material.

A few days later we taped the special for posterity … with Johnny Mathis singing, me conducting, Marvin conducting the *A Chorus Line* overture with me at the piano, and me playing "Nothing" for Priscilla Lopez and "What I Did For Love" for Mathis. Trial by fire! Liza and Carly did songs at the piano with Marvin … and it was me conducting Marvin's act. The show is still out there … somewhere.

During the early days of the run of *Playing Our Song* I was invited to dinner by the lead trumpet player, Dick Perry. Dick was oh so famous for being the lead trumpet on the fabled *Gypsy* recording. He was of legendary stature in trumpet playing and in the New York theatre. I was very flattered that he invited me out. During dinner, he said, "Merm came to the show last week and was *very* impressed with your conducting and your manner with the orchestra. I'm very good friends with Ethel and we spoke of you, and I spoke highly of your abilities on the podium. She is very interested in meeting with you and talking to you about conducting her act. She is planning to do a tour."

I said, "… Ethel Merman wants to meet me … I can't believe it."

He then added, "There is a catch to this … she expects whoever travels with her to be her escort as she likes to have companionship and someone to escort her."

The bluntness of his words made me wary. At this point, I became Jackie Gleason, as Ralph Kramden, "Hummana hummana hummana hummana." I respectfully passed and Pete Matz ended up doing the job. But I was very flattered that Ethel Merman wanted me to conduct for her.

Dick was a wonderful guy and a great player. Later during the run, he told me he'd been offered *Sugar Babies*. I wrote a note to him saying, "Who would want to see a musical with Mickey Rooney and Ann Miller?" I ate my words when *Sugar Babies* became a huge success. Dick saved the note and put it on the stand when we did a recording session for the musical *Colette*.

Sometime later, I took over as MD on *Sugar Babies* from the late Glen Roven. Later on, the show occupied a lot more of my time.

With the success of *Playing Our Song* there were a lot of perks. I conducted a VIP night on Broadway at the Shubert Theatre directed by Pat Birch and hosted by Marlo Thomas and did another gala in Washington, DC with Tony Randall, Phyllis Newman, Kitty Carlisle, and Paul Sorvino. I was getting to work with a lot of different celebrities and becoming known.

Marvin started booking me for concerts with him. This had originally been Don Pippin's job, but Don didn't seem to mind, and he was busy with other things. My first symphony job with Marvin was with the Louisville Orchestra. He would be doing a program of all the music he had written for films. It was a lot of music and all new to me. I had faced some large orchestras, but it was in a studio and not in a pops concert. I brought Michael Keller to play drums and we both took leave of *Playing Our Song*. Marvin played piano and I conducted almost everything. The only thing he conducted was the *A Chorus Line* Overture. *A Chorus Line* didn't have an overture, but it did now, constructed by Marvin, orchestrated by Ralph Burns. It was basically the whole show—all the songs without the interstitial stuff. It was very well done thrilling for the audience and well done.

I played piano on the pianistic parts like "Nothing" and the other little bits. I was intimidated because Marvin always had an enormous Bosendorfer piano on hand. It looked like a tiger with eighty-eight teeth, except the Bosendorfer had an extra octave. It was a serious bunch of teeth looking at me. I was often confused as to where I put my hands. I only muffed that once, going to the wrong octave. I watched Marvin's shoulders move uncontrollably with laughter.

He would often bring some very fine singers along: Karin Wolfe, Cynthia Onrubia, Gillian Scalici, Kay Cole, and finally Valerie Lemon, who became his regular as she was almost always available. One time he brought Anita Darian. Anita was one of the greatest mezzos around. Really delightful to work with her. She would sing some semi-classical piece Marvin had written for Juilliard. He thought it made him seem more serious. One time we did a concert with Kitty Carlisle and her accompanist Joe Moon. Gene Shalit from *NBC News* hosted one event.

One of the most notable occasions was at Boston Symphony Hall with Dionne Warwick and Frank Sinatra. Sinatra put his arm around me and said something unflattering about Marvin. "Why doesn't he just put on a dress and get it over with?" Marvin was doing a vocal check and really sounded like Kermit the frog to be honest.

I did get to watch Sinatra perform "One for My Baby," which was thrilling. I did another show with Milton Berle and Mickey Katz and yet another with Liza Minnelli, Ann Margaret, Johnny Mathis, and, Crystal Gayle.

It was really a treat to travel around as Marvin's conductor. I had worked hard on my technique, and I think that orchestras were surprised that a "Broadway" conductor could do a bit more than just beat time and get through it. With experience and a varied repertoire, I developed more and more technique and really had to pull it together and study a few pieces as we went. At some of the orchestras I would be asked to do something before Marvin's show, and it might be a light classic, usually some Tchaikovsky. It really prepared me for everything I'd be doing.

Back in New York City, there was talk of a strike of the Local 802 musicians on Broadway. They were complaining about not being able to take off and send substitutes in. One contractor, John Monaco, was quite difficult about it and the musicians were griping. The rules were strict, but John was particularly over the top about it. A meeting was called by Gerry Schoenfeld, who ran the Shubert Organization, which controlled most of the theatres in New York City

Gerry basically told me, Don Pippin, Paul Gemignani, Stanley Lebowsky, and all the conductors on Broadway that to avert a strike he was giving the musicians the right to take off fifty percent of the time. I complained openly at the meeting that it was relinquishing control of the quality in the pits and furthermore, since we conductors were members of the local, we too could take off fifty percent of the time. Therefore, we would be able to miss a couple of shows and take more lucrative concert gigs. Up to this time, it had been virtually impossible to miss a show as conductor unless there was some terrible disaster in your family like a death ... or if you were observing a performance with the assistant conducting. Gerry said, "That was not my intention," but all of us said, "Too bad."

That was the beginning of the end of maintaining the quality in the pits and of the ultimate deterioration of the house minimums (number of musicians required). Truthfully, that's what Gerry wanted, and he admitted that he would prefer recordings and *no* musicians. I complained that he hadn't first talked to his own musical directors about any of this and that it was a breach of trust and etiquette. His attitude ultimately led to my decision to leave New York City for good, and to move to California for more lucrative work in films and television. Between the desire of the Shubert's to eliminate live music and the graft that I uncovered, with cash exchanging hands for instrument rentals and that sort of stuff, I was running out of steam, and I had only just begun.

Robert Sher, record producer, called and said that he wanted to resurrect an old Wright and Forrest show called *At The Grand* (this ultimately did make it to Broadway with additional songs by Maury Yeston and Tommy Tune at the helm). *At The Grand* was a show created for Ed Lester for the Civic Light Opera in LA and San Francisco. It had starred Paul Muni and Joan Diener. It had some wonderful songs and was a huge production, but then nothing. Robert wanted me to do new orchestrations or at least be the MD and have several people do the orchestrations for a new recording. Because of *Playing Our Song*, I was the new up and coming MD on Broadway. Bob Wright and George (Chet) Forrest had written or adapted from classical composers many great shows with *Song of Norway* and *Kismet* among them. They were two lovely gents, who had been together since high school. When he was doing *Grand Hotel,* Jack Lee lovingly called them, "The Borodins." Borodin had written the music on which *Kismet* had been based.

Bob and Chet agreed to come visit me at my apartment on 86th St. The apartment had a sunken living room and was high up on the nineteenth-floor, and I was very proud of it. It was a nice place to visit. I was prepared to serve them martinis and wine and canapes. They showed up, the doorman announced them, and they came up, appearing at my door dressed to the nines with suits, vests, very expensive oxfords (saddle shoes) and ready to dine at the Plaza after they left me. They were very old-world gents.

My dog Schroeder was a beautiful boxer/shepherd cross with shepherd coloring, floppy ears, and a tail that could clear a roast off the table. He was gorgeous, friendly, and a well-trained dog. But he came over to the greet "the boys" at the door, sniffed Bob Wright's shoes, lifted his leg, and peed all over them. I was in shock. The boys were laughing. I was happy they were amused.

I ran off to get paper towels and was on my knees wiping off Bob's shoes, horribly embarrassed and shocked at my usually well-behaved and housebroken dog. The boys were laughing hysterically, and said don't be embarrassed and told the story of their Samoyed (a big white fluffy dog) that went with them to someone's home. Their dog took a dump in the center of the white plush carpet without so much as a fart. They were ok with what Schroeder had done, since it was only on the shoes and not the leg/trousers, etc. We settled down and had a couple of cocktails, chatting amiably and discussing the possibilities of the recording. Then Chet announced that they had to leave for the Plaza. Could we go downstairs and get them a cab?

They both suggested that I take Schroeder for a stroll and bring him downstairs with us. We did all the formalities and headed for the elevator and down. I hailed a cab, and we were saying our goodbyes. Then Schroeder came over to say his goodbyes, took a sniff, and peed again all over Bob's shoes as they jumped into the taxi, laughing (I think). Then they drove off to the Plaza and I was left on the street holding the dog. For some reason, discussion of the recording didn't happen again.

Four years later, I was conducting *Sugar Babies* at the Jackie Gleason Theatre in Miami Beach. I was told that someone was waiting for me at the stage door. I went outside and there was Bob Wright (sans Chet, who was in hospital). As he walked up to greet me, he was clearly looking around to see if Shroeder was following me and laughing all the way. He did ask, "Where's the dog?"

They were such lovely gentlemen. I was so delighted when *Grand Hotel* finally happened even with added songs. The best song, "We'll Take a Glass Together" was pure Wright and Forrest.

One of my guilty pleasures was a poker game at Hal Hackady's every week. Hal had a fantastic duplex at 3 E 75th street. The regulars were me, Hal, David Guc, an agent, and his girlfriend Kathleen. We played high/low poker, and it was great fun. David's girlfriend was in *Gemini* and was a pretty young actress. We played at their apartment a couple of times as well. All of a sudden Kathleen was no longer at the game and David said she'd gotten a movie. The movie was called *Body Heat*. Kathleen stopped coming to the games. Kathleen was Kathleen Turner

During the run of *Playing Our Song*. another opportunity arose. Rudi Bennett re-introduced me to one of his oldest friends, Rene Wiegert. Rudi and Rene went all the way back to industrial shows and the show *A Joyful Noise* in stock and on Broadway. Rene had also been present at my piano performance at the gypsy run-through of *Applause,* so a long history.

Rene was MD for *Evita*, which was the most recent of Andrew Lloyd Webber's and Hal Prince's successes. He asked if I wanted to be the MD for the planned open-ended run at the Shubert in LA. I was looking forward to the opportunity of working with Hal Prince again. After all of his successes with Sondheim and my own experience with *A Little Night Music* it seemed like a wonderful idea. The thought of moving to LA and checking out the scene there was very appealing. The idea of sunshine, no winter, and all the other perks also seemed a very good idea. I gave my notice to *Playing Our Song,* which seemed to shock everyone as it was such a success. Leaving Broadway for LA seemed strange to a lot of people—it had only been one year since rehearsals began for *Song,* but this new opportunity seemed like a dream come true. Paul Gemignani was the de facto MD for the Prince office, so he phoned and made it official.

Rene met me at Mathilda Pincus' Chelsea Music Office at 1841 Broadway. He sat down at the piano with me at a music stand with the score to *Evita,* and he played the piano while I conducted. We didn't leave the room till I knew the show cover to cover. I, of course, had been studying the music and attending performances in the pit watching Rene conduct, so I knew his every move. Rene, like Rudi, was all business when it came to conducting—no nonsense (no butterfly goosing).

So, after a very few hours, Rene said that I indeed did know the show cover to cover, and we were off to new adventures. I would be rehearsing the show in LA and Rene would come in to work with the ensemble. Watching him with a choir was watching a master at work. There was some Spanish in the *Evita* lyrics, and he would go through the words without pitch, sotto voce, and at a slower tempo to get all the words pronounced properly. Then he'd add the pitch and cut offs and *voila* … the chorus sounded spectacular. No muss, no fuss.

I could lay down the tempo and the chorus was perfection. Gemignani had hired two rehearsal pianists who were perfect for your standard musical theatre stuff, but totally inadequate for *Evita.* I needed pianists who could improvise, play good "Latin" time, and follow a conductor. I brought in Kathy Rubbicco, whom I had met during my *Playing Our Song* days, and Roger Steinman, whom I had met earlier as well. Both were perfect for the job. Meanwhile, Paul dismissed the pianists he'd hired and hired Steve Reinhardt, who had been MD for *Godspell* on Broadway and was an excellent pianist, with Roger on the second keyboard. Kathy came in a bit later when Steve left. Gemignani also engaged Mike Berkowitz on drums. We hit it off and became "partners in crime" for many years and to this day. I brought Mike to New York a bit later with one of my shows, and he became one of the busiest drummers in New York as well as a very capable conductor in his own right.

At this point in my life, I was still very capable as a rehearsal pianist, and would often sit down and play a lot of the rehearsals. I had good rhythm and would play the dance rehearsals for choreographer Larry Fuller. "The Money Kept Rollin In" was in 7/8 time. Between me and Berkowitz, Larry was happy, Hal was happy, and the dancers were very happy. Kathy was a spectacular pianist and Roger too. It was a great music team.

Rene was very happy, as well, and we were cranking it out at the church on the corner of Highland and Franklin in Hollywood, where so many shows rehearsed. Hal introduced me to the company with the comment, "Larry did a very eccentric thing, quitting a successful Broadway show to join us, but we are very happy to have him."

We all got along famously, and the cast was quite superb. Loni Ackerman as Eva, Valerie Perri (Eva matinees), Jon Cypher as Peron, Scott Holmes as Che, and Sal Mistretta as Magaldi. Rhoda was hired to be in the ensemble. She had worked for Hal on *Candide,* and was also the swing replacement on *On The Twentieth Century.* They were happy to have us both.

Marvin Hamlisch didn't seem to mind that I had left his show … after all, I was working now with Hal Prince, whom he idolized.

Marvin kept me on as conductor for his many concerts. Don Pippin had started that, but Don wasn't so eager to travel around with Marvin and was very accepting of my being his "replacement" for those gigs. He was still solidly ensconced at *A Chorus Line* in New York and was number-one call in New York for so many things.

At one rehearsal where I was standing by the pianist on one side of the church, Hal caught my eye from the other side of the room and clearly wanted to chat with me. I stood by the piano and Hal made his way over. He asked me about a specific spot, suggested something, and I said, "Of course." As he turned around, he said, "One more thing, next time … could you at least meet me halfway?" He meant coming across the rather huge room that he had crossed to talk to me. This taught me a big lesson. and I realized I was acting a bit entitled. I think Hal Prince was a great man.

During the course of learning the show, Rene Wiegert had told me that "Stand Back Buenos Aires" should be very Carmen Miranda in its feel. Mike Berkowitz had evolved it to a much more intricate Latin pattern that was a bit more contemporary, without affecting the existing music or orchestration. I asked Rene if that would be ok, and he readily agreed. We were at a dress rehearsal at the Shubert in LA and playing this with the full orchestra and it sounded pretty great. Rene was sitting on my left in the first row of the theatre with Hal Prince on the right with Ruthie Mitchell, his longtime associate. We had to stop for some technical reason. Hal leaned over to me in the pit and said, "Larry, this sounds *so* great, in New York it sounds so, so Carmen Miranda."

I heard Rene say "Sonofabitch" just loud enough for me to hear.

Of course, he smiled after and enjoyed the humor of it all. Rene was one of the great talents and one of the nicest people in the business.

I started conducting performances and was able to take off here and there for Marvin's concerts. My assistant was Bill Elton, who played trombone. He had been Elliot Lawrence's assistant for several shows and was a very capable guy. No one seemed to mind, and Berkowitz was holding down the fort with his excellent drumming. It was a pretty ideal job. My friendship with JoAnn Kane (Marvin's west coast copyist) was very helpful as well. She was JoAnn Johnson then. She became JoAnn Kane when she became eighth wife to composer/pianist Artie Kane.

JoAnn and her then partner, Sooky Fidelibus, were good friends. They were very ensconced with Disney Studios and film work. They introduced me to a lot of people in the film world, and I was still Marvin's go-to guy, along with Don Pippin. Many doors were opening, and I was learning so many new skills. In California, the movie/TV and recording business were light years different than the very closed world of Broadway. While there was some TV and recording in New York City, that was really based on the west coast where it was a much larger and more lucrative industry.

Evita was a huge success and clearly in for a long run at the Shubert in LA. Andrew Lloyd Webber and Tim Rice showed up. They were not the royalty they are now. Hal was somewhat dismissive of Andrew, but in an avuncular way. Hal was *clearly* in charge, and it was *his* production. I was the MD and was treated with great respect for my position. I was a Broadway conductor who had come to LA to ply his wares. When the show opened in January of 1980, I was twenty-seven years old.

The stage manager for *Evita* in LA had a girlfriend in the chorus. She was the second Evita understudy, and she was ok but not great. However, the stage manager was really pushing for her to go on or at least be auditioned. It was clear that Val Perri would eventually be promoted to doing the role on her own or on another tour. Somehow, the stage manager, who Hal was fond of, was able to swing a dress rehearsal with full crew, costumes, etc. to audition his girlfriend for casting director Joanna Merlin and for Hal. No orchestra. The orchestra would be a pianist and Mike on drums. This was a very big deal.

I was to conduct the rehearsal, but I was never very fond of conducting piano and drums. My piano skills were very much in shape at the time, and I offered to play the rehearsal with Mike on drums. The cast knew the show and we could get through it easily, even more easily with me at the piano. The problem was, we, meaning Mike and myself, were really not too fond of this girl that the stage manager was pushing. She was fine in the chorus, but if it wasn't for her boyfriend, the stage manager, that was as far as she would go. She was not good, and she was far too aggressive in pursuing this job at the expense of others in the cast. It was nepotism in the worst possible manner.

Berkowitz was getting to know me pretty well and sensed something was up if I was offering to play the piano. The girl, pushing too hard up to the very end, brought both me and Mike huge gifts of flowers and snacks before this audition rehearsal. That was simply way over the top. We were both offended and amused at the same time.

We started the show, a complete tech dress, in good faith and were enjoying playing through the score with just us. The first act ended very nicely with the girlfriend doing an ok job. Mike was getting suspicious that it was all going too well.

The second act began, and we were playing along until the number "Rainbow High" came up. Berkowitz had very good ears. He started to grin at me and at the very peak of the song, on its highest note, our stage manager's girlfriend screeched and cracked so badly that she simply eliminated herself from further consideration, even in an emergency.

We got through the rest of the rehearsal unscathed. At the end, Mike said to me, ""Rainbow High" sounds better in the key that Loni and Val sing it, don't you think?"

The stage manager and girlfriend then left a performance early to go to Las Vegas for the weekend. They were no longer an issue for the *Evita* company because they were both replaced immediately.

Marvin was doing the score for a picture called *Ordinary People* to be directed by Robert Redford. The opening of the film was a school choir singing a short piece of music. Redford had filmed a school choir and it really wasn't good enough to use their voices, so they decided to get a better school choir, rehearse, and record, and sync it up. Through a contact on *Evita*, Harold Clousing, I was able to put together a choir made up of students from Hollywood High and some other local schools. One of the singers was Sharon Brown, daughter of comic/actor/singer Johnny Brown.

One day, just after about ten in the morning, my phone rang in my rented house in North Hollywood. It was Emma Samms, Marvin's girlfriend, asking how quickly I could get over to Warner Brothers Studios. My house was literally ten minutes away from the studios on Barham Blvd. She said, "Come now."

I hopped in my car, drove to the studio gate, gave my name, and was led by motorcycle escort to the sound stage at Warner Bros. I had never been on a film lot, and here I was at Warner's. I walked in where the choir was standing with an orchestra and a big screen behind them. Marvin literally threw the stick at me and said, "You conduct!"

The lights dimmed, they told me to put on a headset, and I heard this clicking noise and saw a white band that went across the screen. Gerry Vinci, who was the concert master said, "Wait for the white band [a streamer] to hit the right side of the screen." There would be a flash of light and I'd match up my beat with the clicks on the headset. This is standard film recording technique.

I was totally clueless about any of this. I could hear and see that if I followed the click in my headset, it was neither in sync visually, nor sound wise. It was a mess. I said out loud, "Could we try this again, please, and please turn that clicking sound off."

I looked at the screen and started conducting when the streamer hit the right side of the screen. Watching the mouths of the singers, I made the chorus follow me … just as if I were conducting a live performance of *Evita*.

Everything synced up and we got to the end. The lights came up and everyone in the room started applauding and saying, "Yay Larry! and "Thank you!" There was an arm around me and when I turned my head I was looking into the eyes of Robert Redford, who was thanking me profusely for showing up. (Apparently Redford and Hamlisch had been getting close to blows because it wasn't syncing up.) Since I didn't know anything at all about film recording, I had just done what I always did, and it had ended any and all arguments. I recorded several more cues of just music and that was the beginning of my career in Hollywood. My name appears no where at all in the credits for the film. However, I still get a small royalty from the special payments fund for my contribution as conductor.

I continued conducting *Evita,* meeting a lot of people, and doing a lot of concerts for Marvin. One night, Hal Prince invited me to a party at his father-in-law's home. His father-in-law was Saul Chaplin, film composer and producer. I was so excited to be invited along with the principals from the cast.

When I arrived, I was happy to see Larry Grossman, the composer of *Goodtime Charley* and *Snoopy*. He was working on new projects with Hal. Hal's wife Judy was very kind to me as well. While I was sitting in the living room, Danny Kaye walked in with his wife Sylvia Fine. When everyone else went to the piano while Saul or Larry played, Danny Kaye asked if he could bum a cigarette. I sat with Danny Kaye while he bummed cigarettes (much to the chagrin of wife Sylvia) and we talked for hours about flying and Chinese food, which were both passions of his. That was a treat for me. I had seen him in all those films and of course on Broadway in *Two By Two*.

I was getting homesick for New York. I was still traveling for Marvin, but basically, I was just doing what I did in New York in sunny weather and I missed the comforts of home. At that moment in time, I didn't feel I had the skills to compose/arrange in Hollywood and I was more at ease with the comforts of Broadway. I started asking around if there were any Broadway shows in search of an MD.

John Monaco was a busy contractor on Broadway and told me of a show that was being produced/managed by Joe Harris. Joe was one of the most respected general managers on Broadway. The name of the show was *Onward Victoria*. It was written by some unknown and untried writers and had had a workshop. The score was by Keith Hermann. I heard a demo and thought it showed promise. I read the script and said pretty much what Max Bialystock said when he read the script for *Springtime For Hitler*: "The show will close on page four."

I'm sorry to say I was so negative about it, but with untried authors it really didn't look too good. However, I admired the score and thought that would give it some value and it was a way to get me back to New York with someone paying me to do it. The director was Julianne Boyd and the choreographer at that time was Arthur Faria. Arthur was an up-and-comer and showed promise. Victoria was going to be played by either Linda Purl or Dixie Carter. Linda was a rising name and Dixie was an old Broadway hand who was transitioning into lead roles. I signed on and went back to New York without realizing I was really burning bridges a bit. I was anxious to move forward, but I had effectively terminated my relationship with the Prince office. I had cut short my transition to LA and was going back to New York because I wanted to be back on Broadway.

We had auditions for *Victoria,* and it was between Dixie Carter and Jill Eikenberry. I voted for Jill. Arthur Faria quit, and Danny Levans became the choreographer. Danny Levans was a dancer with the Richard Thomas ballet school and company and had an important role as the young choreographer in the film *Turning Point.* Rudi Bennett's daughter Marissa was his assistant. That was a happy coincidence as she was like a kid sister to me.

The show was troubled with disagreements among the staff and Danny withdrew. Marissa went with him. They hired Michael Shawn as the new choreographer. Michael had been a Michael Bennett dancer.

Beth Austin, my old pal from *Oliver* at Gateway Playhouse in Long Island, was hired as the secondary lead. Michael Zaslow was hired as the male lead. I was told that the dance arranger was Don Johnston, whom I knew from my brief job as an orchestrator on *But Never Jam Today.* Keith Hermann chose Larry Fallon to be orchestrator.

Larry Fallon had been the orchestrator for *Seesaw,* but almost all of his work had been replaced by the work of Larry Wilcox and Jonathan Tunick, without credit. He was a recording arranger and had very little experience with theatre. Wanting to work with one of the known and seasoned Broadway orchestrators, I was disappointed, especially since I knew how tenuous this project was.

I had a meeting with Larry and Keith, and asked Larry what his plans were for instrumentation for the show. The show took place in 1865, and was about Victoria Woodhull running for president against Ulysses S. Grant. I pointed out ... many times ... that she hadn't won. Larry informed me that he was planning to use some brass and four or five saxophone doublers, along with strings and rhythm. I said very gently that it was 1865. "Do you think saxophones are appropriate?"

He said rather tersely, "That's why I'm the orchestrator and you are the conductor."

"Not anymore," I said without a moment's hesitation and I told Keith that this would not work out.

I hated putting Keith in this position, but Fallon's attitude was unacceptable, and he had to go. I also came from the school that the buck stopped with the music director. There was one head to the music department and that was the MD, who was following the wishes of the composer and functioning as emissary for the music team. This was 1980, before music supervisors and music coordinators were the norm.

After much talk, I suggested Michael Gibson as orchestrator. Michael was coming up—he had done *Grease, Over Here* and some other little shows and was eager to do it. He had also worked on *Oh Kay,* which closed on the road. Michael was hired and off we went. I cajoled Michael Berkowitz to move from LA to New York to play drums. There was no out-of-town tryout, just a very extended preview period in New York.

As the show progressed through its rehearsal period, I realized that it had little to no chance of success. The people involved were just too inexperienced and despite the very good musical score by Keith

Hermann and the skills of the music department and the designers, including the fabulously talented Theoni Aldredge, this wasn't going to be long lived. Don Johnston was a very talented guy and we became friends. I had several friends in the cast.

The director, Julianne Boyd, was inexperienced with a show this large. Michael Shawn was doing the best he could with the inexperienced script/lyric writers. I suggested my friend Hal Hackady come in and fix some lyrics. He did, but that was too little too late. The choral arrangements by me and Keith were quite nice. We also had an old pro, Ted Thurston, in the cast, and Lenny Wolpe played a nice character part. So, there were a few high spots to help us get through the rough one's.

There were many, many previews. The audience applauded wildly at the production numbers. The score had some nice attributes, but it really just didn't land. One night, I saw Kander and Ebb come into the theatre as I was getting situated in the pit. I slumped down to the bottom of the pit, hoping not to be seen. But the long arm of John Kander tapped me on the shoulder and said, "I see you." I couldn't hide. Fred Ebb's partner, Ed Aldredge, was the stage manager on the show. We all knew where we were headed. At one performance, Lehman Engel, the revered music director, educator, and head of the BMI workshop, appeared by the pit to say hello to me. It was raining outside and he asked if I would store his overwrought raincoat in the oversized pit. I said, of course. He pointed to my thick score on the podium and said, "That is one of the largest scores I've ever seen."

I said, "Lehman, that's the *first act*."

At the end of the show, I received a note from Lehman saying he didn't stay for the second half, and would I have his raincoat sent to his address?

I had decided that I would dress at home on West 86th street and trek down to the Martin Beck on 45th, so I never made it to my dressing room on one of the higher floors. This turned out to be a blessing. Don Johnston told me that he had been offered a show called *Copperfield* by Al Kasha and Joel Hirschorn. Don Pippin was supposed to conduct but was now at Radio City and didn't want to leave. Both Don's had suggested me to Rob Iscove, the director/chorographer, as possible MD and vocal arranger. I met with Rob Iscove, who agreed that I would be perfect. I accepted the job. The show was starting rehearsals late February '81 for an April opening on Broadway with a pre-Broadway tryout in St. Louis.

This was now November 1980. I had absolutely no expectation of *Victoria* running. Just to be sure, I gave my notice prior to the opening in December at the Martin Beck. Beth Austin asked me what I'd do if the show ran. I was incredulous at her question, but truly, when you are working on a show, you hope for the best.

During the preview period I made a trip to London (my first) with Marvin Hamlisch on the Concorde, traveling with Michael Keller, my drummer from *Song,* and Marvin. On the flight were Derek Jacobi, Isaac Stern, and Elaine Stritch, all of whom I was introduced to at baggage. Marvin's girlfriend Emma Samms (a Brit) was with us.

We did a concert at the Carlton Towers Hotel with me, Marvin, and Keller. Marvin took us all to Annabelle's, the fashionable disco in Berkeley Square. Then the driver gave me a tour of London around Buckingham Palace and dropped me off at Heathrow where I saw patrons having a pint at eight a.m. in a pub at the airport. I got on a plane to New York and was back in time for the afternoon rehearsal and the performance that night.

Onward Victoria opened mid-December 1980. My opening-night guest was Marvin Hamlisch, who came to Sardi's with me and said, "It's not that bad." The reviews came out, and Sardi's emptied rapidly. In his review on television, Stewart Klein said, "*Onward Victoria* has great vocal arrangements and great costumes. Would you pay $22.50 for great vocal arrangements and costumes?" That was the one and only official performance of *Onward Victoria*. I didn't even have to go to the theatre to clean out my dressing room, since I never got to use it.

Somewhere between the opening of *Onward Victoria* and New Year's Eve, I was asked to conduct for Connie Francis, who was a *huge* recording, nightclub, and TV celebrity in the late '50s and onward. Connie asked me to come to her home in Essex Fells, New Jersey for a rehearsal. Essex Fells is well known for being the home of a great many Italian Americans.

Connie sent a car for me, as there were storm clouds all over New York and it looked like a nor'easter was coming in soon. The car took me over the GW Bridge and to her home. The driver was wearing an earpiece, very much like the Secret Service.

I was escorted to the door where Connie greeted me in pin curlers, eating a bowl of pasta. I followed her to the kitchen where she offered me a glass of water and said, "Follow me." We trudged through the living room, past a big swan fountain looking very much like Club Bene in New Jersey, or Leonard's of Great Neck. She took me through to her bedroom, where there was an upright piano at the foot of the bed. There was a boombox next to the bed with a microphone and Connie lay down on the bed with me at the piano. She grabbed the mic and put the pasta down. I start playing the piano: "*Who's sorry now? Who's sorry now?*" For the un-initiated, that was a big hit song for her.

I went through all of her songs, pounding away at the foot of the bed and this went on for several hours. The storm clouds were looming, so I suggested that I'd better get back.

Connie said, "There's plenty of room if you need to stay."

I mumbled something like, "I'm good," and her driver got me back to Manhattan ust in time to beat the rain and snow that followed.

I conducted for her at the Waldorf with the loudest drummer I've ever heard (hers), and Mike Berkowitz played percussion. She asked me to conduct for her again, but my schedule with Broadway was interfering. Many years later, one of my best buddies from Bayside, Neil Schulz, now a successful cardiologist in Ft. Lauderdale called to tell me that his patient Connie Francis said to be sure to say hello. Despite all the jokes and Italian connections, she was very kind to me, a great artist and a wonderful singer. Back to Broadway!!!

Chapter Four

I found out with great delight that the orchestrator for *Copperfield* was to be Irwin Kostal, the same Irwin Kostal who had orchestrated *West Side Story* with Sid Ramin, as well as *Forum, Sail Away, Tenderloin* and my beloved first musical, *Fiorello*. Irwin had won Academy Awards for *West Side Story* and *Sound of Music* and, of course, had done *Mary Poppins,* as well. I was thrilled. While on the west coast with Marvin for a concert, I rang Irwin up and asked to meet. He invited me to his home where I met him and his lovely wife, Sylvia.

We hit it off instantly. He was flattered that I thought to meet him before we started. Little did I know that in short order he and Sylvia would become surrogate parents to me and surrogate grandparents to my own children later on.

Back to New York to begin rehearsals for *Copperfield.* The rehearsals were to take place at the Minskoff Studios. There was a lovely cast, with Carmen Mathews, George S. Irving, Mary Elizabeth Mastrantonio, and a very young Christian Slater as the understudy for young David Copperfield. Christian's mom, Mary Jo Slater, was a very busy casting agent in New York City.

Woman Of The Year was rehearsing across the hall with Jack Lee as MD. I ran into Bob Moore, who was directing. He told me that

Jack had had a heart attack and had to leave the show. Bob asked if I could get out of *Copperfield* and take over for Jack. Bob thought I could handle the personality of leading lady, Betty (Lauren) Bacall. Michael Gibson was the orchestrator and was recommending me, as well. John Monaco was the contractor for both *Copperfield* and *Woman Of The Year* and wasn't so keen on my moving over to the other show.

I phoned Don Pippin, my guru and advisor, and mentioned this to him. Don was at Radio City at the time as their MD. He was uncharacteristically negative to me about this and said, "You don't want to deal with Betty Bacall." He had done *Applause* with her and had some issues. In fact, he was really negative about it, saying that he had recommended me for *Copperfield* and it would reflect badly on him if I withdrew.

My feeling was that if they wanted me badly enough on *Woman Of The Year,* they would deal with all of that. The director and orchestrator wanted me. John Kander would've been happy to have me. I was taken to lunch at Sardi's with Bacall and Bob Moore and was seated across the table from Betty.

At this point, I was coming up on my twenty-ninth birthday and was weighing all of the positives and negatives. The positives were: John Kander, Bob Moore, and a very likely successful run with a hit show. The negatives would be negative impact on my relationships for bailing on a show in rehearsals, stopping my working relationship with Irv Kostal, and getting into the pit with a leading lady who ate conductors for breakfast along with anyone else in her path. Before I could make a proper decision, Don Pippin told me that he was leaving Radio City, and stepping in. Career crisis totally averted. I knew that it was the best thing that could've happened on so many levels. Apparently, Don was already vying for this position, which accounted for his negative response to my questions.

As we began rehearsals for *Copperfield*, it was decided that we would shoot and record the music for the TV ad for the show before we had our first orchestra reading in St. Louis. The first time I would be working with Irv Kostal would be in a recording studio in New York, recording the music. Irv wrote the chart, we met at a studio with the eventual pit band for New York, and I began conducting. On the first break, Irv said two life-changing things to me: "Y'know, when you conduct, you are standing on one leg. You should go to a chiropractor and get an adjustment." And then he said without any provocation, "You are easily the strongest conductor I have ever worked with in the musical theatre." That was extraordinarily flattering considering the people he worked with.

He then asked me who I had studied conducting with. I told him that Rudi Bennett was my conducting mentor, and he was using the teachings of a Russian conductor, Nicolas Malko. Irv put his hand on my shoulder, and with a slight tear in his eye and said, "I was Nicolas Malko's last conducting student." At that point we bonded forever, and I can honestly say that the rest of my life changed in that instant.

My relationship with Irv grew during the preparations for *Copperfield*. I knew this show needed major help in the routine of production numbers. Don Johnston was excellent in working with Rob Iscove in making all that happen; however, the songs needed opening up. Al Kasha was the lyricist, and Joel Hirschorn (a lovely man) was a good songwriter. They were pretty open to whatever I brought to the table. I don't recall either of them being interfering or demanding. They were trusting Rob, me, Don, and especially Irv, to deliver. Irv had done the Disney film, *Pete's Dragon,* and other stuff with them. He was a proven entity.

I proceeded to make rather elaborate vocal arrangements to build up the numbers. There was one particular number: "What Do We Do With A Copperfield?" which was not unlike "Oliver" in the musical *Oliver.* In fact, there were a lot of similarities to *Oliver* in terms of what was going on. Joel/Al wrote a song called "Is There Anyone?" that was a tad too close to "Where Is Love?" But we chose not to bring it up and leave it there. They also wrote a song called "Circles" that was a little too close to "Chim Chim Cheree" ... but not close enough. I don't mean that in a sarcastic manner. I rather liked this show and thought it had possibilities. We were scheduled to open at the Anta theatre (now the August Wilson) across from the Alvin (now the Neil Simon) where *Annie* was playing. I figured anyone who couldn't get into *Annie* would see *Copperfield* across the street. That didn't turn out to be the case, but I had a positive attitude.

I built up the "What Do We Do?" number to a giant climax where they threw little David Copperfield off the top of the set to all the chorus boys waiting below. Aside from singer Dick Pugh, they were a bunch of tall Jewish singers and dancers. At one performance, when understudy Christian Slater was thrown, Dick Pugh shouted for all to hear, "Throw Christian to the Jews." That was one of the highlights of *Copperfield* for me.

While out of town, director Rob Iscove was making major cuts in an important scene that led to a big song. I was not at rehearsal, preferring to stroll the streets and shops with my mischievous drummer, Mike Berkowitz. Don Johnston was holding down the fort playing piano. When I came in for the performance, I was told that the cue for the song had changed. I asked Don what the cue was and he said, "They changed it so many times, I don't remember, ask Peter Lawrence." I asked Peter, the stage manager, and he said, "One of my assistants was minding the store, ask them." No one seemed to know. I even went to Mary Minestrone (our nickname for Mary E. Mastrantonio, our leading lady). "I don't recall," she said. "Don started playing and we sang, but I'll look at you when the time comes."

We got to the scene during the performance, and it was starting to sound like a song was coming on. I stood up at the ready with the orchestra, who had bows up and reeds to the mouth. But the scene seemed to go on for a while with no cue. I looked at Mary. She shook her head, no. My mind was starting to wander and the orchestra was losing interest. I turned my head for a split second and then I heard Mary on stage, directing at me, "Psst psst psst!" You never saw a baton move that fast anywhere.

The music started, and those of us in the know had a good laugh. Of course, the audience knew nothing except perhaps for wondering why this show was so slow.

Rob spent two weeks in St. Louis working on the bows, and every time I asked what's up, he said, "Go shopping, we're working on the bows with Don. We'll get to it."

Anyway, this went on for two weeks with few changes to the show. I had a wonderful time with the cast; Berkowitz and I were quite mischievous. We had been working together all the time since *Evita* in LA. One night, everyone was drinking and partying and hanging at the bar, when Mary Minestrone announced a party in her room. We were staying at the American Hotel in St. Louis, working at the American Theatre (no longer in existence).

We showed up at the party. There was an enormous amount of drinking and smoking (of all substances, meaning tobacco and weed), and there were a lot of people in the room. Finally, there was a knock at the door, and I being the music director and authority figure for the moment, went to the unopened door and said, "Yes? Who is it?"

The answer comes: "House detective."

Many ran to the bathroom flushing their joints down the toilet, and there was much hubbub.

When it was relatively clear, I opened the door … with the smell of weed/tobacco wafting out the door. There stood a very young, attractive fellow, who said, "Neighbors are complaining of loud, popping sounds, and I have to ask you to stop that." It turned out that Mary M loved popcorn, had a popcorn maker in her room, and that was popping away furiously … which was disturbing the neighbors.

The house detective said that something smelled good, and that he was off duty in about twenty minutes, so we invited him to join us a bit later. Berkowitz and I were drinking quite heavily, along with the others, but for some bizarre reason … felt nothing. Perhaps it was the anxiety of our tryout with the show … and our youth. The party continued with rehearsals the next day and no hangover. Unfortunately, that result was a one-time event and is still a mystery.

Copperfield moved to New York, and we were no longer feeling too secure. The boys (Al and Joel) wrote a new song and, we (Irv, me, and the actors, including George S. Irving) were summoned to hear it. I said to Irv that it sounded like a college football song and he responded with, "For the losing team." George, the loveliest and most polite man in show biz said, "This is a piece of shit." And the number died its death right there.

In a panic, Al and Joel said that "Is There Anyone?" sounded too much like "Where Is Love?" and it had to be changed. Irv and I pointed out that changing it would involve virtually every piece of underscoring in the show … so that idea went away, too.

We were at an orchestra rehearsal for an opening song called *"Boys,"* which was to be sung by Carmen Mathews. She was a lovely woman and a delight to be around. Unfortunately, she had been in more flop musicals than even Karen Morrow (another beloved Broadway singer). At the orchestra rehearsal, Al Kasha turned to Irv and said, "Irwin, that is the most horrible arrangement you've ever written."

Irv, totally unflappable, said, "What don't you like?"

Al replied, "When Carmen says, 'Go to war,' the trumpets should go *ta ta ta ta.*"

Irv dictated the notes to the trumpet and we played the number from the top. Then Al said,

"Irwin, that is the finest arrangement you've ever written."

Irv winked at me.

Rob was released from his directing duties but not really replaced … he was still working on the curtain calls. We made a giant cut in one of the numbers, "Something Will Turn Up" and eliminated 150 bars of dance music, which now needed a different transition. We had a performance in a few hours, so I announced that we would perform the old number tonight, and then have an orchestra call the next day to put in the new orchestration. I phoned Irv and the copyist office with the changes. Chris Ambrose at Chelsea Music was handling the show and I told them the plan.

Irv was a famously fast writer, to the point of deification. I was conducting the show that night when Berkowitz, at the drums, suddenly started laughing and pointing at his music. I looked down at my score and saw that the *new orchestration* had been copied and inserted in the books. The cast was doing the old version, and the orchestra was about to cut 150 bars of music. There was no keyboard in our instrumentation, so there was no way to call out to the piano player to continue playing the old version. We were about to crash and burn in the middle of a preview performance, so the orchestra played the ending as corrected, while the entire cast kept singing and dancing on stage with no accompaniment except Berkowitz playing after beats and holding himself back from laughing out loud.

The number ended with everyone on stage in their final pose, to no applause and a stupefied audience. However, there was more to the act. Despite the smoke coming from my ears and the frustration, I still had an act to finish. We got to the end of the act, and I was fuming and about to give a piece of my mind to Irv and the copyists. I saw Irv coming down the aisle in a peacoat (it was cold outside). Irv was six-foot two and imposing. He was walking straight towards me with his hand up in the air and said, before I could speak, "If you hadn't shouted 'oh fuck' into the open mics, it would've been ok." Then he added, "Drinks at Victor's across the street after the show on me." We had a very good laugh.

Alan Jay Lerner was brought in by the producers to doctor *Copperfield*'s book. At a production meeting, he suggested some changes to the plot.

I, being the youngster in the room, said, "Excuse me, isn't this Charles Dickens?"

Indignant, the producers said, "You are talking to Alan Jay Lerner, the author of *My Fair Lady and Camelot.*"

And I quickly added, "Yes, and *Lolita, My Love.*"

A hush came over the room, and Alan put his arm around me and said, "The kid is right." He left the production and we died a natural death…not that he could have saved it anyway. In his review, Clive Barnes said that *Copperfield* had great bows. (I'm not making that up.)

Copperfield was, however, a turning point in my life, as that's where I met my mentor, Irwin Kostal. One day, I was conducting a rehearsal and Irv said, "You are an excellent conductor and you write excellent vocal arrangements that indicate a lot of compositional talent. Why don't you come to LA and I'll teach you to write? Then you can conduct *your* shit instead of this shit." (These were important words and ultimately life changing.)

Shortly after Copperfield closed, my marriage to Rhoda was falling apart, so I moved into an apartment on West 57th Street. The next few months are quite a blur and really a gap in my memory. I think I needed some time off, and I had enough money in the bank so that it didn't matter too much. Work wasn't happening, and I didn't seem to care. I likely had several concerts with Marvin Hamlisch, which were always ongoing, and that was enough work to keep me out of trouble. The year 1981 sort of whisked by rather quickly.

After a brief separation, Rhoda and I decided to stay together. We had been married for ten years and it seemed the correct thing to do. We had wanted children, which hadn't happened, and we felt it might be a good thing. We went for medical advice, though there was a decided lack of interest from both of us.

My savior, Don Pippin, called and said, "I ran into Harvey Schmidt on the street." Schmidt and Jones had written *110 in the Shade*, *The Fantasticks*, *I Do I Do*, and *Celebration* and were very respected. Don said they were doing a new musical called *Colette*, and that he had recommended me as music director. Don was still doing *Woman of the Year*, and was giving me all of his hand-me-downs. I was happy to be the recipient.

I was invited by Harvey to his beautiful town house on West 75th street. He and Tom and his pianist Ken Collins *auditioned* the score for me to see if I'd be interested. I was a great fan of theirs and loved the music and lyrics, so was really excited. I bid them farewell and walked up to my apartment on 86th Street. When I walked into my apartment, the phone rang with both of them on the phone asking if I'd do them the honor of being music director for their show. It was so flattering and of course I said yes. The next day a little gift arrived…a Limoges pencil box. It was simply a gesture of welcome aboard. Harvey Schmidt was a very old-world gentleman.

Harry Rigby was the producer of *Colette*. Harry had been kicking around producing from the early '50sn and was always involved in interesting projects, most notably, *Make A Wish, No, No, Nanette, Irene,* and a revival of *Good News*. He had strong loyalties to many talented people. Ralph Burns was very fond of him, and as I mentioned earlier, invited me to do *Sugar Babies* when Harry asked him to orchestrate. Ralph said he would do it if I would be music director. I was busy with *Playing Our Song* at that point, and really didn't want to tour, as they had planned to do.

I had a lot of regard for Harry. He was always interesting, with lots of plans and innovative ideas for casting. He invited me to Charlie's on 45th Street to meet Debbie Reynolds, who was talking to Harry about playing Colette. Not necessarily the best casting for the role, but she was Debbie Reynolds, much loved, and would probably sell tickets. Next thing I heard was that Debbie was not doing it. They were looking around. The director was going to be Dennis Rosa, who directed the successful Frank Langella *Dracula*. The choreographer was going to be Carl Jablonski, who had assisted Ernie Flatt for years. Ernie was Harry's first choice, since he had done *Sugar Babies*. Carl was very facile. He had been a dancer in the original *My Fair Lady,* and was a very nice fellow. The design team was stellar, beginning with the famous Raoul Pêne Du Bois. Hilary Knight designed the adverts/poster, as he had done for Harry many times before. The music team was going to be me, Larry Wilcox as orchestrator, and David Krane as dance arranger.

Larry Wilcox was a tremendously gifted orchestrator with many credits, too many unsuccessful shows (not because of him), and many uncredited successes. He was a ghost for Ralph. Ralph had turned this one down as his movie career was flying high. David was a regular on the dance arranger scene and was amassing many credits. Larry had done many large sections of *A Chorus Line.* He had an alcohol problem (like Ralph). However, he was great fun, brilliantly talented, and a pleasure to work with.

We had auditions and many of the top dancers on Broadway were hired for *Colette.* There was a great singing chorus, which included Rhoda. And Rhoda was also given a very small role from the ensemble.

We auditioned Patricia Morison, Ellen Hanley, and several others for the role of Sido, Colette's mother. I was delighted to meet Ellen who had been in *Fiorello* and knew Irv. It was nice to chat with her. She wasn't quite right for the role, though, and we moved on to Patricia Morison who was very well loved and had been the original female lead in *Kiss Me Kate.* She'd done other shows as well but KMK was her calling card. We also auditioned Marta Eggerth, a Hungarian-born opera singer who had been in a few films. She appeared on Broadway a lot with her husband Jan Kiepura. They were known affectionately as "Ham and Eggerth."

After much ado, Marta was hired, because Patricia was too similar to our chosen leading lady, Diana Rigg! Diana was the glamourous

Emma Peel from the British TV show *The Avengers*. All teenagers of my generation, and our fathers and sons, were in love with Diana Rigg.

A meeting was arranged with me and Diana at my apartment on West 86th. She showed up, kicked off her heels, and was standing toe to toe with me in my living room. She was very close to six feet tall in her bare feet. We bonded quickly with much humor, and I ran through all of her songs. Like most Brits trained in theatre, she had perfect rhythm and could carry a tune well enough. Clearly, she had the acting chops. Diana was a very commanding presence and great fun to be around.

I realized, though, that she needed some vocal work. To maintain eight shows a week while carrying a musical is a large load. I hooked her up with my mentor/friend Rudi Bennett, who was teaching voice (very successfully) and could handle a presence like Diana. They hit it off immediately, and soon Rudi was coaching Diana, which made my job much easier. She was so musical, and she regarded me as her go-to, reliable friend and musical mentor.

John Reardon and Marty Vidnovic were hired as her two suitors (husbands). Reardon was a delight, and Marty had been in the chorus at the Kenley Players when I'd started out. Ron Raines was hired as standby for Reardon and the first husband. This was so weird, because Ron is blessed with good looks and a fantastic voice, and Reardon was his mentor. But, as standby, Ron had nothing at all to do except hang around.

Marti Stevens was hired to play the sometimes girlfriend of Colette. She also had little to do in the show, but Diana gained a very classy and delightful drinking buddy. Marti was a major talent, but like Ron, had practically nothing to do, but go out after the show for cocktails.

Reardon was a charming and talented man. I had trained the chorus to give him back-up on a song called "Come To Life." For the last chorus he sang the lead with the choir behind him. I mentioned, "John…you are not singing with the chorus."

He said with a huge smile, "I'm not *in* the chorus."

When I asked why he was singing behind the beat, he smiled and said, "Maestro, have you considered that it might be too fast?"

It was all said with love and affection, we both laughed and to prove his point, he invited me to dinner. He was a great asset to the show.

Marti Stevens had been the muse of both Marlene Dietrich and Noel Coward. She was also great pals with Don Pippin, so we got along famously. This was some cast of characters. It was a gorgeous-looking cast, great singers and dancers, great score, great team. The script was a little arch, and Dennis Rosa started treating it like an operetta from the late '30s. Apparently, his success with *Dracula* had been a fluke, saved by the presence of one Frank Langella. So, there was trouble in paradise.

I decided to do some very "posh" vocal arrangements with my great singers, and all I will say is that they were very grand and sounded quite impressive. There was much to work with, and Harvey seemed really pleased with what I brought to the table.

Rehearsals plodded on at 890 Broadway. These were the studios that Michael Bennett owned, and were the favored place to rehearse. They were on 19th Street and Broadway, which was convenient to nothing. However, some nice restaurants popped up, and it was a good time and place to be. I suggested to Harvey that we put a little bass button (ending) on one number, with just the bass playing the final note, and he said in his big Texas drawl, "Larry, that's like a frog pissing on a blotter." He was right. But as traditions go in the theatre, we did it anyway.

115

Diana would invite me and some others to dinner. Her assistants would make a lovely meal, and there was always far too much wine and port. We also had the company of Diana's little daughter, four-year-old Rachael, later to become Rachael Stirling, a very successful actress.

We had a long pre-Broadway tour at least *planned*. Our first stop was the Fifth Avenue Theatre in Seattle, followed by Denver, LA, San Francisco, and then the Kennedy Center and New York. We didn't make it past Denver ...

The orchestra rehearsals in Seattle went very well. Larry's orchestrations were brilliant and everything seemed to fit into place, though I ended up doing a few bits and pieces of the orchestration. Larry was running behind and farmed two numbers out to Jim Tyler (a great writer in his own right). I offered to do bits and pieces of underscore following Larry's lead, so he didn't have to get any more help. I really wasn't that experienced yet at writing, but having conducted and been around Ralph Burns, Irv Kostal, Michael Gibson, and Phil Lang, I had learned enough to help out. All was good! We had a marvelous orchestra including Beverly Mann Statter, the original harpist on *The Fantasticks,* who had semi-retired to Seattle. She was delightful and played so well. Ken Collins was my associate and pianist. He was a major asset to the production.

We were about to have our first dress with orchestra at the enormous Fifth Avenue Theatre. I had dinner with Harvey, Tom, Harry Rigby, and Mitch Brower, who was our company manager initially. Alan Wasser was the GM on the show.

Very carefully, I announced that without an audience the very first dress rehearsal would be alarming. I told them that the orchestra would be excessively loud, because they were new to the music, and adjusting their ears to the acoustics, and that without the bodies in the seats absorbing the sound, it would be *way too loud*. But if we held them down, the next performance would be too soft, and it would be difficult to get a proper balance. In those days (1982), sound design was a couple of mics in the pit for enhancement, and body mics and area mics for the stage. It wasn't what it is today, with everyone on a separate mic.

They all agreed to hold their tongues and to trust me, understanding that we'd need a couple of performances, including dress rehearsal, to settle. At the very first downbeat of the overture that night, every person in the auditorium came running down the aisles screaming that the orchestra was too loud. ...so much for my good advice.

Harry Rigby was getting totally fed up with our director, Dennis Rosa. Diana was also fed up with Dennis, and she had contractual approval. So, Dennis was fired. I pointed out to Diana and Harry that Dennis had been so secretive that not even stage manager Bob Vandergriff was sure how the show was to work technically. So, Dennis was rehired. I told Harry that once we got through the opening night, Dennis wouldn't be needed, and Diana agreed.

As soon as we got through the opening night, you could hear Harry's eerie voice saying, "You're fired," ... and off he went. We had no director. *Colette* was running every night without a rudder. We just kept running the show. Apparently, they were bringing everyone in to see the show and make suggestions: Arthur Laurents, Grover Dale, some others ... and then finally Martin Charnin. Marty had been brought in on so many troubled musicals and had never saved any of them. But like Abe Burrows, just bringing him in seemed like throwing a life saver to someone who had fallen off the *Titanic*. Marty Charnin confided in me as music director that he was going to throw everything up in the air and see where it landed. I wasn't looking forward to that at all, not in the slightest. Unless they were going to bring in someone who knew what they were going to do, I wasn't in the mood for rehearsing every day and ending up with something worse. Besides, Diana was spectacular in the show, the music sounded great, and they just needed to rework the book a great deal ... not throw it up in the air. Tom Jones needed some real guidance on the book, and a director with authority.

Diana didn't really like Marty anyway, and after much noise, he went away. His success was with the musical *Annie,* period—and that was really Mike Nichols. So ...

Early in rehearsals Harry Rigby excitedly told us that Sir Robert Helpman was going to come in and play the part of Colette's best friend and sidekick, Jacques. This was the same Robert Helpman from the movie, *The Red Shoes.* He had become quite a popular director in the UK, and we were told he was a tremendous asset. Well, Carl Jablonski was staging all the dance numbers and framing the ensemble around "Sir Bobby's" first entrance. Sir Bobby was not going to grace us with his presence until the second week of rehearsals, since he was off on holiday in Spain, or something like that. So, it was "Bobby will make his entrance from stage right with a grand jeté and a pirouette and ..." The lyric was "that master of dance known as Jacques, Jacques, Jacques." Bobby would do a somersault and *voila* ... he would be present.

One day I looked in the corner of the room and there was standing a very short, very old-looking, seventy-something-year-old man smoking a cigarette and coughing his brains out. He was wearing a cape and one of those Spanish hats with the balls dangling all around it ...it was *Sir Bobby!*

We were screwed. Carl's disappointment was visible when he realized that Sir Bobby would have enough to do just walking on the stage—albeit slowly. I have to say he was one of the nicest men and sweet as he could be. He couldn't dance at all, but he could act as if he had actually said something very important, and make an exit speaking nonsense and get applause. One good thing Marty Charnin said was not to pander to Bobby's age or lack of rhythm, and just pull him through the musical numbers, so he wouldn't appear to be doddering. I did that and Marty was absolutely correct. It helped (a little) ... and Bobby was charming.

One night we had a lovely party at Diana's digs with most of the cast, or at least the principals. Bobby pulled me aside and sat me down at the edge of a bed in one of the rooms. He said, "Harry has asked me to take over as director, what do you think?"

The truth is he was very capable in this area and probably could've done something good for the show. However, it was clear that the show needed some heavy re-writing before he could do anything splashy or visually creative. I said, very measuredly, that he had been a successful dancer at the ballet, made an indelible impression in *The Red Shoes,* and was a well-respected director resting on his laurels. Why would he want to "go out" with a show, that at this point was probably doomed to a very short run at best? He agreed and thanked me and stayed on as that master of mime, "Jacques, Jacques, Jacques."

Choreographer Carl Jablonski, with some inappropriate advice from the dance arranger, turned the sexy song "La Vagabond" into a bunch of beautiful women scurrying like rats. We had the most beautiful and sexy girls in tuxedos, dancing to music written in a 7/8 meter. But, the choreography turned a very good song into an awkward mess.

When Diana was on stage, it was golden, especially when she was paired with Bobby, John Reardon, and Marty Vidnovic. Marty and Diana did a soft shoe in their underwear to a song called "Ooh

La La", that was glorious. It was Diana at her best, and Marty being a charming song and dance man. We needed more of that. At one point, Tom Jones announced that he was taking over as director, and Diana said, "No you are not."

Then John Mauceri showed up to watch the show. John was a protégé of Bernstein's whom I had known when he was MD for *Candide* in New York. He finally ended up as the very successful MD for the Hollywood Bowl Orchestra. But at this time, he was working for Roger Stevens at the Kennedy Center, who had put up a huge amount of money for the show, and was ostensibly the co-producer (and money). After the show John invited me up to his room for a private dinner and discussion of the show.

He told me that he thought the show was not very good. He said that the music was excellent and in good hands, that the choreography was ok and, in some cases, not bad, and that Diana was superb … but that he was going to advise Roger Stevens to pull the plug and close it down. He told me this in confidence, and I kept it that way except, of course, for Diana, who was already in on it, in any case.

I had become very friendly with Diana and would visit her in the dressing room before the show and chat while she prepared. At the interval, her dresser John handed me a huge foaming drink, which was clearly alcoholic. I said, "Diana, it isn't really customary in the States to drink at the interval" (intermission). She threw her head back, laughed, and said, "Well darling, I'm not going to drink alone."

She was a delight to be around and would invite a select few to drink and dine with her. Unfortunately, Rhoda, who was playing her daughter onstage, wasn't included in this group. Rhoda would hang with other members of the ensemble while I was hanging out with the leading lady, as well as Marti Stevens, Diana's drinking buddy.

We were moving on to Denver without having changed *anything* at all in the show. The show that opened in Seattle was virtually the same show that opened in Denver—and in fact was the same show that ultimately closed in Denver.

There was one scene where Diana was doing a pantomime with Marti Stevens. It was an Egyptian-based theme, with Diana dressed like Cleopatra. At the peak of this "dance/pantomime," Diana would grab the clasp to her asp-covered brassier and expose her breasts to the audience. as apparently the real Colette had done. The audience let out a mild gasp, seeing Mrs. Emma Peel expose herself, and then the lights would black out.

When we got to Denver where the show was in its last throes of life, while Diana was making up in the dressing room, margueritas in hand, I suggested that even though Diana's exposing her breasts was a highlight of the show, it was perhaps keeping people from bringing their families and may have been killing any chances of the show moving forward (along with all the other issues that plague a failing show). She said, "You are absolutely correct, darling. I will by-pass the expose."

That night, as I was conducting the music that led up to the big flash, she waited for the music to peak, grabbed the clasp in front of the "asp," looked straight at me in the pit, and shouted, "My tits are too good for Denver!!" as I segued into the next bit of music.

Diana was a very naughty, but delightful Dame! When she was bestowed the title of Dame by Queen Elizabeth, I wrote her a note that said, "You've always been a great dame, when did the queen notice?"

Sometimes in both Seattle and Denver, Larry and Barbara Wilcox (the orchestrator and his wife) would be invited along with Diana and entourage. In addition, Barbara's aunt, or cousin (I wasn't clear) Illsley was around. She was clearly a wealthy woman and very kind. I invited her to sit in the pit next to me on several occasions. She was known to the cast and they welcomed her as Barbara's older relative.

Illsley invited the entire cast for a fantastic party at her home in Seattle on the water, which was absolutely gorgeous. We became great pals and she would invite me, Rhoda, Larry, and Barbara to one of the restaurants she owned. It was always fun and she became a bit of a mascot to the company. Years later, when I was working at Benaroya Hall in Seattle with the Seattle Symphony, I noticed the smaller hall next door dedicated to her: Illsley Nordstrom Hall. She apparently owned the Seattle Sea Hawks, as well as Nordstrom stores. I have to admit that I was a little naïve about who she was. Looking over the details of her life, this "older" woman, Illsley, was younger than I am right now as I write this. At age twenty-nine, everyone over forty appears to be ancient.

Colette closed without much ado in Denver, leaving us all unemployed. It was difficult to say goodbye to Diana, Illsley, and the rest of the cast.

In 1994, I was music director for a gala in London, celebrating Diana and several other celebs. She saw me backstage and enveloped me in a huge embrace, as Patrick Macnee (from *The Avengers*) watched with quizzical eye. She said, "Patrick, Larry and I did *Colette* together."

He turned to me and said, "You were wonderful in it."

It was quite the gala with Michael McDonald, Michael Bolton, Deniece Williams, Elaine Paige, Robert Goulet, David Cassidy, Petula Clark, and especially Ann Miller. Dame Diana told me she was hysterical watching me conduct for Ann Miller. Annie flung her feather boa in my face at every opportunity, while singing *Everything's Coming Up Roses*.

Over the years, I managed to say hello to Diana several times before she passed a couple of years ago. She was a great "Dame."

Chapter Five

I was unemployed with very vague rumors of resuscitating *Colette* floating about, but that wasn't very likely. It was back to New York with little and nothing to do, but that wasn't unusual after coming off a show.

I was invited to dinner at Trader Vic's, a restaurant in the bowels of the Plaza Hotel. It was famous for its kitschy drinks and ersatz Chinese/Polynesian food. A fun hang. Harry Rigby invited me with others from *Colette*. I don't really recall the entourage. In the course of conversation, Harry told me that Glen Roven, the conductor of *Sugar Babies* at the Mark Hellinger, was due to take vacation for two weeks. Usually, the assistant conductor, Bill Grossman, would take over. Harry was feeling a bit puckish and wanted to upset the apple cart with Glen, so he asked me if I'd like to cover Glen's vacation.

I was an established conductor on Broadway and not exactly an assistant conductor. But I was in need of income, and what would be the harm in taking over for a couple of weeks? Glen and I had been friends since meeting up in San Francisco when I was doing *Snoopy* in 1975.

He was almost exactly five years younger than me. He claimed to be the youngest conductor in Broadway history, but that was not so. Alfred

Newman had conducted a Gershwin show when he was seventeen. However, Glen, Al Newman, and I were probably the youngest guys in Broadway history—for whatever that is worth in a trivia contest.

Harry announced I would be taking over the podium for two weeks while Glen was gone.

Glen was none too happy about it as I wasn't his choice, and he had an assistant to cover his absences. However, no one was being penalized financially and I was getting paid.

I started observing the show, watching Glen or his assistant Bill conducting, with Ann Miller and Eddie Bracken, Mickey Rooney's vacation replacement. The show had a lot of cues because of all the sight gags and one-liners. Fun!

However, it seemed I would be stepping into the show the night Mickey returned without having seen him do the show. No one seemed to care much what Mickey thought or did, as long as he was under control. And Mickey couldn't have cared less who was in the pit because he was going to do what he did. Annie Miller was a bit more particular, but as long as her dance numbers were ok, she wouldn't make too much of a fuss.

Glen was a bit petulant with me, but he was going away and when he came back, I'd be gone. He was in no danger of losing his job and truthfully, two weeks of *Sugar Babies* was enough for me.

The show was very funny and entertaining, a fast-paced burlesque show. I was delighted to be working and so I learned the show. The band had been basically a good band but the show had been running for several years and they were on automatic pilot. Because of that, the tempi had gone awry and the orchestra was somewhat indifferent about it. It was *very* fast and no one was paying attention. It was punching a time clock.

I was delighted to find out that my friend Jane Summerhays (Sheila in *A Chorus Line* on the international tour), was doing the Soubrette role and covering Ann Miller. We were good friends, and I knew Jane would pass the word in the company that I was competent and knew my business.

This was put to the test.

I was summoned to Ann Miller's dressing room where she said, "Larry, I'm sure you are very capable or Harry wouldn't have hired you, but Glen is my friend and is upset. I'm going to have Bill Grossman conduct my numbers." I smiled and said, "Sure, if that's what you want." I assumed Glen had asked her to do this because he thought I might walk out and say forget it. It was a bit of a pain in the butt, but when the music got to her spot, I would hop off the podium, Bill would hop on, and then we'd switch again several times in the show. This did seem absurd, but I wasn't going to walk out or be difficult.

Mickey Rooney didn't give a hoot who was in the pit. He and I were fine. The orchestra was on such automatic pilot that it didn't matter who conducted, although I had my ideas how to get it back into some semblance of reason. It was just too fast.

The next performance, Ann Miller was out of the show and Jane was going on. They asked Jane if I should conduct and she said, "Absolutely, I know Larry, and he'll be terrific!" Jane was one helluva tap dancer and singer. She sang and danced the show like the star she was, and I was on the podium from the overture through the exit music. Because of Jane's performance and my preparation, it was a very good and smooth performance. Mickey singled me out on my bow as opposed to his usual perfunctory manner.

The next night, Annie Miller was back at that theatre, summoned me to her dressing room again, and said, "I heard everything was great last night, Glen's my friend but would you conduct my numbers at today's matinee?" I smiled and said, "Y'know Miss Miller, [everyone called her Annie and I was being totally passive aggressive], I don't want to cause trouble, so let's have Bill conduct your numbers." She was confused and I left the dressing room.

Bill and I did the switcheroo as we had done the first night. The cast was a little bewildered as everything had gone so well the night before.

Between shows, I went out to dinner with Jane for a nice catch up. When I returned to the theatre, I was summoned to Annie's dressing room and she said, "Can we stop this shit? Would you please conduct the entire show tonight?"

I did, everything was fine, and we had a delightful two weeks.

There were strange happenings in the orchestra pit. The show had been running for three years-plus. When there is a page-turn in the music, the inside string players are responsible for turning pages and usually they drop out for a few beats while the rest carry on. That means you get half the strings playing every now and then for a few seconds. With a show running this long, there were few substitutes in the pit and it seemed strange to me that they were relying on the music. I jumped off the stand and found out that they had cookbooks on the stands and were just reviewing new recipes. All the page turning involved cookbooks, and not the music.

I let my displeasure be known. I was only a temporary conductor, but I was on the ascent in the Broadway world, and the players didn't want to be on my wrong side. I let the band have it for jumping a scene-change cue before I gave the downbeat. They heard the cue from the stage and started playing before I took a breath. I was reining in the show into musical-theatre standards. If Mickey was going to rush the show, the rest of the cast wasn't going to. Harry Rigby was pleased, the dance captain was pleased, Annie Miller, and eventually Mickey were pleased.

Jane Summerhays's good will and support helped me a great deal with the company. I left after my two-week stint and *Sugar Babies* continued to run on Broadway without me. I moved on to finding other means of employment.

Florida producer Jan McArt hired me to conduct a Toronto production of *The Pirates Of Penzance* with Andy Gibb and Barry Bostwick. This was Jan's production from Florida, not the Joe Papp version but a somewhat unauthorized rip-off of that production from Central Park and the Public Theatre. Andy and Barry had done the earlier tours for Joe Papp.

We couldn't use their orchestrations, staging etc., so I was hired to re orchestrate, which I did, never once referencing the Papp version. I went back to the Gilbert and Sullivan originals. Andy and Barry did what they did. Caroline Peyton who had replaced Pam Dawber as Mabel was a first-class singer/actress.

Joe Papp's people tried to catch us out for using their materials. When they sent their conductor Don Jones to see it, I showed him the parts I was using and that we were not doing Joe Papp's version.

It was Gilbert and Sullivan and they had no case. I enjoyed the show, the mostly Toronto-based cast, and the orchestra, which was made up of Toronto's finest. It was a very good production all round.

I made lifetime friends with my Canadian associate and pianist, Stephen Woodjetts, and the very good first flutist in the pit was Barbara Ackerman. It turned out, Barbara had grown up just a short distance from me on Long Island and at the same time. Stephen, Barbara, and I were a little bonded triumvirate. I was blessed with two friendly pals to dine and drink with. It was a very pleasant time and I enjoyed conducting music that didn't need a drummer to hold it together.

Canada was a new experience, and I seriously considered Toronto as an alternative to New York. It was a bit smaller and had many of the advantages of a major city but was a bit more European in attitude. Having traveled a bit at that point, I was considering something other than New York as a home. I was a New Yorker but it was changing and appealing to me less and less.

Shortly after *Pirates*, Director/Choreographer Pat Birch asked me to be involved with an original musical called *American Passion*. Stuart Ostrow was the producer. I invited Stephen Woodjetts to assist me with this project. The only highlights were that Robert Downey Jr. was in the cast and that one of the girls in the cast, while having a drink with me and Stephen in our shared accommodations, pulled out a switchblade to show she was a serious street girl. She was. Stephen promptly gave his notice and asked if he could go back to Canada ASAP. He did!

We were trying out in Cambridge, near Boston. I asked my friend Bill Cox to come in and replace Stephen. He came to Cambridge to take over and I escaped. Much later, during my tenure with the tour of *Sugar Babies,* I was asked by Pat and Stu Ostrow to take a look at the Off-Broadway production of *American Passion* at the Joyce Theatre.

After I saw the show, which was a pretty hopeless venture, Pat asked what I thought. She was thinking of quitting during previews. I told her that if she quit during previews, Stu would blame her for its failure, and if she stayed through the opening night, he would blame the bad reviews on her work. She decided to stay. With *Grease, A Little Night Music, Pacific Overtures,* and *Playing Our Song* on her resume it wasn't going to ruin her reputation. Stu did blame her for its failure, but it was just a bad idea to begin with.

Rhoda and I were still talking about having a baby. *Sugar Babies* was closing on Broadway and was going to do a major tour. Glen Roven was asked to do the tour and according to Harry Rigby asked for an extraordinary amount of money. Harry said no and asked me. I had little happening at that time, and *Sugar Babies* was playing major venues. First was Chicago for at least a month or two. It seemed ideal. Then a layover for Christmas and New Year's and major stops. It seemed ideal. I said to Rhoda, "I'm going to go on tour, collect some big chunks of money, and then we can plan a baby."

I left for the initial opening in Chicago. The orchestra was wonderful, the cast was excellent, Mickey and Ann were delightful, and onward. When I came home for the Christmas break, Rhoda informed me that she wasn't really sure about having a baby. We had been married for twelve years at this point. When she told me that, the marriage had ended. If not officially, it had ended in my mind. We didn't discuss much else and I went on the road, looking forward to the tour: Columbus, Miami, St Louis, New Orleans, Toronto, Atlanta, Boston, Philadelphia, Chicago, Denver, San Francisco, and ultimately LA.

I looked forward to getting to Toronto and seeing my friends there. I enjoyed the city. We were playing what had been the O'Keefe Centre, which was now called the Hummingbird Centre. It turned out that Ann Miller hurt her wrist or leg and needed time off. She was replaced (temporarily) by Carol Lawrence. Carol was an old pro who done so many musicals. I knew her slightly, from playing piano on her act with Bill Cox conducting. We got along great, and she did the show very professionally. She wasn't Ann Miller, but she did her thing, and it was fun.

Annie returned and when we got to Boston, we found out that we were to do a cast recording. There had not yet been a cast album of *Sugar Babies*. Famed conductor Milton Rosenstock was the music supervisor and orchestrator Phil Lang, was asked to do a new overture.

I am a strong believer in Broadway tradition and since this was a cast recording, if not the original Broadway cast, I suggested to Harry Rigby that he ask Glen Roven to conduct. As much as I wanted to do it and it had become my show, I thought it was a piece of history and Glen, being a friend, should do it. Glen was asked and perhaps not knowing that it was me who had suggested this, once again asked for an extraordinary sum of money. Harry said, "Uh uh." The recording was masterminded by record producer Robert Sher and was finally done, with me conducting at the RCA studios in New York City. It was a delight to be part of this recording. All done on a day off during our Boston run. It turned out to be an excellent cast recording and is highly regarded as such.

While *Sugar Babies* was in Boston, *La Cage Aux Folles*, the new Jerry Herman/Harvey Fierstein musical, was trying out with Don Pippin as MD. It was a surefire hit with Arthur Laurents directing and Scotty Salmon doing the choreography. Don invited me and Annie Miller to see the show. It was a giant success and during the "can-can" on stage, the audience went wild and there was a standing ovation in the middle of the show. I stood up too, but Annie just sat there. When I sat down, I asked, "Don't you like it?"

She said, "I saw the original."

I said, "You mean the Cole Porter musical with Gwen Verdon?"

She said, "Honey, I saw it with Toulouse Lautrec."

She was wickedly funny sometimes.

We showed up at a cast party after the show and Don boldly introduced me to Arthur Laurents as the music director for the planned LA production following the Broadway production. Arthur didn't take too kindly to being told anything, but he smiled and knew that I had Jerry's approval, on Don's recommendation. This was many months in the future.

I opened *Sugar Babies* in Atlanta while I was being romanced by another producer to conduct *Marilyn,* directed by Kenny Ortega. This was planned for an almost immediate Broadway production . I took time off from Atlanta and participated in the auditions (for no fee while my contract was being negotiated by my then-agent Yvette Schumer). My contract hadn't been signed and I was already participating in the prep of the show. When I overheard the very peculiar Aussie producer discussing other music directors' names with the casting director, Barry Moss, I promptly announced my non-participation in the project and went back to Atlanta for the last performances of *Sugar Babies.*

Marilyn ended up a disaster and a little schadenfreude is part of all of our lives. Especially in show business.

Later, on days off from the tour in Philadelphia, several of us decided to train up to our homes in New York City. Getting off the train at Penn Station, I would subway or taxi uptown with one of the Sugar Babies, Kaylyn Dillehay. It turned out we lived around the corner from one another. She was on 87th and I was on 86th. We enjoyed chatting and found out that we had almost worked together many times. In fact, when I'd come into the show on Broadway, she had been on vacation. Later on, when I was absent from Atlanta, she had been asked to be a vacation, temporary replacement. We figured out that she had almost been on several shows that I was involved in. This was a bit of kismet as she thought the road was a good place right now too.

After this flurry of work, the recording, the little bout of auditions with *Marilyn* (the musical), Kaylyn and I started spending more time together. We were both suffering from marriages that were similarly on the rocks.

The tour continued through Denver, San Francisco, and ultimately Los Angeles. One day, at the Pantages in LA, Ronnie Field, the choreographer, was visiting Annie. I had been rehearsal pianist on the *Applause* bus and truck in 1973 and so Ron said, rather flirtatiously, having known me at age twenty-one as a rehearsal pianist, "Larry, you haven't changed one bit."

Me, now the wizened, experienced MD of thirty-two said, "You haven't changed either."

Annie said, "Oh boys, stop that shit."

Had to love her.

The best thing that happened in LA: After conducting a performance of *Sugar Babies* at the Pantages, I felt a tap on my shoulder. I turned around and Irv Kostal was standing there, and said, "You were planning to call me, I hope, and this is Peter Matz."

The time had come for me to continue my friendship and studies with Irv and Peter Matz, who was a giant in the pop music and theatre music business. Irv and I continued our friendship, and he immediately took me on as his protégé. He wasn't really working much anymore, but he was president of ASMAC, the American Society of Music Arrangers and Composers. He invited me to their luncheons.

The first luncheon was at a well-known "hang," Tail O' the Cock at Coldwater Canyon and Ventura Blvd. When he brought me into lunch there was a very long and crowded table with the likes of all the older Hollywood composers, arrangers, and conductors: Van Alexander, Billy May, Frank Comstock, Les Brown. Frank De Vol, Allyn Ferguson, Ray Charles (of the Ray Charles singers), Jon Charles, Herschel Gilbert, Mauro Bruno, Pete Rugolo, Vic Mizzy, Vic Schoen, and Hank Mancini (who was still very active). There were many others too, all having lunch together. This was an ASMAC luncheon. As Irv said, it was a chance for everyone to get together, shoot the breeze and talk about anything. Very informal and collegial. This was my entrance to the world of Hollywood TV and film music with all of the old regulars.

Meanwhile, I was officially offered the San Francisco and LA production of *La Cage Aux Folles,* and gave my notice to *Sugar Babies, which* was running at the Pantages Theatre.

I went back to New York and Rhoda and rehearsals for *La Cage* knowing that in about six months' time, after San Francisco, I'd be in LA, more or less permanently.

La Cage was a *giant* success on Broadway. It was pro-gay, and it was the right time. It opened on Broadway in August 1983, and we were opening in San Francisco in the spring of '84.

San Francisco was an openly gay town. It was the Wild Wild West and a truly wonderful city for everyone. Everyone was welcome. A real party town.

Rehearsals in New York were at 890 Broadway, the Michael Bennett studios. In those days, I always showed up at rehearsals in my best Paul Stuart suit, shirt and tie, handkerchief in the pocket. Very dapper.

Walter Charles was playing Albin and Keith Michel was playing Georges. I knew Walter slightly from earlier times. He was a wonderful singer/actor and a great guy. Keith Michel was a well-loved Aussie, who was just charming, and great in everything he did. The cast was quite superb all the way around and I knew many of the dancers.

Jerry Herman was thrilled to have me there, as Pippin's hand-picked choice. On the first day, when Arthur Laurents was introducing everyone in the cast and crew, he said, "Our music director is the esteemed Larry Blank, who is unfortunately not one of us," (meaning I was *heterosexual* with … ohmigod … a *wife* … who was a *woman*!!!)

I must've turned bright red with embarrassment, because Jerry Herman sidled up right next to me and said very loudly "Well, I like him." That's how rehearsals began and continued for the entire four-week rehearsal period.

Unfortunately, I was forced to use a pianist I had sacked from the *A Chorus Line* tour. He was an excellent pianist who had a very troubled personality. If you were to look up the definition of passive-aggressive, this was your man. But he had formidable skills and was well liked by some, especially Arthur. I was stuck with him. This pianist had originally played some of the rehearsals for the Broadway production. He knew all the dance music, including the dance music that had been eliminated during the out-of-town tryout, and would sometimes remember it at the oddest times—like, during a run-through I was conducting.

Arthur would glare at me and say, "What are you doing?"

I would respond very bluntly, "The stick doesn't make any noise."

Don Pippin persuaded me not to walk out or display any anger, which was Arthur's intention in goading me. He was trying to get me to storm out or bluntly argue with him in front of the cast. I had too many friends and supporters in the room, including Keith Michel, who had become a friend and was very aware of Arthur's behavior. I knew what I was doing, and I had the support of the composer, the music supervisor, and the producers, Barry Brown, and Fritz Holt.

It didn't hurt that Allan Carr was the lead producer and was Marvin Hamlisch's manager and that I had his support as well.

The haranguing and abuse Arthur directed at me was daily and un-relenting. It was only the quiet coaching from Don Pippin that prevented me from lashing out and giving Arthur cause to have me sacked.

Arthur was one of the most talented men I ever met. He was also a loathsome human being, and his talent didn't redeem his despicable behavior to many. A totally disrespectful man. He was hideous to me and to Laurel Lockhart, who played Mme. Dindon. I stayed calm, knowing my business, despite being insulted regularly.

I was looking forward to San Francisco where I had a love affair with the orchestra, who knew me from *A Chorus Line* and *Sugar Babies*. Between the pianist, Arthur, and choreographer Scott Salmon, who sucked up to Arthur, it was rather unpleasant. My being totally unrattled, bothered Arthur even more, and the cast rallied behind me. Brad Wong (BD Wong) and Cady Huffman were members of the ensemble. Eric Underwood (one of the *cagelles*) was a good friend as well. I was rid of the disruptive rehearsal pianist. I had a wonderful orchestral rehearsal with the fabulous San Francisco band at the Golden Gate. A pleasure.

We had a new finale written just for this company and a lot of time was put into it. It was not really an improvement, but it was an attempt by Scott Salmon and Arthur to be closer to one of the drag bars in France, like Michou, in Montmartre. It took a lot of time and orchestra rehearsal.

At the orchestra rehearsal in San Fran, the band was playing the crap out of it. It was as good as any orchestra in the world. The lead trumpet, Bill Wagner, was a giant and he couldn't be beat.

I played the new finale for Arthur and Scott, and Arthur said, "If you conducted with more intensity it would work."

I turned to him, handed him the stick, and said, "Show me."

He smiled and backed way off because I wouldn't take his abuse. He dropped his harangue and the stick as well.

Later on, when we were setting up in the pit, Arthur came down to the pit rail and said something like, "if you knew what you were doing this would be ok".

It was so offensive that the orchestra gasped out loud. He walked away and I started to climb over the pit rail into the auditorium at the Golden Gate Theater. Fritz Holt was standing there and said, "Larry, please don't walk out." Fritz was co producer for *La Cage*.

I said, "Fritz, I'm not leaving, I'm going to hit him." I was absolutely serious.

Fritz, one of the great gentlemen of the theatre and a stage manager/producer of the first order, thought quickly and said, "In that case, let me get him and I'll hold him." He caught me off guard and I started laughing, he started laughing and the crisis was averted. I suspect that Fritz then had some words with Arthur to get him to back off.

We got through techs and dress rehearsals and were at our first public performance at the Golden Gate. Jerry was sitting in the third row. Mary Martin was sitting a few rows back. Keith Michel was renting her San Francisco apartment and she had come to see him. Everything was going smoothly. There were wonderful performances, flawless lighting, fluid scene changes, and the sound was excellent.

We were getting to "Chez Jacqueline" in the second act where there were crucial scenes. Then the set … *jammed up*. I had a specific music cue when the set cleared to make the transition, but it was not going to happen and we were stuck in a vamp. The stage manager, Jan Beroza, was flashing me on my headset but I need both hands. I looked into the camera that was on me for the offstage singers and for Jan to see my cues, and I gave her the thumbs up that I saw it. Then I turned to Don Chan on piano and said out loud, "Start playing the "La Cage" song," and waved the band out. Don Chan and drummer, John Gates were playing the tune so that we weren't stuck in a vamp, but the set was still stuck. I turned to the orchestra while Don and John were playing and told them to be ready to come out of the vamp into the music on my cue.

I saw the set coming around to where it was supposed to go. (this is after about two or three minutes of nothing happening except the piano/bass/drums playing the tune.) I saw the get unstuck, gave the entire orchestra the cue, and the scene change continued … to much applause from the audience and a huge smile to me from Jerry Herman. We could've been in that vamp for three minutes.

The show continued to the end and a happy finish. Backstage, Arthur Laurents came up to me and said, "Larry, I apologize. I was completely wrong about you. Thank you for that save."

I said, "Arthur, will you call the company together and say that to them?"

He said no, and I said exactly what any person would say to a response like that, and I walked away.

He never warmed up much beyond that, but the abuse stopped. He had done enough damage to me during the rehearsal period. Once Arthur went away, it was a pleasure to do the show every night. The show got excellent reviews and it was a very happy time.

Four years later when I was conducting *Mack and Mabel* at Papermill Playhouse, Arthur came up to me after a performance he attended and treated me like an old friend, as if none of this had happened. However, the damage had been done and despite his talents as a librettist, I can never feel much of anything towards him except dread. When Mary Rodgers was asked about Arthur Laurents, she was quoted as saying, "Call me when he's dead."

When *La Cage* opened in San Francisco it was just before my thirty-second birthday and the San Francisco run was a pleasure. I treasured the time I spent with Keith Michel, and Walter Charles doing the show. The rest of the cast, and the orchestra were sublime. Unfortunately, the specter of AIDS was rising. We all were hearing of the "gay" disease that was causing concern and there was occasional word about someone getting very ill and dying. *La Cage* celebrated love, and it didn't matter whether it was between men and women, or men and men, or women and women.

We were scheduled to move from San Francisco to Los Angeles at the end of the summer, which was really too bad, because the show could've run for a very long time in San Francisco. The celebration of the gay movement (of that time:1984) was elevated because of *La Cage* and there was a great demand for tickets. Although I was "not one of them," I was part of the celebration and appreciated being part of the show. Jerry Herman always made me feel special and a major contributor to its success. Because of *La Cage* and my relationship with Don Pippin, I would continue working with Jerry till the end of his life.

At the end of the San Francisco run, Keith Michel departed for the Broadway production and was replaced by the Broadway Georges, Gene Barry. Gene was a beloved TV star. He had started out on Broadway as a singer in some major flops. Then he went to Hollywood and after the film *War Of The Worlds*, stayed in Hollywood for a big career with an occasional musical in summer stock and tours.

Gene was a little insecure about his singing. During the run, I accompanied him on a couple of TV shows: Merv Griffin and Johnny Carson, and for a couple of galas. He had done a nightclub act and aside from having a certain lack of natural rhythm he was ok. Some people have said that he was homophobic. I certainly didn't see or hear anything from him that would indicate that was true and he would have been excoriated by everyone had this been so. He might have made a thoughtless comment that was construed as such, but I don't believe it was out of anything but a lack of thought behind it. He wasn't the actor that Keith Michel was, but he deserved a lot of kudos for his contribution to the success of the show. It was his very bravado and sincere warmth that made the other performances shine. Gene was a good man despite any negative comments from others.

The show moved to the Pantages in Los Angeles. I had many friends in the pit. It wasn't the love fest we had in San Francisco, but still very pleasant.

The best part of *La Cage* was becoming friendly with our lead *"cagelle."* Randy Doney and his partner Alton Ruff became friends for life. Alton became my business manager until his passing and Randy still a great friend. Larry Fuller, choreographer from *Evita* was a mutual friend of theirs along with Sandy Roveta. We all became friends for life.

My marriage to Rhoda had finally fallen completely apart. I was seeing Kaylyn although we lived separately. Carrying on my joy of learning to fly from so many years before, I was doing a lot of flying. My flight instructor was Alan Johnson (not the choreographer), but my bass trombone player in the pit. I was achieving higher pilot ratings, and ultimately became a CFI (certified flight instructor). Not that I wanted to teach, but it was an accomplishment in the hierarchy of flight ratings. Eventually, I bought an airplane and then another. It was right up there with buying a boat. An expensive indulgence.

Because of my instructor rating, I was able to give Kaylyn lessons, along with her "proper" instruction from the experienced Alan Johnson. Whenever it was possible, we would fly on days off. Kaylyn was dancing in various shows at the Grand Dinner Theatre and local venues as well as some industrials and TV.

I was also working on getting more writing experience and spending time with Irv Kostal. Through Irv and various ASMAC events I was meeting people. Because of being on the west coast, my relationship with Marvin Hamlisch had become perfunctory although we occasionally were in touch about something or other.

Sadly, with the AIDS epidemic and other factors, *LA CAGE* wasn't the success it was in New York and we had dwindling houses. It was clear that the show was going to close prematurely.

I was now living alone in Hollywood, spending time with Kaylyn. However, my income was about to go away. I had managed to save some money and had enough to live on. Due to the behavior of Arthur Laurents, I was pretty well emotionally beaten up by the end of the run. I decided I was going to back off from doing musical theatre for a while and focus on a little down time and some flight instruction. Being a flight instructor is not a way to make a living, but it was something. I flew a bit, partied a lot, and did some flight instruction to pay for my flying habit.

I was living in an apartment on Laurel Avenue in Hollywood down the street from the Comedy Store and Greenblatt's Delicatessen. On Mondays, Greenblatt's served new Beaujolais wine at twenty-five cents per glass! I would order four glasses at a time. Thinking back

... they were overcharging, but it was fun with a few friends and an overwrought deli sandwich. Slowly, I was running out of money, but I was happy to be doing nothing for a minute. It's not that I was depressed or anything like that, I was just taking a rest from what had been a constant working situation since I'd had graduated high school in 1969. It was now 1985.

One day, the phone rang and it was my old friend, Jack Lee. Jack was a well loved and respected conductor on Broadway. He had been very supportive of me since the beginning of my career playing piano at that gypsy run-through of *Applause*. He said, "I'm coming to LA with the tour of *My One And Only* with Tommy Tune and Sandy Duncan. How would you like to play second piano?"

I said, "Jack, I am so sick of doing musicals and dealing with characters like Arthur Laurents, I don't know if I can do it."

Jack said, "You will have no responsibility at all except the piano part, no Arthur Laurents—just me."

"Well, I don't know, Jack. I don't want to be stressed."

"Stop this shit," said Jack, "and get back in the pit where you belong and we'll have fun."

Well, thanks to Jack—another life changing moment. I was recovering from post-traumatic stress disorder from dealing with Arthur Laurents and Jack helped my recovery. I'm joking, but the experience on *La Cage* had really worn me down and even now almost forty years later, it still stings.

I worked on the piano part, which was really beyond my piano chops after having been in the pit conducting for so long. But I worked hard at being able to play it decently. I was happy to get in the pit with so many friends. Joe Soldo was first reed and contractor, and it was a lot of my good friends from *La Cage*.

Kaylyn announced that she had been going to auditions and she had been hired as a replacement dancer in *My One And Only*, so we'd be working together. It was a tour, so inevitably she'd be going on the road with the show. I was only booked to be in LA. However, it was an extended stay at the Ahmanson.

I enjoyed being in the pit and seeing so many friends backstage, a lot of dancers and singers I had known over the years. I had known Tommy Tune from his friendship with Lucie Arnaz and Sandy Duncan was very warm and friendly. It was nice to show up at the theatre and it was nice that Kaylyn and I were working together. I was also still working on other music, getting invited to recording sessions, and getting more familiar with the LA TV scene and working around the fringes of TV music.

Most importantly, Jack Lee had brought me back into the fold and I was back in show biz. To paraphrase *The Godfather* ... Just when I thought I was out of it...*they sucked me back in.*

We had a nice run with *My One And Only*. Lucie Arnaz came in to replace Sandy Duncan, who left to go back and spend time with her family. Lucie and I had a nice reunion. Lucie would continue with the tour.

Kaylyn went off on the tour and I was on my own in LA. Almost immediately, my phone rang and it was music contractor Mel Rodnan for *My One And Only* telling me that the second pianist in Louisville, KY was not working out so well. Could I fly out ASAP?

I said sure. Kaylyn was on the road, and I had a place to stay and a paid holiday in Louisville. I sat down in the pit and after hearing a few bars, I turned to the concertmaster and said, "Pass it on, the piano has been tuned." I was glad that Jack welcomed my totally irreverent sense of humor. The next few months, I would go back to LA and the phone would ring and it would be Mel or Jack saying, "How fast can you get to Denver?" and so on. So Kaylyn and I got to visit.

Jack managed to get me booked as the "regular" for the tour's stop in San Francisco. I still had a union membership in Local 6 in San Francisco from my earlier days there, so it seemed a good fit. In the meantime, I took off for a few weeks and was the music director for a production of *A Chorus Line* at the San Jose Civic Light Opera.

At some point I went back east to visit family. My parents were still in Bayside, with my father failing but still at home.

I used my airplane and flew into LaGuardia with my little Piper Cherokee. Over the radio, New York approach said … "Piper 5375Lima, what are your intentions?"

I said, "Business."

The response was, "Ha!"

I flew up the Hudson River and air traffic control told me to turn right when I saw the runway (which you do from the Hudson River at 5,000 feet). It seemed that I turned right at 96th Street and apparently the runway does line up with 96th Street in Manhattan.

It was an exciting time. I visited my family and somehow, I don't remember how, I ended up at Caldwell Airport in Caldwell, New Jersey. Kaylyn was in Detroit with *My One And Only,* so I planned to fly there to visit and then continue back to the west coast.

I took off on visual flight rules from Caldwell. New Jersey to Michigan is a relatively easy trip that takes some all-day flying but is otherwise a normal flight for a light private plane. I was an instrument-rated flight instructor, so I was fully qualified to fly in mild weather and in the clouds under instrument flight rules. The weather report was basically ok, with some precipitation. It was winter and there would be some instrument flying but nothing abnormal.

Of course, in a commercial jet you'd be above all the weather, but in a little *pee popper* Piper or Cessna aircraft, you have to navigate through some clouds.

I took off and almost immediately in Pennsylvania I was in clouds and some very light precipitation. I was talking to air traffic control and they said it would be ok, but I asked to climb to a higher altitude to see if I could get over this little bit of rain. As I climbed, I saw the temperature drop and a little bit of ice was forming. In a light private plane, ice is not something you can deal with. There is no anti-icing equipment and you have to get out of it ASAP.

My plane was quickly becoming inundated with ice and I was in very serious trouble. I had to get out of this. There was no way up and the only way out was to land. I was covered with ice, couldn't see anything, and was on instruments.

Williamsport is what's called an uncontrolled airport, meaning, there is no control tower but you do what you need to do. You announce your intentions on a prescribed frequency and you listen to other people at the same airport. At least it wasn't going to be busy in this kind of weather. The only approach to the airport was called an NDB approach: a non-directional beacon. That means, they have a broadcast signal and you have a device in your airplane that says, *We are over here*. It would be the equivalent of flying to the Empire State Building because it's broadcasting a radio signal, but you *can't see it*.

You have a chart that says what the altitude is, if there are any tall buildings and when you can descend. All determined by the pilot. I was in a non-radar environment, so air traffic control only had vague information. I was clearly on my own.

I located the beacon and flew by needles/instruments towards it. Very gently, I began my descent, hoping I wouldn't misjudge my distance (all by instruments) before my plane fell out of the sky because of ice. I hoped I wouldn't hit trees (which I couldn't see).

, I descended very calmly with the noise of the plane and no help from air traffic control. They did ask if I was declaring an emergency and I said no, I was on the approach. As I descended, I heard *POW POW POW.* When I looked around, I realized that the temperature was getting warmer and the snow/ice was turning to rain, which meant the ice was melting very slowly, flying off, and hitting the tail of the plane.

Coming out of the clouds, I saw the trees well below me, and I was in clear sky below the clouds and above the trees. My windshield, however, was totally covered with ice, so I could only see out of the small side windows of my plane and had to turn the plane sideways to look around.

I spotted the runway in the distance about four miles away. It was covered with a light layer of snow. No planes had been on it, so I would be landing on a snow-covered runway in a little pee popper airplane in the middle of nowhere with no guidance from ATC or anyone at the airport.

I went through all the emergency procedures I had learned as a flight instructor. To eliminate the chance of fire or worse if I lost control on the snow/ice, I knew I had to turn everything off before I landed so that no fuel would be flowing. My plan was to make a normal landing and kill all power just before I touched down (still not able to see out the front window since it was layered with ice).

I made my descent using my side window to spot the beginning of the runway and used full flaps (so I could fly as slowly as possible). Landing roughly at/or above sixty MPH, I killed all power, straightened the plane, touched down perfectly, and rolled down the runway. Starting to slow down in the snow, I tried to keep the plane straight … slowing, slowing, slowing, slowing, and slid off the side of the runway into the snow. My plane was totally intact with everything off. I got out of the airplane as quickly as I could, looked around and saw no damage, and leaned against the side of the plane not sure whether to laugh or cry.

I heard some laughing and looked over to see a huge hangar, a small Allegheny Airlines aircraft, and two pilots laughing. Allegheny flew commuter flights to Williamsport. Later, it was to become US Air. The two pilots brought over a small tow truck, helped my trusty pee popper Piper Cherokee into the hangar to dry out, and took me to a very nice dinner with as many beers/glasses of wine I could handle. I was very grateful for my good fortune. That night, I checked into a local motel and got a good night's sleep.

The next day was beautiful and sunny. What I had encountered had been a freak snowstorm over Lycoming County. I completed the journey to Detroit to tell Kaylyn the story.

Chapter Six

Not long after this, Kaylyn phoned me in LA to let me know that she was pregnant. Our first child, Jamie, was born nine months later. This was as close as I ever came to becoming religious.

We were both very happy as this was something we both wanted, but Kaylyn decided to dance as long as she could with *My One And Only*. I was in LA and still occasionally showing up on the tour when they asked. One night, when I was visiting in Chicago (not playing in the pit) we attended a party at Tommy Tune's digs. Kaylyn and I had confided in my old pal Lucie Arnaz and she very cutely announced, "Guess who's gonna have a baby." It was very much like an episode of *I Love Lucy*. So … the cat was out of the bag.

Kaylyn continued to dance until she finally said it was enough. She had been getting dizzy dancing and was suffering a little nausea in the wings. So she gave her notice. Meanwhile, Baayork Lee contacted me and asked me to be the music director for *A Chorus Line* in Tokyo and Kobe, Japan. It was going to be with Tony Teague, Donna McKechnie, and Rita O'Connor. Donna was an old friend by this time and I was happy to be returning to my old friend *A Chorus Line*. It was a superb company and Michael Bennett and Bob Avian visited rehearsals.

It was clear that Michael was unwell and there were rumors he had AIDS. He and Donna were very friendly and it was clear something was up, but no one would dare say it.

The show was going to play San Francisco; Portland, Oregon; the Fifth Avenue Theatre in Seattle, and then off to Tokyo. After Tokyo there'd be a short run in Kobe.

Kaylyn was very pregnant at this time, and we decided she'd stay at home for the little, short US part of the tour and then would join me for the trip to Tokyo. She was less than six months pregnant, and it all seemed a safe thing to do.

During the US part of the tour, I had my usual love fest with the band at the Curran in San Francisco, but a little less so in Portland and Seattle. Both are wonderful cities with great musicians but the orchestra contractor at the time was not as conscientious as they are these days.

When I was in San Francisco prior to Japan, I had received a rather strange call from Marvin Hamlisch. He was about to go into rehearsals for his new musical, *Smile.* I had originally been asked to do it when the lyricist was Carolyn Leigh. Carolyn died suddenly and the show went through machinations and was now being co-written with Howard Ashman.

I hadn't been as involved with Marvin since I'd made my move to LA and he had workshopped *Smile* with Bob Billig and Fran Liebergall handling the music and Mike Berkowitz on drums.

Marvin had been a little strange lately. He'd had an on again / off again working relationship with drummer Michael Keller, whom I had brought on board with *Playing Our Song.* Then I brought Berkowitz on board and then I was on and off with Marvin. Pippin was on and off too, but mostly on because he was Don Pippin.

In any case, I received this call from Marvin asking if I'd be interested in conducting *Smile*. Because I was just about to leave for Japan, I hemmed and hawed.

I put in a call to Don Pippin for advice and he started laughing and said that Marvin had called him and asked him the same thing. Meanwhile, Mike Berkowitz had suggested Paul Gemignani, whom he had been working with and Marvin had called Paul as well. I had seen Marvin do this with orchestrators on *Playing Our Song* where he asked two or three orchestrators to orchestrate a song and then picked his favorite. Well in this case I wasn't really available, Pippin wasn't interested, and Paul was both interested and available. Marvin had the coup of getting Gemignani, Sondheim's conductor.

No conductor of a musical ever caused it to sell more tickets, so it really didn't matter too much. Everyone else had jumped ship on *Smile*, including Michael Bennett, who had originally planned to be involved during the Carolyn Leigh days.

I was off to Tokyo where on landing I was sent directly from Narita Airport to an orchestra rehearsal. I was totally exhausted. The rehearsal was being conducted by Mori Shibuya, a lovely man with great communication skills and very smart. Mori was my translator and soon became a friend. He was the music director for Tokyo Disneyland and had been the translator/orchestra contractor for an earlier incarnation of this tour. His musical skills weren't quite first rate, but he hired the right people to surround him along with the best musicians in Japan. His young assistants were Akira Miyagawa (now a major star in music in Japan and Megumi Chinju (now very successful in music theatre in Japan as well). Both were very helpful to me at the time. Megumi was playing rehearsals as necessary.

I got on the podium with Ed Shea on drums and Dan Strickland on piano and we were able to get things moving very quickly. The band was excellent and as good as any of the first-rate orchestras in the world. Aside from language barriers, it was a fine experience. This was to be repeated in Kobe, where I had a different set of musicians equally as good. We travelled with certain players like the percussion and the harpist, Aiko Erie.

I recall that one time, I was having a chat with Donna McKechnie before the show. The stage manager came in and said, "Larry-san."

I continued talking and a moment later I was bracketed by a stage manager on each side politely moving me to the podium as I continued to talk. They were virtually people movers. They were on schedule even if I wasn't.

The band in Tokyo was backstage and off to the side. As on Broadway, they were not seen as they are in normal theatres in the pit. We were permitted to wear anything we wanted as we were totally unseen. The very last night, one of the wind players came to fetch me. He was fully dressed in a tuxedo. He brought me to the bandstand where the entire band greeted me in full dinner jacket attire. It was a sign of respect for me, and I was very touched and flattered. Mori had become a good friend and introduced us to his American friend, Larry Billman, and his wife and daughters. Larry was a great dancer/choreographer and responsible for a lot of the shows at Disneyland California, Orlando, and Tokyo.

We had a lovely time in Japan, and I seem to recall being there at least a month if not longer. Kaylyn was now approaching seven and a half months.

Marvin was on the road with *Smile* and booked me for a few concert dates. I recall I had one scheduled for October 16th and 17th,

1986 in Washington, DC. Marvin would be doing *Smile* in Baltimore at that time.

On October 14ᵗʰ, Kaylyn was in the hospital in labor. After much ado, labor was induced a little further and after trying for a long time Jamie Erin Dillehay Blank was born by C-section on October 15ᵗʰ. Then I got on a plane to DC to do the concert with Marvin and Mike Berkowitz on drums. I think we pushed the C-section just so I could make the plane.

Jamie was a beautiful baby girl at nine pounds, six and 1/2 ounces.

It was a bit awkward as Marvin and Mike were dealing with *Smile* and I was conducting the concert as per normal in the past. It was fine but not likely I was going to be doing much more of this with Marvin. I was grateful to him because he had given me a great deal of work and recognition, a major-hit Broadway show, and many, many concerts with great symphony orchestras when I was very young. My move to LA had initiated a change and I didn't really mind. I was thirty-four years old and I had guest conducted virtually every major orchestra in the US as guest conductor for Marvin Hamlisch.

Back to LA.

My mother rang me up and sent me a check for $5000.00, which was a lot of money. She told me not to take any work and to stay with Kaylyn and our new baby for a month. It was a blessing, and I was happy to take the money and not have to work. In 1986, $5000 went a very long way.

Shortly after, though, the need to make money reared its head. I got a job writing a little show for Disney (the parks, not the film studio) and then a new theatre was coming to life. The California Music Theatre was being created by director Gary Davis and his business partner Lars Hansen. They were ambitious. They phoned me and said, "We are planning *Most Happy Fella, She Loves Me, and The Desert Song.* Which one would you like to do?"

Without hesitation, I said, *The Most Happy Fella.* I had done the show in my first season of stock at Kenley Players, and I really wanted to do something with some meat in the music and do a good job of it. They allowed me to engage Joe Soldo as the orchestra contractor and hire an A+ orchestra to do the show with the full orchestration. I had the best players in town along with John Raitt as Tony, Linda Michele as Rosabella, Larry Guittard as Joe, Wayne Bryan as Herman. Lisa Robinson was Cleo.

My old friend (from *A Chorus Line*), Patti Colombo, was the choreographer. We were able to hire all of the best singers/dancers in Los Angeles and it was a glorious production musically.

The reviews reflected that as well, though it was rather ambitious for a local theatre company, and I don't believe they had a chance to make any money with their ambitious plans.

I established a nice relationship with John Raitt. My good friend Jim May (cousin of my high school buddy Clifford May) was associate. He was connected with John, and it was a perfect choice.

I enjoyed the show tremendously and was so complimented when Ray Charles, (the other Ray Charles from the Ray Charles Singers) rang me up to tell me how excellent the choral singing was. It was a great joy and a wonderful production, but I had other fish to fry and didn't do anything further with the organization.

They hired some very good people but their later productions were less prestigious and eventually the organization went away. I was sad to hear that. Gary and Lars had great plans. Unfortunately, Los Angeles really doesn't seem to sustain theatre for too long. Not since the days of Edwin Lester and the Civic Light Opera had there been an attempt with continuing musical theatre in LA. Sad that it failed.

Shortly after that I did an industrial with John Raitt. We were having a deep-dish pizza on Chicago's Gold Coast, when a gentlemen recognized John and sat down with us. It was Bill Cosby, who despite his later reputation, was absolutely charming and on his way out, picked up the bill for us.

John was a very big Broadway star in his day. I always enjoyed talking to him and he was a very friendly and warm guy. He knew his stuff. His daughter Bonnie would hang around in his dressing room and was always very sweet too. She wasn't yet *the* Bonnie Raitt, but she was still Bonnie Raitt, John's daughter. And a very nice girl.

While I was busy with *Most Happy Fella*, Kaylyn was hired to choreograph *Best Little Whorehouse* at the San Jose Civic Light Opera. Kaylyn took baby Jamie with her. After *Fella* closed, I went to play rehearsal piano and entertain our baby daughter. On our return, we had just enough time to schedule our wedding with Irv as best man. 6-month-old Jamie was clapping in the wings.

And then ... the next call came from Don Pippin.

He had been asked to supervise *Teddy And Alice,* a musical about Teddy Roosevelt and his daughter, Alice Roosevelt Longworth. Hal Hackady had put lyrics to some Sousa marches adapted by Richard Kapp plus some original tunes by Kapp and Hackady. There was talk of Gene Hackman, but we fortunately secured Len Cariou, who was quite wonderful and a great guy.

Pippin was going to supervise. The show was being funded by some big money in Tampa and they were supposed to use John Head (trumpet player and conductor from Atlanta) to do the show. But they needed some Broadway people to put it together. We went into rehearsals, and I knew instinctively that we would never see John Head once I established myself as the MD in the room.

That is exactly what happened and quite correctly. I asked Jim May to assist me. Donald Saddler was to choreograph, and Pippin had set it up so Kaylyn would not only be a swing dancer in the show but Don Saddler's assistant. Donald was a charming, Old-World gent. He had lasted in the business for a very long time because of his warmth and business sense, winning a Tony for *Wonderful Town*, with an assist from Jerry Robbins on the opening number, and a Tony for *No, No, Nanette* with an assist from Mary Ann Niles and Ted Cappy. He had been on a lot of shows over the years.

Gordon Harrell was the dance arranger and Jim Tyler the orchestrator. A great team. Pippin was happy I was involved and basically did some vocals and then left me to do the show.

I'll never forget the first rehearsal day with director Stone (Bud) Widney. Bud had been Alan Lerner's buddy and associate on many projects most notably *Camelot* and *Lolita, My Love.* He had done some directing and was mostly a very nice fellow. But he went on for hours and hours and hours talking about Teddy Roosevelt and the history as we all dutifully sat there listening—Ron Raines, Len, Beth Fowler, Nancy Hume, who was Alice, and all the rest of us. Don Pippin raised his hand and Bud said, with great respect, "Yes Don."

Don said, "What key and how fast?" which broke everyone up.

We went to lunch and began rehearsal on return.

The show was opening the Tampa Bay Performing Arts Center. Orchestra was coming from all over Florida. I'm still in touch with first-trombone Jeff Thomas, who is principal trombone for the Orlando Phil.

Teddy And Alice had a stellar design team of Robin Wagner, Theoni Aldredge, and Tharon Musser. It had all the people who make hit shows. What it didn't have was a good-enough book, music, or lyrics to make a hit show. It was all good, it just didn't gel. But the performances were good and the show was slick as could be.

When we were staging the end of Act One the day before we left for the Tampa tryout, Kaylyn came up to me and said, "Don Saddler left the room and doesn't seem to be coming back. What should I do?"

I said, "Stage the finale."

So, she did with everyone waving an American flag. The number was called "Wave The Flag" and was based on Sousa's "Stars and Stripes Forever" with Len singing lyrics devised by Hal Hackady based on the famous piccolo part. It was very corny but there was something kind of good about it all. Eventually this evolved to a giant cannon being erected (literally over the audience) to end Act One. Lighting designer Tharon Musser quipped that this was the first "taste free" musical on Broadway.

We headed to Tampa to the new theatre, which was still very much under construction. Despite fumes, wet paint, unfinished floors, and such, we got the show open. A bunch of kids in the show played the Roosevelt family. Karen Ziemba, Andrew Leeds, and Richard Blake were members of the cast and went onward to bigger and better things. But the show was a bit noisy and not together.

My father had been put in a senior citizens home near my mother so she could spend time with him. He died (not unexpectedly) while we were in Tampa. I came back for the funeral before heading back to Tampa to work on the show.

The producer Hinks Shimberg fired Bud Widney and brought in John Driver (who was known as an actor). I never figured this out.

John did tighten up some story lines and focused a very few things. The show wasn't that bad; it just wasn't that good. They decided that after Tampa it would go back into rehearsal and then open at the Mechanic in Baltimore for its further pre-Broadway tour and then at Broadway's Minskoff in November.

Little Jamie was traveling with us, and we had a nanny. Just as rehearsals began, Kaylyn advised me she was pregnant again. We decided to alert everyone as it was early days. She was swing, dance captain, and assistant choreographer, so it was a good thing. She was only a few months pregnant, and being tall and slender and in hoop skirts, it was going to work as long as she could dance.

The show was tightened up a bit in Baltimore. I did a few little orchestrations with Jim Tyler's blessings. He had farmed out some to Michael Gibson and Chris Bankey. There was an important piece of underscoring that Gordon Harrell insisted I do. I always appreciated Gordon's faith in me. He was very supportive and encouraging. It gave me great confidence. I had not yet done anything important enough to give anyone confidence in any of my orchestrations, but I had been around and knew what made an orchestra tick.

I did have one very funny experience.

While at the 890 Studios (we had learned of Michael Bennett's untimely passing from AIDS while rehearsing) … a guy in a tuxedo came in and said, "Where's Larry Blank?"

I recognized him immediately as Larry Kert. He came over and said, "Harvey Evans and I are rehearsing a tour of *La Cage* downstairs and Arthur Laurents says you are the one who can help us out."

I went with Larry and said hello to Harvey, whom I knew from an earlier show. The pianist/MD was having trouble with one of the songs and I played and coached them through it. Straightened it out (so to speak – since despite Arthur's efforts I was still not one of them). It was nice to be asked. Didn't change my feelings about Arthur Laurents by one digit.

Back to *Teddy and Alice*.

We got to Baltimore and the show was better but still not the giant musical they had hoped for. I wouldn't know how to fix it. It just wasn't that important enough and didn't really have anything to say. It just seemed that Teddy was rather indulgent with his outspoken daughter Alice. Despite the Sousa songs, some clever lyrics, and an ok book with great performances by all…it just didn't quite work.

One day I sent Jim May into the lobby with the children and a keyboard to work on the songs. I walked in and he was playing the Mr. Rogers theme, "It's a Beautiful Day in the Neighborhood," and Jim was saying to the kids, "Hey kids, do you know how to spell unemployment?" I couldn't help but roar with laughter and love Jim to pieces.

Despite all, this show was a good time for our family. Our daughter Jamie had her first birthday at the Mechanic Theatre with the cast learned to walk backstage at the Minskoff, taught by the kids in the show. On opening night Don Pippin handed me an envelope. He had given me as a gift, his entire fee for vocal arrangements for *Teddy and Alice,* saying that it was a welcome for the upcoming baby and for all the hard work I had done while out of town with the show.

I was moved to tears as was he. He said, "You've been with me on the two hardest days of my life."

I said, "What?"

"First, telling you how good I think you are. Second, having to pay you for it."

He was a generous soul and had given me so much.

We opened to a bunch of mixed reviews late November and were creeping along. The producer was willing to pour money into advertising. But *Cabaret* was at the Imperial and had to move and kick us out of the Minskoff. There was no way to move the show *and* pour money into advertising, so we closed in January. Kaylyn stayed in the show as long as she could with Theoni letting out the hoop skirts one notch at a time. At nearly 7 months, Kaylyn finally had to replace herself as swing dancer but was asked to stay on to run all the replacement and understudy rehearsals until the show finally closed, 3 weeks before giving birth.

In the meantime, Don Pippin called and said that *Mack And Mabel* was going to have a major revival at the Papermill Playhouse. Would I like to be music director as well as write whatever new orchestrations were required? Lee Horsley (TV's Matt Lincoln) and Janet Metz were to star as well as my friend Ed Evanko, who had been in the tour of *A Little Night Music*. My associate was to be Kay Cameron who was a friend from various projects around town.

Our son Michael Benjamin Blank was born at Long Island Jewish Hospital on Feb 10, 1988, sixteen months apart from Jamie. We were staying with my mom in Bayside and Kaylyn's mom Pat had come in to help. I had rehearsals and two months of performances at Papermill. Kaylyn, her mom, and the two kids went back to California to settle in while I was making the bacon in New Jersey. I was able to take up residence at Hal Hackady's apartment. He always had room for me on his living room couch. It saved me a lot of dough and I was able to do the job.

I did a lot of work on *Mack and Mabel* and a lot of new orchestrations at Pippin's insistence and to Jerry's delight. They added the "Hit 'Em On The Head" ballet and the music that I did for Papermill is now the official version. It eventually all went to the production that ended up at the Piccadilly in London a couple of years later. I somehow ended up being a major contributor to the orchestrations for *Mack and Mabel*.

Richard Riskin contributed a lot to the ballet and was the dance arranger for that huge number. Scott Salmon was the choreographer along with Robert Johanson as the director. Angelo Del Rossi was the producer at Papermill. He was very helpful to me in my early years ... hiring me to play auditions when I started out. It was really coming full circle.

My guardian angel, Don Pippin, was recommending me for orchestration jobs. Rudi Bennett was giving me conducting advice and friendship and Irv Kostal was looking over my shoulder at my scores and telling me how to make it all better. My skills on the podium always came to the fore and I was so grateful to these guys for giving me so much support.

Through my efforts and especially the efforts of Don Pippin, I was getting a lot of opportunities to write music, orchestrate, and arrange. Irv was more or less retired, but he was always talking me up to people and I was clearly his protégé. He involved me heavily with ASMAC as a member of the board, mostly for me to be part of that community and the LA community. He was very inclusive. Meanwhile Pippin was recommending me to people, and it was paying off. I was getting hired for little industrial shows as a conductor/arranger. Don hired me to orchestrate the NFL Superbowl show. There was so much music needed for various things like that. Through Mori Shibuya and Larry Billman, Kaylyn and I were offered a job working on *Sessue*, a musical in English about Japanese actor Sessue Hayakawa. The star of the show was Masitoshi Nakamura—a big name in Japan. The music was written by Masao Yagi.

We went with almost two-year-old Jamie and ten-month-old Michael. They had organized babysitters for the kids while Kaylyn choreographed, and I was arranger/MD. Mori had Akira lined up to help with the orchestrations. He was an amazing talent and could knock stuff out and it was very good and frankly, very American. He had been assisting Mori on the shows at Tokyo Disneyland and was extremely facile. Yagi was enamored with American jazz and pop tunes and was amazed that I understood "Japanese" music. Truly, the Japanese tunes he wrote sounded like Russian/Jewish folk tunes. Mori pointed out to me if you look at the map you will see how close Russia and Japan really are. He wrote show tunes for the most part and it was all just my cup of tea.

We had an all-American cast, except the two Japanese principals, Masitoshi and the leading lady, Tomoko Mariya, who was a very well respected, young Japanese actress. Old friend Ed Evanko was in the cast as well. We were scheduled to run for a month or so at Theatre Apple in Shinjuku. Aside from the long hours and then dealing with small children it was a lot of fun.

They rented an apartment for us in Yokohama which was an hour by train from Tokyo. It was a bit of a trek before and after rehearsals but during rehearsals, Yagi or a hired car would take us back and forth. We were treated like royalty and constantly being watered and fed. The day after the show opened, the babysitters disappeared, and Kaylyn was left totally alone with the kids. I was commuting to conduct the show. It was very interesting and disappointing how everyone disappeared after they got the product. Before … they couldn't do enough. I realized this is pragmatic Japanese culture.

On a day off from rehearsals, Mori was desperate that Kaylyn and I come to Tokyo Disneyland early in the morning (before they opened for the day) to see a rehearsal of his musical theatre show at the park. Mori loved American musical theatre and it was quite a spectacle.

The band I had on *Sessue* was ok. We were scheduled for a month or so at Theatre Apple in Shinjuku.

My assistant was a very young Japanese lad with a lot of talent. There was one scene in the show in Japanese and I could never understand the cue ... so he would poke me. He was ambitious and his ambitious pokes became more pugilistic before the time the show came to an end. That was the last time I was in Japan, circa 1989.

Back in the US, Don Pippin was hired to replace Abe (Glenn) Osser as music director for the Miss America Pageant. That was a very big job. Abe, a major influence on TV music who was one of the finest arrangers of his time going back to Paul Whiteman's band, couldn't understand how he was being replaced after forty-six years as MD. He was eighty-six. Don was in his early sixties.

Don brought me, Gordon Harrell, Harold Wheeler, and Nick Archer on board to handle music. I was getting a lot of responsibility and a lot of work. Scott Salmon was the choreographer.

Abe Osser had been so ensconced at Miss America that on Don's first broadcast there was a subtle attempt to sabotage him.

We were on the stage of the Trump Plaza, where the show was being done and I saw the stage manager getting ready for the countdown out of commercial to the main theme. We had a pit-sized orchestra on stage. Ed Shea was the percussion, Ray Marchica on drums, and Nick Archer on piano. Don was talking to the orchestra, and *no one had given him a warning*. Me, having been busy in Hollywood and doing a lot of TV, was more attuned to the studio stuff, and I saw the stage manager counting down from ten to the cameraman.

"Don! Get your hands up! Get your hands up!" I shouted at him. "Don! Five, four, three…"

He realized we were on two, one—and the band hit the downbeat.

The rest of the show went flawlessly. Crisis averted.

I was now becoming a full-fledged orchestrator and getting jobs to write. Don had been going to London once a year and sometimes twice a year to music-direct charity galas for producer Barry Mishon.

Barry had been an "estate agent," which is UK talk for real estate broker. But he had the theatre bug in him and had started producing these galas. Hooking up with some charity, he would put on a "Night of a Hundred Stars," resurrect a lot of the MGM stars (all retired), bring them over, and put on a stage show recreating famous numbers using much of the West End talent. It was a brilliant idea and Barry's intentions were good. He would somehow get people to donate hotels, air fares, theatres, and musicians, or rather get the charity to back this and promise to offset these expenses with the profits from the ticket sales. More often than not we got a very impressive show, but the charity would take a loss to put it on. It gave Barry a bad rep, but his intentions were solid. He did many of these over the years and I inherited many of them from Don or worked with Don when he was available.

These shows introduced me to all the talent in the West End and made me a familiar visitor on a yearly basis. Over the years, this and later work on *Friday Night is Music Night* helped to establish me with the British audience and management.

The first show was *Stairway To The Stars* at the London Palladium with Tony Martin, Gloria De Haven, Virginia O'Brien, Jane Russell, Lorna Luft, Van Johnson, Dorothy Lamour, Arlene Dahl, Dolores Gray, and the Nicholas Brothers. Great stuff and this was just the beginning. I orchestrated several numbers and conducted for many of the stars. Because of Don and others, I was getting bigger and better bits of stuff to do. I was also becoming known as the guy to go to for the movie musical numbers and for becoming friendly with some of the old, retired stars, plus Miss America with Don.

During rehearsal with Harold Nicholas, I commented that the drummer was losing his time.

Harold turned to me and said, "You can't lose something you never had."

I've kept that in mind whenever I lose my patience.

Marvin Hamlisch phoned and said, "Do you think you can coerce your friend Irv Kostal to do some orchestrations for the Academy Awards?" Marvin had been hired to be the MD by his producer friend, Allan Carr. I phoned Irv, who said he was actually retired … but he was not going to turn down the Academy Awards, in any case.

What I didn't know was that he (Irv) told Marvin he would do it only if Marvin gave me a few cues to orchestrate as well. Marvin gave me a few short cues to orchestrate for the Academy Awards.

All I can say is that I put everything I knew into those cues, and they were successful.

They were just minor things, but the orchestra and the other arrangers, Chris Boardman and Pete Matz noticed.

Unfortunately for Irv, Marvin gave him the big "Snow White" number with Rob Lowe, which was also noticed for being pretty cheesy. Irv's work was excellent, but the whole concept was quite a mess.

But … I had written for the Academy Awards. I felt like I was actually an orchestrator and arranger more than just a Broadway conductor.

Kaylyn had been working part time, first at Alfred Music Publishing near us in Van Nuys, and that opened some opportunities for me to help them with their computers. As compensation, Alfred was able to buy me a computer and that was a great perk.

I had a new, current Mac and it enabled me to compete with my contemporaries.

I did need steady work to support the family and I heard that *Phantom Of The Opera* was planned to open in LA for an extended run. I immediately wrote to Hal Prince and asked him if there was a spot for me. He wrote back right away and told me that they were gung-ho on hiring an opera conductor but that he would throw my name in.

Hal, ever loyal to people he had worked with and liked, told me that the associate-conductor position was open.

I was well established as a Broadway conductor and especially in LA where I had conducted *Song, Evita, Sugar Babies,* and *La Cage.* However, "pride goeth before a fall," and I had a wife and two children and a lifestyle to support. I said I would accept the associate-conductor position, and Hal being the gent he was made it so.

I knew it would be difficult for me. I received a call from David Caddick, the music supervisor, who had asked me to come to his hotel for a meeting. He very directly told me that he'd been told by Hal to hire me for the associate-conductor job, that he knew I was over-qualified for the job, and that he was concerned because of my reputation (outspoken, volatile, a bit hot-tempered). He basically made me promise to behave.

Nonetheless I was pleased to have a job on a big Hal Prince/ Andrew Lloyd Webber musical and I flew to New York to participate in rehearsals with Michael Crawford, Dale Kristien, and Reece Holland (who had been a "*Cagelle*" in *La Cage* with me).

I came to rehearsals in my usual suit ensemble and Hal greeted me warmly. The music director they had hired was not much of an opera conductor but had some coaching credits and was rather grand. He had conducted tours of *Les Miz*, and *Showboat*. He talked the talk and was personable enough with the powers that be but made it clear that I was not a welcome addition to the team. However, Kristen Blodgette was David Caddick's associate and musical right arm. I had befriended Kristen when she was a pianist on *Jerry's Girls* in San Francisco during the *La Cage* run. She was very kind to me and smoothed things over. Hal, of course, was always the great gent he was known to be.

The second day, Caddick asked me to dress down as I was dressing better than anyone else in the room—my first sign of trouble. I was already too grand for this room. I laid low and was very unhappy. They realized quickly I wasn't going to make a good rehearsal pianist and I was basically hanging around to learn the show. I don't remember much about the rehearsal period, but I did spend time learning the show and getting my head around it for the inevitable performances I would have to conduct.

There were some nice people in the cast but Crawford was distant to all. He was a big star at this point, a long way from the squeaky kid in the film of *Hello Dolly* and his fame in the UK as Frank Spencer in *Some Mothers* (a Brit TV sit com).

We made it to LA for orchestra rehearsals and I had to play a very minor second keyboard part, which was mostly programmed and easy to play. Jeffrey Silverman was the very good first pianist and a fast friend. Mickey Nadel was the local contractor and Mel Rodnan (old friend) was the show contractor. Mickey was wary of me because of our relationship (or lack thereof) on *Sugar Babies* and *La Cage*. The pit band was not perfectly cast and knowing the Brit sensibility of the creative team from the UK, he was going to have some problems.

Two trumpet players were hired. The lead trumpet was a strong player … but not for *Phantom*. However, the second player was perfect for *Phantom*. They needed to be switched.

Along with the lead trumpet, the strings were not really right for the sensibility of the show. The string section was what I called the "Cash Date String Section." There were a few very good players, but there was a lot of featherbedding going on with Mickey's friends.

The woodwinds and horns were excellent. The percussionist was Jerry Williams, one of John's brothers and an excellent player. The bass was Steve LeFever, who was an excellent bass player and perfect.

Orchestra rehearsals were unnecessarily slow and torturous. The conductor treated the orchestra as if it were the pit band for the Pumpkin Potts, Iowa Opera Theatre. He would go through string runs as if it were a theory class, and really didn't know how to rehearse a professional orchestra. It sounded terrible and it was oh so slow.

I overheard David Caddick saying he wanted to sack the trumpets and the percussionist and complaining (rightfully) about the strings. Even though I was being treated like the bastard stepchild no one wanted, I decided to counsel David with my thoughts as a local. I explained the situation with the trumpets, and he asked me to see if I could intercede with the players. I did by suggesting to the lead trumpet that he pass on the important parts without stepping down. I also advised David that Jerry Williams, was one of the finest percussionists in the country and that if he had objections, he should keep them to himself or open up the wrath of the entire LA music community. Jerry was and is a great player—he just had to be asked to do something specifically, then it was solved. The biggest problem was really the miscast strings and a conductor who was much more inexperienced than he professed to be. It was very tiresome and tense for everyone.

As I was sitting by myself at the Ahmanson one day, waiting for rehearsals to begin, Hal Prince sat down next to me, put his arm around me and said, "How are you?"

I told him about my career in Hollywood, etc. etc.

He then said, "Larry, what are you doing here?"

I said, "I have two young children and I need to work."

He gave me a hug and said, "I get it."

Not another word was spoken, and he ran off to rehearsal. I tremendously appreciated that Hal had gotten me hired.

I was told by David Caddick that I would be conducting Act One at the Saturday matinee right after the opening. (I was clearly being auditioned.) I said to him very firmly that I didn't do "acts," but I'd be happy to conduct the matinee on Saturday. He looked at me with an *It's your funeral* stare and said ok.

I did my homework and was fully prepared to conduct the show. We went through previews uneventfully and the big opening night, but I'd had no rehearsals with the orchestra and I was going to conduct a full performance of *Phantom of the Opera* with Michael Crawford at the Saturday matinee. I was a well-established conductor, thirty-seven years old with a lot of experience and credits and I was being auditioned. This wasn't in my mind; it was a fact.

Privately, I reflected that for *A Little Night Music and Goodtime Charley*, I had walked in without rehearsal and conducted on tour and on Broadway. I'd taken over *Very Good Eddie* on Broadway a year later. I'd conducted a sitzprobe of *A Chorus Line* without knowing the cast. I'd walked into the pit on *Sugar Babies* with Ann Miller without

ever having seen Mickey Rooney do the show … plus all the shows I
had done on my own. For _Phantom,_ I had done my homework and
knew the show. However, I was rattled by the pressure that seemed
to be being put on me.

I was hired at Hal Prince's request. They were looking for justifica-
tion to replace me.

I got on the podium and Mickey Nadel came in and said to me
in front of the brass and horn section, "I'll bet you five dollars that
you don't get through it."

Brian O'Connor, the first horn player, who was a fellow airplane
pilot and had played in the pit with me on my other shows, stood
up and said to Mickey, "I'll take that bet if you make it a hundred."

Mickey left rapidly.

The show began.

And having done my homework along with having an orchestra
that really wanted me to succeed, I sailed through the first act.

At intermission, I walked up the stairs from the basement where
the Ahmanson orchestra pit is located. At the top of the stairs was
Michael Crawford in cape with his brains hanging out (the makeup
for the phantom). He offered his hand and said, "Astonishing." I said
thank you and he said, "Everything is perfect," and smiled through
his bloody lips at me.

David Caddick strolled by and said, "Going well."

I went back to the pit and did the second act, which went equally
well. Admittedly. I was a little less secure with the last half of it but I
didn't fluff anything and it was a very good performance. The cast and
orchestra applauded me, and I was summoned to the stage manager's
office to meet with David Caddick.

In very measured tones, David said to me, "For a first time, not bad." He made a few comments, and I don't quite remember my exact words, but they were not "thank you." I said something on the order of, "I haven't been treated well and I just conducted the first time without an orchestra rehearsal and without a hitch. It was a great deal better than *not bad.*" And then I added, "If you want to fire me, fire me."

I wasn't fired and that was that. As time went on, I went from conducting two shows a week to three, four, and sometimes five times a week. I would get paid a bit extra, but the regular MD wasn't penalized when he didn't conduct, so he took off frequently. I was in many ways the de facto MD for Phantom as I was conducting so much.

Crawford was clearly very happy when I conducted and really, that's all that mattered. I invited lots of movie people to see me conduct and it was a good credit to have. Eventually, I became so fed up with the situation that I would send in a substitute to play the keyboard chair. In essence I became the alternate conductor.

One peculiar incident happened right after *POTO* opened in LA.

An event was going to happen at the Century Park Plaza hotel in Beverly Hills honoring someone at Warner Brothers who was departing the company. It was someone very important and they were hiring Michael Crawford, Sarah Brightman, Andrew Lloyd Webber, and the entire orchestra from *POTO* to play the event. They were flying in Mike Reed, the original conductor of *POTO* to conduct. Andrew would play the piano for Michael and Sarah, and I was playing second keyboard. We had very little to do, except, "Music Of The Night" for Michael with Andrew Lloyd Webber playing the piano with the orchestra and then Michael and Sarah would do "All I Ask Of You" with Andrew Lloyd Webber at the piano and Mike

Reed conducting. We would also do the "Phantom" number with Michael and Sarah.

Having the leads from *Phantom* along with Andrew Lloyd Webber was a very big deal at that moment in time. Hottest ticket in theatre. We were all making a small fortune and it was on our day off from the theatre, so everyone was happy to do it.

Pianist, Faith Seetoo (just out of university) was on piano for the spots without Andrew Lloyd Webber, and I was playing the second synth part.

At the last minute, Michael Crawford said no way, he wasn't working on his day off. So now it became a solo for Sarah Brightman. Sarah would do it all. First the "Phantom" number, then "All I Ask Of You," solo, and then Andrew Lloyd Webber would join for "Music of The Night."

At the rehearsal Andrew stood up from the piano and started shouting at all of the busboys setting up the tables for the event, "If this noise doesn't stop at once, we will cancel the concert."

The hubbub stopped for about thirty seconds when everyone heard the screaming. However, since the majority of the help didn't speak English, Andrews's screaming meant very little. Un-translated, idle threats have little meaning. Mike Reed and I looked at each other across the abyss and laughed.

That night we gathered on the stage of the Century Plaza: the orchestra and Mike Reed with Sarah and Andrew Lloyd Webber waiting in the wings. We were supposed to be revealed later, because the audience didn't particularly know there was an orchestra. The gold lame curtain in the main ballroom was down with a band of around thirty crowded on the stage.

One by one Clint Eastwood, Robert Redford, Faye Dunaway, and on and on ... every major star in Hollywood was on the stage on the other side of this gold lame curtain. We didn't see *any of them*, just heard their voices. We were trapped behind the curtain, not making any noise to be the surprise of the evening. One star after the other. It was a bigger event than the Academy Awards honoring whoever was leaving Warner's. I remarked out loud that it was all a scam and it was just Rich Little (the famous impersonator of the stars). From behind that curtain, we never saw anyone.

Finally, they announced Sarah Brightman. Mike Reed was conducting, Faith was at the piano, and I was at the second keyboard synth, with the pounding electronic bass notes for "The Phantom Of The Opera." The orchestra was revealed ... Sarah was singing, and the audience went nuts with applause. It was apparently a real treat to see/hear the largish orchestra out of nowhere on their night off.

We got through that, and Sarah sang "All I Ask Of You," warbling her high notes with the orchestra soaring through it.

Andrew Lloyd Webber was known to drink a bit too much and, on this occasion, he appeared quite well lubricated. He sat at the piano facing me (the stage was quite crowded) and played the opening vamp for "Music Of The Night" ... or at least attempted to play the opening vamp. Aside from bad aim, it really sounded like he was wearing mittens. Faith (just out of school and perhaps a bit naïve) got on the piano bench and pushed him over to the side. I thought I heard her say under her breath, "What are you doing?"

Andrew, knowing he was a bit under the weather, was falling off the edge of the piano bench. Fortunately, the audience was listening to and watching Sarah center stage. Andrew went down off the edge of the bench, quickly recovered, and exited stage left, wiping his mouth with a handkerchief. The number ended with a tremendous ovation, and we were done.

During the run of *Phantom,* I would wake up in the morning, and Kaylyn would go to work at her job, so I would take the kids to pre-school, do other jobs (writing/rehearsals), and pick the kids up from pre-school. Kaylyn would come home, I'd go to *Phantom,* come home close to midnight, go to bed, and next morning start all over again. Occasionally, I would get a call to go to the UK, or a call from Hamlisch to conduct some concert because others weren't available. This was my life.

One day, Jamie was sitting with Michael at breakfast, and she said to Kaylyn, "Mommy, do you have a baby in your belly?"

This was out of nowhere.

Kaylyn turned to me and said, "I'm one day late."

On April 30, 1990, Danielle Gene Dillehay Blank was born. The band threw a little party for me one day and gave us a little baby outfit that said PHANTOT OF THE OPERA.

Sadly, almost one week to the day before Dani was born, Kaylyn's much-loved father, Gene Dillehay, died suddenly. He had been ill, but his sudden passing was a blow. I feel fortunate that the night before he died, he was on the phone and I put both Jamie and Michael on to speak to him. Gene was in hospital, and my instincts told me something was up.

Meanwhile, I was writing little bits for *Tiny Toons Adventures* (a celebrated animated series), wrote more stuff for Disney Parks, conducted a TV show (*Aladdin*) with Richard Kiley, Barry Bostwick, and Donna Mckechnie, and did some new orchestrations for Robert Goulet for a tour of *The Fantasticks.* Through Richard Kaufman at MGM (a fellow theatre conductor I had met in San Francisco doing shows for Ed Lester), I was hired to compose some music for *In the Heat of the Night*, the Carroll O'Connor TV series.

I wrote some pizzicato (plucked) strings for a chase cue. A girl was running from the police in Atlanta in high heels … so I wrote the "High Heel Chase," and it seemed to me the pizzicato strings, suggesting the clicking of high heel shoes on the pavement, were appropriate along with a wailing sax solo and a guitar (the norm for *In the Heat of the Night*).

When the line producer heard the pizz strings, he said to me, "What are those bumps???"

I realized that I had gone into the tunnel of no return with music beyond his comfort zone, and I said, "History," and quickly eliminated those bumps.

Somewhere in this time period, I needed help to finish an arrangement. Joe Soldo (woodwind player extraordinaire and contractor) suggested I contact Mort Stevens. Mort had composed *Hawaii Five-O* and was head of music at CBS Television in its heyday. He had done much television and film work. He was a contemporary of Joe's and had been Sammy Davis Jr's MD at the beginning of his career. Sammy was really responsible for Mort's career, insisting he compose the music for Sammy's early TV opportunities. Mort became quite a superstar at that time, and I knew him as the conductor for the Broadway musical *Mr. Wonderful*. He was a good buddy to Jerry Goldsmith and John Williams, and had also been great friends with Kostal, who knew him from early days.

Mort was more or less retired on his ASCAP and happy to be asked to do anything for fun. He and his wife Annie and their children, Lisa and Mark, became good friends in time. Mort and I bonded instantly, and he became another mentor to me. He taught me much about orchestration and practical application in television music.

When I was given my opportunity to score an episode of *In The Heat Of The Night*, I had no idea of how to write a music cue that showed a guy's face responding to something terrible (the discovery of a dead infant), though the audience doesn't know that till after the commercial. I asked Mort, "How do you show that something terrible has happened, when the camera is simply on the guy's face showing horror, then cut to commercial?"

I had written this rather bucolic piece of music for Bubba, a friendly police officer on vacation in the woods with his dog. Then the dog comes in yelping and brings Bubba to see what he's discovered, and you see a close-up on Bubba's face and his reaction.

Mort said, "Oh, that's an easy one. When the camera zooms in on Bubba's face, you need an oy-vey chord."

What's an oy-vey chord???

He said, "You play your nice music and land on a beautiful C chord. The cello plays an arpeggio down the notes of a C chord and other notes in a C scale ... and when it gets to the bottom, it lands on a big fat A flat (which is not in the scale of a C chord), and *voila*, oy vey."

This taught me a huge lesson in composition for film and was very practical. Mort had also been great friends with Kostal, who knew him from early days.

Shortly after I met Mort, he was diagnosed with terminal pancreatic cancer. I spent a lot of time with him and visited him in hospital until he died in November 1991. Kaylyn and I stayed in close touch with his widow Annie until the day she died.

Mort was a tremendous influence on my approach to music and orchestration. A lot of his music is played all the time, especially his iconic theme to *Hawaii Five-O*. His license plate on his BMW was EEGBAE—the musical notes to the Hawaii Five-O theme.

Back at *Phantom* ... the regular MD was very happy when I wasn't there, so they let me off to do another Barry Mishon show celebrating

174

My One and Only, with Sandy Duncan and her husband Don Correia, along with Donna McKechnie, Harold Nicholas, Bertice Reading, and Georgia Brown. Kaylyn was helping with rehearsals and was asked to come in as a replacement for Frances Ruffelle when she bailed at the last minute. This was a great thing for Kaylyn, and I was happy she was getting recognition for her great performance.

While we were in London, Diana Rigg took me and Kaylyn to dinner at Orso's in Covent Garden. During dinner, her husband Archie Stirling appeared, as did some paparazzi who photographed us. Next day in the papers it was reported "Diana Rigg reconciles with husband Archie Stirling with Yank friends at Orso's." Unfortunately, the reconciliation didn't last.

Michael Crawford left Phantom LA in April 1991. Robert Guillaume had stepped in for a while before that, but Michael came back and then left permanently. He was replaced by Davis Gaines.

One time, I decided to skip a matinee. The second cover was on for Dale Kristien and midafternoon the stage manager phoned saying, "How quickly can you get here?" I raced to the theatre in maybe twenty minutes and was told to put my tux on. Apparently, the MD was so upset by the performance the second cover was giving, that he refused to conduct the second act or the performance that evening where she was appearing. Truthfully, she wasn't the best choice, and she had a very bad cold, exacerbating the situation. I calmed her down and conducted the second act with a very late start.

At the denouement before the evening performance, I was asked specifically by the stage manager what I thought of the MD's behavior regarding this incident.

I said, "Aw c'mon, you don't refuse to conduct because a performer isn't up to your standards. It was totally inappropriate behavior and telling the girl that she stinks [which he did] doesn't help at all and is unconscionable."

Don't ask for whom the bell tolls … it tolls for thee.

Barry Mishon asked me to come back for another gala with Pippin, *A Cole Porter Centennial* in June 1991 at the Prince Edward Theatre. I took a leave from Phantom for a couple of weeks. On that engagement I met Michael Feinstein, and we have remained friends and colleagues ever since.

At the performance, Don Pippin was set to conduct the overture, but we couldn't begin because we couldn't find the pianist, which was really delaying the curtain. Suddenly he appeared, quite flushed and nervous, and he jumped to the piano and started playing. Meanwhile there was some hubbub around the theatre. It appeared that the piano player had been receiving a blowjob in the basement of the theatre when a dresser walked in on them. He was dating/living with one of the artists.

As is usual in the theatre … *hubbub, hubbub, yata yata, blowjob, yata yata, blowjob, hubbub, blowjob, blowjob,* was going around the theatre with everyone giggling a bit under their breath.

The show went on and was quite good, with various artists doing their thing. During the 2nd act, Sammy Cahn, Rita Moreno, and Alexis Smith were standing in the wings Pippin was on the podium so I was standing with them. All of a sudden, the girlfriend of the pianist was on stage, singing a big number (and very well).

Sammy leaned over to me and said, "Larry, is *this* the girl with the blow job?"

Without missing a beat, I said, "Sammy, listen to that cocksucker sing."

Lovely Rita and Alexis were laughing so hard that they had to be hushed by the stage manager.

In the same show, novelist Harold Robbins's ex-wife was asked to sing "My Heart Belongs to Daddy." She was a would-be singer and had been singing in cabarets around LA. I had coached her in her Century City apartment, and after hearing her sing, I said, "This key is no good for you," and I transposed it. She was a semi-professional and not happy about the key change, but I had to be realistic and put it in the right key for her.

Later that day, she phoned and said, "My frock [dress] won't work in that key."

It became our backstage mantra for many shows. My frock won't work in that key.

There were a lot of wonderful people in that show and it's available as a CD, but now also streamed, I'm sure.

I came back to *Phantom* and conducted a performance. At the interval/intermission, I gave a note to one of the players, and the lead clarinetist went off on me and started screaming at me with the audience hearing it. I calmed him down and we got the second act started. It was totally unprovoked and bizarre. I was really rattled by this outburst.

The next day I received a call from Alan Wasser, the GM on the show, telling me that my services on *Phantom* were terminated. Alan was an old friend from *Sugar Babies* and *Colette* days and thought it was an inappropriate dismissal. It wasn't happening because of the unfortunate incident with the clarinet player the night before. That had just opened the door. It was because the stage managers had sandbagged me with the second cover incident. I was told it was because of my criticism of the conductor regarding the second cover.

In time, I would find out that my job had been safe as long as Michael Crawford was the phantom. Once Michael left, there was no one to protect me. Alan felt terrible about the whole incident, and instead of getting two weeks' pay, I was given four weeks, and told that I didn't have to return to the theatre to collect my things. I was history.

I was quite shocked and strolled for several hours away from the house. I was even more shocked when I was ready to come home, and didn't have my wallet or phone. We didn't walk around with cell phones in 1991. After all that disappointment, I was really upset that I had to walk home now, too.

Later, Michael Crawford hired me as his music director. In time, no one really remembered that I'd been sacked from *POTO*. They remembered that I was there and that I was Michael Crawford's music director.

Being let go of my *Phantom* obligations was actually the best thing that could have happened to me. I was able to focus on being a composer/orchestrator. I pursued it with a vengeance.

Chapter Seven

Pippin was calling me and recommending me for a lot of things. The *Miss America Pageant* became a regular job, writing a lot of notes. There was much more material on that show than meets the eye. Pippin was trying to update it and he succeeded. Harold Wheeler did some arrangements, and I learned a lot by looking at his scores.

Producer Don Gregory, who had produced *Copperfield,* called and set me up as music supervisor on a production of *42ⁿᵈ Street* at Harrah's in Lake Tahoe, where I hooked up with Director/choreographer Chet Walker. I did some arrangements for Jason Alexander for the Jerry Lewis Telethon, and a few arrangements for a musical called *Stardust,* with lyrics by Mitchell Parish. I orchestrated a show called *Laughter Epidemic,* directed by Christian Slater, who was now an adult. Through choreographer Richard Sampson, I ended up writing music for some shows for Princess Cruises, which turned into more work. I conducted for Donna McKechnie and for George Hearn. Through Pippin, I hooked up with David Gest (who was later married to Liza Minnelli briefly), and conducted several star-studded gala events for him. I conducted for Shani Wallis and became music director for what I called "Disease of the Month." If there was a gala/fundraiser for some disease, I was the music director.

I hooked up with producer Laurie Grad (Abe Burrows's daughter) and her husband Peter Grad and was music director for the Alzheimer's Association yearly shows. They were impressive for the TV celebrities they got on board, and I did that for a long time. If there was a TV name, they were on it doing tab versions of the scores for hit musicals. Naturally Laurie chose *Guys and Dolls* for the first one.

I was doing bits and pieces of orchestrations for everyone and conducting whenever someone called. I ended up doing galas for SIDS (sudden infant death syndrome), SADS (sudden adult death syndrome), AIDS, colorectal cancer, heart disease, and so on. Michael Crawford called me to work on some material with him. Composer Harvey Cohen asked me to do some orchestrations for episodes of the *Batman* animated TV series for Warner Brothers. I conducted for the esoteric rock group Queensryche on the MTV Awards.

Pippin called me to do orchestrations for the opening sequence of *Catskills on Broadway* with a five-piece band. I didn't want my name associated with such a show on Broadway, so I'd had it removed from the music. It turned out to be a surprise hit, and the critics singled out the opening sequence as being a highlight. Of course! A little arrogance goes a long way.

I conducted for Lorna Luft in Sparks, Nevada at the Nugget. Chinese acrobats with baby elephants opened the show. Each night, Lorna and I would walk by the elephant enclosures to go backstage. It seemed that every time Lorna walked by the elephants, they would rear up, pretty much like when Frau Blucher's name was mentioned in *Young Frankenstein.* It made us both laugh a lot.

I conducted for the esoteric rock group Queensryche on the MTV Awards.

My professional life was filled with lots and lots of little bits and one offs. Nothing to complain about at all. Just a lot of it.

I had become friends with British singer/actress Georgia Brown. She was the original Nancy in *Oliver* and was a bit tough personally, but a great singer and a great gal. Georgia had been born Lillian Klot in Whitechapel and was great friends with *Oliver's* composer, Lionel Bart. She was a nice Jewish girl from the east end of London. She had a hard time after her husband divorced her and was living on Coldwater Canyon in LA. I would go over for tea and biscuits and play piano for her for the conversation and warmth. I enjoyed playing for her and having a surrogate "mum" nearby.

Barry Mishon asked me to be music director for *Mr. Wonderful,* a tribute to Sammy Davis Jr. in London. Some great people were on it including, Cy Coleman, Charles Strouse, Clarke Peters, George Hearn, Ken Page, and Georgia Brown. My associate was a young wannabe music director just out of university named Michael England. Mike was from Manchester and was very eager.

One day, I came into rehearsals very tired and unfortunately with a big hangover from hanging out the night before, as one does when in London. He said, as a good young associate should, "Can i get you anything?"

I said, "All I need is a cup of coffee and a blow job."

He replied, "Get your own coffee."

With that response and the laugh that followed, we bonded, and he got me the coffee and a biscuit. He is now a very successful MD/conductor in the West End. I think at this point he has others getting *his* coffee.

On the *Mr. Wonderful* show, Tony Martin sang "The Tenement Symphony," which was a trademark for him. Tony had been a super star in the '40s and '50s and one of the highest-paid performers in Las Vegas history. He was married to Cyd Charisse and had been married to Alice Faye earlier. Tony was a bit of a PITA (pain in the ass). He had been a musician, so he knew everything and how he wanted it to go. He was telling me how to conduct it. "Do this in two, do this in four, do this softly, do this loud…" and on and on.

With people like Tony, I had learned to be as accommodating as possible and to do what they wanted the best I could. I was at this point quite facile, and really not too concerned. Watching this rehearsal from the front row were Marvin Hamlisch, Charles Strouse, and Cy Coleman, who were all making an appearance on the show as were as the Nicholas Brothers. After Tony had finished beating me up in the rehearsal of "Tenement Symphony," I walked off the stage with Marvin, Charles, and Cy all saying, "Good job, you handled him well," etc.

Marvin said, "How did you put up with that?"

Without even thinking, I answered, "I put up with you." Cy and Charles both roared with laughter.

Marvin conducted a song he wrote for Sammy for the Academy Awards called "Come Light the Candles," which Elaine Paige was to sing. I wrote the chart. Marvin and Elaine were very pleased with it. Cy played the piano with Sammy Cahn doing special lyrics in tribute. Marvin played "Mr. Bojangles" for Harold Nicholas. Georgia sang "Lost in The Stars" with my arrangement. I also orchestrated an overture for the event.

Marvin came up to me in front of Theatre Royal Drury Lane and said, "I know you are based in LA, but I'm doing a new show called *Goodbye Girl* with Marty Short and Bernadette Peters. I would like you to conduct it and be music director."

I said "Marvin, I really appreciate it and I would love to do it, but I really can't uproot my family and come to New York at this point in my life."

I could see in his eyes that I had forever shut the door on my relationship with him. I did conduct for him in concert some more later on. and I did a little work with him at the end of his life. But I had, without intention, really hurt his feelings and that was that. He acted as if nothing had happened, but I saw in his eyes the closure of our earlier relationship. Marvin had been an important part of my life and I was sad to have this ending but conducting another show in New York was not in my future.

Sadly, this was Georgia's last performance. When the show was over, we were standing in line for some royal reception, Princess Alexandra or something like that, and Georgia said, "See you in a couple of weeks for tea and biscuits." After returning to LA, I heard on the radio that Georgia had died in hospital in the UK. It still makes me so sad to think about that. She was only fifty-eight.

The concert over, I flew back to LA sharing a double-seat with my friend, George Hearn. I was amazed to see George close his eyes over Scotland and not open them until we were within an hour of Los Angeles. I wish I could sleep like that on long international flights.

I came back to being asked to do an arrangement for the Harold Rome song "Wish You Were Here" for Michael Feinstein's upcoming recording. Michael had insisted I do this. It was a big deal for him to ask for me with the likes of Ralph Burns and Billy Byers available, but he was supportive of me as an arranger and trusted me.

The producer for the recording was Brooks Arthur, who had produced the recording for *They're Playing Our Song.* He had also produced several recordings for Neil Diamond, Janis Ian, Peter Allen, Van Morrison, and comic Adam Sandler, among many others.

"Wish You Were Here" was the title song from the 1952 musical and had been a huge hit for Eddie Fisher. Michael was going to do it as an homage, but with a new arrangement and orchestration. He had fleshed out an arrangement, as he often does at the piano. It was transcribed, and we talked about it at length. We had both worked out a counterpoint, and Michael played the changes he liked. I decided at one point to quote the strings from Eddie Fisher's chart, but only for a moment.

Brooks and I had a meeting, and he asked for something from the original arrangement that I really didn't care for, as it was very arch and really sounded like a direct quote. But Brooks insisted that I include it quite forcibly, in an *or-else* manner. I did, but begrudgingly, as I knew it wasn't right.

I prepared a little mockup. Remember this was 1992, so a little mockup was a lot harder to do than it is now with all the keyboards and computer programs. We sat down with Michael and played it for him. When it got to Brooks' "or else" figure, Michael bristled, as I knew he would, and Brooks said instantly, "I told you not to include that."

Michael, sensitive soul that he is, knew that it was Brook's pet fill, and told me when we had a private moment that he knew I never would do that. When it got to my little homage, Michael laughed, and it remained in the chart.

We recorded with a superb orchestra hired by Bill Hughes. My chart was a huge success and I was forever grateful for that opportunity, which helped push me forward. Billy Byers was at the session. Billy had also been a protégé of Irv Kostal's from the '50s. He said to me, "You know how warm and fatherly Irv is to you now?"

I said that he was…very much so.

Billy said in his very gruff voice caused by cancer surgery, "When he was your age in the '50s, he was a total prick, but we loved him, and he taught me and Johnny Mandel so many things." Billy really enjoyed sharing this with me, and we had a good laugh.

This chart for Michael put me on the musical map, at least with Billy Byers and some of the musicians in LA. It was a game changer for me, and I am forever grateful to Michael for the chance.

A few weeks later, while Irv and I were driving to lunch together, Irv pulled his Cadillac to the side of the road. (A Cadillac was a sign of affluence for his generation.) He put in my cassette of "Wish You Were Here," and we listened to the end. When it had finished, he turned to me and said, "You don't need me anymore. You wrote a triple counterpoint, and if I showed you where, you'd never be able to do it again." He added that my natural abilities, and especially my conducting abilities, which he openly admired, would help me as my career moved on.

Irv had given me a boost when I needed it most. I was forty years old and embarking on an arranging career a bit later than I'd intended. I was truly moved by his support. He had become a surrogate father to me. He and Sylvia were surrogate grandparents to the children.

Don Pippin, Irv Kostal and Rudi Bennett were my three guardian angels, who gave me unending support throughout my career. It had never gone unnoticed by me how important mentors are and how important it is to be mentored. I knew that ultimately; it would be my turn to do the same for others.

Michael Feinstein started calling me regularly to conduct his symphony concerts. I really enjoyed working with him, and it was a treat to be doing so much Gershwin. Michael had spent time and money on his music library. He had an endless library of great arrangements done by great writers. It was also so much fun to be back on the symphony circuit. I was known by many of the orchestras, and it was nice to reconnect. The rehearsals were enjoyable, and then there was instant realization and performance, rather than the long, drawn-out rehearsal period on a new show. It was instant gratification, and Michael is so musical.

Through Michael, I developed a nice friendship with Marilee Bradford. She worked at MGM, alongside Richard Kaufman. They were planning *That's Entertainment III* with Marc Shaiman doing the music, and Marilee strongly recommended me to Marc. Marc had been Bette Midler's MD, after Barry Manilow and others, and was good friends with Billy Crystal, who'd brought him to Rob Reiner. Rob was directing many films and gave Marc a lot of pictures to do. Marc, like Marvin Hamlisch, had a facility at the piano and a good feel for film scoring. I worked with him on a picture called *North*. Rob Reiner said to me and fellow orchestrator Jeff Atmajian that he thought Marc had become quite a good film composer. He really was. Scoring films is a learned skill/craft, and Marc was becoming facile. With time, his orchestration ears got even better too, and he could easily lay out a chart and give it to us orchestrators to flesh out further. He knew his business. On *TEIII* (as it was called), Marc and Jeff did a fabulous overture. I was given a lot of cues and asked to make it sound like the famed Conrad Salinger. Salinger was the premiere orchestrator of Hollywood musicals in his day. It was a big compliment to be asked to replicate his work.

I had studied a lot of the MGM scores, had worked with a lot of the MGM people, and was constantly doing galas with the remaining "stars." I seemed to be the go-to guy on this type of stuff, and I was so grateful to Marilee for setting this up with Marc. John Mauceri conducted the score for *TEIII* with the Hollywood Bowl Orchestra. I had a long-standing collegial relationship with John as well.

Marc was always using Jeff Atmajian, Brad Dechter, and Mark McKenzie to do his "film" cues, but as time progressed, he was giving me a lot of the crossover Broadway stuff and production numbers. If there was a song in the score, very often sung by trumpeter/singer Jack Sheldon, I would get the assignment.

Marc started calling me regularly to do bits and pieces in his films, especially when it was more show bizzy and needed arranging he didn't have time for. I was grateful for the work and occasionally I would get a "plum" cue when everyone else was up to their ears.

On the main title in *City Slickers II,* when Marc's name appeared I had four French horns and trumpets and trombones blowing out the main title. When Billy Crystal's name appeared as the director, I had three trumpets in Harmon mutes sounding very much like toy trumpets. It was a little joke intended by Marc, but I carried it to the extreme. Billy, turned to me in the booth and said, "Larry, did you orchestrate this? Fuck you," and giggled.

Those of us from New York always go to the dreaded "fuck you," when we are having fun with familiar people ... and often, when we really mean it. I have learned to be very sparing with my fuck you's as they tend to be terminal in the wrong situation. With passing years, I tend to use it more and more sparingly. People have trouble detecting affectionate one's from the real one's.

Don Pippin was conducting *The Red Shoes,* Jule Styne's final show, at the Gershwin. It was orchestrated by Sid Ramin and Bill Brohn with dance music by Gordon Harrell, a great team. There was lots of ballet music and a big orchestra, but it was not a good show. Not to belabor it, it had its issues. The music was orchestrated well, but it was not the greatest score. The orchestra was playing their butts off with all the ballet music, and the cast was singing, all good things. But the show was a turkey.

Jim May and I were sitting mid-theatre, Don's guests for the show. In the middle of the show, a girl sitting behind us lost her dinner and the champagne that washed it down (must've been prom night). None of it got on us, but we were surrounded on all sides by rivers. We were trapped in our seats. The woman behind us was cursing at young Miss Sweet Sixteen, because she had soiled her fur coat. Jim, on the other hand, was shaking with laughter. No one was watching the show on stage, cause our show was much, much better. Jim's shoulders were going up and down with uncontrollable (but quiet) laughter. Finally, we got to the interval, and an usher came up to us and asked if he could show us to other seats. Unable to control my total disgust I said, "Yes please, two down front at the Majestic" (where *Phantom* was playing). Jim was out of control now.

We came back for the second half, since we were guests of the conductor, and afterwards, we went to the French restaurant across from the stage door—*Tout Va Bien,* I think, next to the Mark Hellinger. Don joined us and Stanley Donen, *The Red Shoes* director, was sitting alongside. Apparently past his prime, Donen had taken a bad show and made it far worse.

"Don't tell me this as bad as that *Onward Victoria* show you did at the Martin Beck," Pippin said to me.

Unable to stop myself, I said, "Ok, I won't tell you."

"It can't be *that* bad," he said.

And someone at the bar, overhearing the conversation, said, "It's much worse."

It's difficult to hear bad things about a show you are working on, but we had a very good laugh. Don had never had a flop of this magnitude. Admittedly, I was far more experienced with less-than-successful shows. Even a few years later, Don would say, "It wasn't as bad as *Onward Victoria*."

At this point, 1994, I was conducting regularly for Michael Feinstein. I shared the podium in San Francisco with brilliant composer, David Raksin (who wrote "Laura"), and we became friends. Along with being on the board at ASMAC, I was doing orchestrations for a whole bunch of films for Marc and other composers. I was always busy doing arrangements for various theatrical productions, as well. Usually, it would be a one-off for a revival that had a new dance number. This stuff kept me very busy. I got some TV work on several of the animated series that were happening, many bits and pieces. I did the yearly Alzheimer's shows, as well as my other periodic *disease of the month* galas.

Much of our home in Sylmar, California was destroyed in the Northridge Earthquake in January of 1994. On a whim, I had purchased earthquake insurance, so we were covered for some of the damage. The kids were little, and it was quite a scary event. But everyone was ok, and that's all that mattered. We found a contractor to rebuild our home, and we traveled up the coast with the kids to let the repairs happen.

The trip was fun, but we came back to find the house wasn't repaired at all. It took a while for the significant, massive repairs that were required, but it also allowed for some major renovations in the process. Even with all the new upgrades, the house ended up being worth not much more than we'd originally paid for it. However, we now had a new kitchen that could sleep ten. We used it only for meals.

The first phone call we received after the quake was from Irv Kostal, making sure we were ok. The phone lines and electricity were out for a quite a while, so this was several days after the quake. He hadn't been affected at all, living in the hills near Laurel Canyon.

Irv's wife Sylvia had died in April 1993. He was quite bereft without her, having been married since 1929. He decided that he had to do something for ASMAC, so he planned a concert with a lot of big names called "A Musical Affair to Remember" for March of 1994.

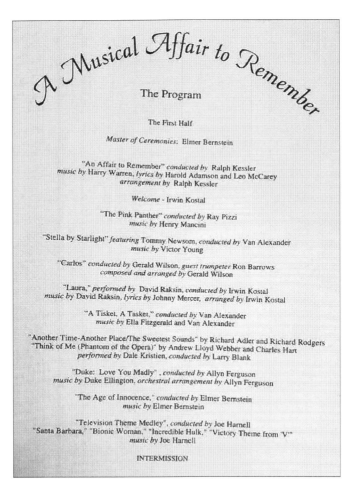

A Musical Affair to Remember

The Program

The First Half

Master of Ceremonies: Elmer Bernstein

"An Affair to Remember" *conducted by* Ralph Kessler
music by Harry Warren, *lyrics by* Harold Adamson and Leo McCarey
arrangement by Ralph Kessler

Welcome - Irwin Kostal

"The Pink Panther" *conducted by* Ray Pizzi
music by Henry Mancini

"Stella by Starlight" *featuring* Tommy Newsom, *conducted by* Van Alexander
music by Victor Young

"Carlos" *conducted by* Gerald Wilson, *guest trumpeter* Ron Barrows
composed and arranged by Gerald Wilson

"Laura," *performed by* David Raksin, *conducted by* Irwin Kostal
music by David Raksin, *lyrics by* Johnny Mercer, *arranged by* Irwin Kostal

"A Tisket, A Tasket," *conducted by* Van Alexander
music by Ella Fitzgerald and Van Alexander

"Another Time-Another Place/The Sweetest Sounds" by Richard Adler and Richard Rodgers
"Think of Me (Phantom of the Opera)" by Andrew Lloyd Webber and Charles Hart
performed by Dale Kristien, *conducted by* Larry Blank

"Duke: Love You Madly" , *conducted by* Allyn Ferguson
music by Duke Ellington, *orchestral arrangement by* Allyn Ferguson

"The Age of Innocence," *conducted by* Elmer Bernstein
music by Elmer Bernstein

"Television Theme Medley", *conducted by* Joe Harnell
"Santa Barbara," "Bionic Woman," "Incredible Hulk," "Victory Theme from 'V'"
music by Joe Harnell

INTERMISSION

The Second Half

Master of Ceremonies: Dudley Moore

Music from "Bedazzled," *performed by* Dudley Moore, *conducted by* Pete Rugolo
music by Dudley Moore

"Mahogony Bird", *performed by* Wayne Shorter, *conducted by* David Blumberg
music by Wayne Shorter, *orchestrated by* David Blumberg

"Oklahoma/Carousel," *performed by* John Raitt, *conducted by* Larry Blank
music by Richard Rodgers, lyrics by Oscar Hamerstein II

Theme from "Round Midnight," *performed by* Herbie Hancock
music by Herbie Hancock and Thelonius Monk

Theme from "Harlem Nights," *performed by* Herbie Hancock
conducted by Garnett Brown Jr.
music by Herbie Hancock, *arrangement by* Garnett Brown Jr.

"Remembrances" from "Schindler's List,"
performed by John Williams and Tamaki Kawakubo
music by John Williams

Pass the Baton - *Intro by* Tony Thomas

"Wonderful Life," *conducted by* Vic Schoen
music by Dimitri Tiomkin

"ET" Flying theme, *conducted by* Larry Blank
music by John Williams

"Gorillas in the Mist," *conducted by* Maurice Jarre
music by Maurice Jarre

Thank you to all the performers, composers and arrangers
for the beautiful music performed this evening
and to you, the audience, for your appreciation

This was a big deal for ASMAC and for Irv and Irv really promoted me as conductor. He gave me the *ET* "Flying Theme", despite John Williams being present for the event. When I approached John, I said, "I'm embarrassed to be conducting this with you here."

He said, "Larry, everyone knows who you are, and I know who you are, and I'm pleased you are conducting it."

John's a great gentleman. He played piano for his beautiful music from *Schindlers List*. John knew, too, that I had been a protégé of his friend Mort Stevens, and we had met at that time. He is a very generous and talented man.

I also conducted for John Raitt, singing the "Soliloquy" from *Carousel,* and Dale Kristien singing an arrangement of mine. That was quite a treat, and of course, I knew John from *Most Happy Fella* a few years before.

Maurice Jarre and Elmer Bernstein conducted their works, and David Raskin sang "Laura," while Irv conducted. These were world class film composers, and John Raitt was famous for *Carousel.*

At the next ASMAC meeting, it was discovered that the concert had operated at a loss. Irv wrote a personal check to cover it, so that ASMAC wouldn't be penalized. I learned a lot of lessons from Irv.

While I was continuing to do a lot of little jobs, I didn't have a steady paycheck. I was freelance and every job was a one-off. Sometimes there was a nice paycheck, but it was one job at a time.

Kaylyn had had a steady job at Disney since 1991. It was a regular paycheck with benefits, and the perks of having a silver pass to Disneyland, which is great with three little kids. Her salary covered a lot of our bills, but we were dependent on my getting some nice arranging or conducting jobs to supplement. Sometimes it was great and other times, not so much.

I received a call from a film composer, Terry Plumeri. He said he needed an orchestrator for a TV film he was doing. As was usual with this sort of thing, it was a cash job for the orchestration, down to the music copying, and the musicians on the job. We all had to make a living and supplement our income the best we could. Terry told me that he had $250 per day for orchestration, and the recording would be the following Saturday, one week away. He told me that as he wrote it, he would fax me the music on a simple sketch, and I would orchestrate from that. At that time in 1994, most of the music was written by hand. The computer programs were developing, but it was much faster to go by hand. It takes a lot of hours to put the notes in whether by hand or computer.

While the money he offered was low, I had a family to support. With a few days at $250 per day, it would be a nice supplement. This was Saturday and the recording was a week away. I assumed that even if it were five days to orchestrate, it would be a nice pay day, regardless of the amount of work I had to do.

Monday came … no music was sent. Tuesday came … nothing. I called Terry and he said, "Don't worry, it's coming." Wednesday, Thursday, nothing. On Friday, my fax machine started vomiting pages and pages of sketches. I started orchestrating by hand (for an orchestra of about forty musicians) and turning out the pages. Kostal had trained me, and I was very fast. I was writing on music paper in ink (no time to sharpen pencils) and cranking it out. The music kept coming, and by Saturday morning I was finished. The copyist was sending messengers to get the pages and was copying in a frenzy.

On Saturday, I showed up at the session. The orchestra was in place, the director was present, and they started recording all the music for the film. This was a major television movie with familiar faces and a familiar director. Everything went very well, and we finished. Terry thanked me and handed me a check for $250.

I said, "Terry, I did the whole movie overnight for you."

He said, "I told you it was $250 per day."

Naturally I started arguing and said, "It was five days' worth of work and I managed to get it done despite your late delivery."

He said, "I paid what I promised, and you knew the deal."

I told him to never to reach out to me and again and if he saw me on the street to cross to the other side.

He said, "You are threatening me!"

And in the inimitable style of Mel Brooks, I said, "You betcha."

Well, he never darkened my door again and now he is no longer with us. It takes all kinds and I learned my lesson.

On November 23, 1994, my phone rang and it was Irv Kostal. It was the day before Thanksgiving. Irv was going to have Thanksgiving with one of his daughters, his son, Irv Jr, and some grandchildren. We were planning our usual turkey with the kids, and another family or two to share the chores.

Irv invited me and Kaylyn to lunch at the Daily Grill on Laurel Canyon and Ventura Blvd. This was a usual hangout for us and many others. The food was good and it had a nice atmosphere. Irv asked that we pick him up, as he didn't want to drive. He'd been suffering some minor heart issues. Irv was about six-foot two and a hearty Bohemian from Chicago.

At lunch he ordered a cocktail, which was extremely unusual for him. He would drink at dinner, but I had never seen him order a drink at lunch. Not even a beer or a glass of wine. He suggested we all have a cocktail. So, we did. There was some small talk. He complained about missing Sylvia, and he was unhappy that he couldn't play golf much anymore. This was unusual, too, because he was usually very cheerful and upbeat.

I asked his advice about some business and all of a sudden, he said, "You are forty years old and have a family. You do not need my advice regarding business or anything else. You are a grown man and can make your own decisions."

He had never spoken to me that way before, and since he was virtually a surrogate father to me, I almost broke into tears. I knew that wouldn't be appropriate, so I bucked up, took his dressing down, and changed the subject. We enjoyed our meals, although I was quite shaken by his tone with me. It was just so unusual.

After lunch, he asked that we drive him back to his home up the hill on Laurel Canyon. When we got to the house, he invited us in. He started walking us around the whole house, showing us things we had seen before and walking into various rooms and pointing out things. I had a sensation that something was wrong, and that he perhaps was having some kind of mini stroke or lapse. He was very articulate, but it was just strange.

He told us that he was expecting fellow composer, Shirley Walker, who was going to interview him for an article in some film music magazine. He asked if we wanted to stay. We begged off, saying we had to start preparing for Thanksgiving the next day. He walked us to the door and asked again if we wanted to stay. We walked to the car and he said, "Next week is Kaylyn's birthday, I'll take you to dinner, ok?" We said sure and wished each other Happy Thanksgiving.

Two hours later, my phone rang, and it was Scherr Lillico, who was our event planner and general major domo at ASMAC. She said tearfully that during the interview, Irv had closed his eyes and fallen over dead from a heart attack. We both were weeping, but I have to admit that I wasn't the slightest bit surprised, because of the events that happened at and after lunch.

While my mother was still very much alive, I felt I had lost my father again. It was a big blow.

I had several mentors in Hollywood. Another was Pete Myers, who was a very busy writer, and sometimes Artie Kane, who had been a very active pianist, composer, and conductor.

Irv had always been my go-to, whenever I didn't know how to do something or questioned my abilities. He would show me techniques to get out of trouble musically. He knew every trick in the book and would tell me without hesitation.

Myers's attitude was always supportive, too … but as he said to me once, "Does Macy's tell Gimbels?" He meant it affectionately, but he was still active in the business.

I was very sad when I realized that I wouldn't have Irv on the other side of the phone or at our many lunches together.

It was fortunate that I had a lot of work coming up. David Gest called and asked me to be MD for The International Achievement in Arts Awards. This was a big deal show at the Dominion Theatre in London. It would feature lots of great performers, including Kirk Douglas and Anthony Quinn dancing à la *Zorba*.

Alan Bates was presenting an award to Quinn. Ginger Rogers, Doug Fairbanks Jr., and John Mills would be on stage. Ann Miller was singing "Everything's Coming Up Roses." The night would feature Michael Bolton, Elaine Page, David Cassidy, Robert Goulet, and many others. Robert (RJ) Wagner was hosting.

Goulet showed up at rehearsal and I started chatting. I knew he was a great friend of Pippin's. I mentioned that I had been Irv's protégé and that Irv had just passed. Robert was taken aback and became very teary. They had worked together many times on *The Garry Moore Show* and on a TV *Brigadoon*. I hadn't known, but he warmed up to me because of Irv.

David Gest and Celia Lipton
Present
THE INTERNATIONAL ACHIEVEMENT IN ARTS AWARDS
'A Night of 200 Stars'

Honouring
SIR ANTHONY HOPKINS
SIR JOHN MILLS
ANTHONY QUINN
GINGER ROGERS
For Distinguished Achievement in Film

DAME DIANA RIGG
For Distinguished Achievement on Stage and Television

SIR PETER HALL
For Distinguished Achievement in the World of British Theatre

PETULA CLARK
THE FOUR TOPS
For Distinguished Achievement in Music

Hosted by ROBERT WAGNER
Sponsored By American Airlines And American Eagle

Produced and Written by David Gest
Executive Producer Celia Lipton
Directed by Tristan Rogers
Musical Conductor Larry Blank

Legal Firm: Shelden, Kulchin, Rosen, Florence & Jones
Public Relations U.K.: Fiveash & Hill, Nick Fiveash & Graeme Hill
Public Relations U.S.A.: Dale C. Olson & Associates, Inc., Dale C. Olson
Assistants to Mr. Gest: Joanne Lichtenstein, Sue Sketchley & Jan Douglas
Transportation Coordinator: Elizabeth Applegate
Travel Agents:
Adventureland Travel, Mary Jane McDonald
Royal Palm Travel, Leigh Tucker
Security: Willie Green

Benefiting 🎗 Great Ormond Street Children's Hospital Fund

He was going to sing "If Ever I Would Leave You" and "Impossible Dream." I got to the podium for the rehearsal and there was no conductor part. He said, "I know where it is."

I said, "Where?"

He said, "On the sofa in my living room in LA."

Great.

He said, "C'mon, you know how it goes."

I started conducting, and the intro was exactly as it was on the original cast recording of *Camelot*. I was in heaven.

He started singing, "If ever I would …"

I cued the orchestra on "leave you," … and it was a Las Vegas bossa nova. He laughed, because he knew it would take me by surprise. The routine was the same, just a bossa nova.

Fortunately, "Impossible Dream" was pretty straightforward. Robert was a very nice guy, easy to work with and a lot of fun.

This show was a big PITA (pain in the ass) because of all the artists, all the music, all the variables, and David Gest's total craziness. However, *everyone* was there, on stage and in the audience. It was quite the star-studded event. And, of course, Diana Rigg was honored as well.

I came back to LA to do a whole bunch of work on various projects, and I was asked to preside at Irv's memorial with an orchestra, and to conduct several of his arrangements. Sid Ramin spoke, and I was so flattered when he included me with Peter Matz, Billy Byers, Johnny Mandel, and himself as Irv's protégés. What an honor to be included in that group.

Shortly after this event a board meeting was held at ASMAC, and they elected me president.

It seemed to me with my election as president of ASMAC, that I had finally achieved my goal of transitioning to becoming an accepted arranger/orchestrator in the Hollywood Scene. Not to make light of it, but ASMAC was basically just a club for arrangers. It often tried to be more than that, but it was a club with a nice elite membership. Many of its members were successful people from an earlier era. People joined it to hang around and learn a bit, but it was mostly about lunches and the yearly Golden Score Award.

ASMAC had been losing money for years, and my goal was to put it back in the black. I scheduled luncheons which we called *Honoring Our Own*, meaning honoring members of the organization. This allowed me to bring in people who were more current and active in the business. I knew a lot of people, so I used those connections, too.

It took a lot of time to keep ASMAC running properly. Scherr Lillico, who ran an organization called The Proper Image, was important in keeping the profile up. I told her that if I was king of ASMAC, she was queen. She really took care of the workload for luncheons and invites, and was important to the success of the organization.

Meanwhile, I was also trying to maintain my career. I was working a lot with Michael Feinstein, conducting many concerts for him with symphony orchestras. Marc Shaiman was still calling me, and with Harvey Cohen, we orchestrated a substantial portion of *Forget Paris*, a picture with Billy Crystal with lots of Big Band music. I got a lot of recognition for that.

Marc asked me to do an arrangement of "The Way You Look Tonight" and "I Have Dreamed" to be played by a dance band for the film *The American President*. They would use one or the other of the arrangements. The scene was supposed to be the widowed president (Michael Douglas) and his date (Annette Bening) dancing and falling in love.

Director Rob Reiner wanted the Marine Band (the official White House band) to play it, then he'd shoot to that. I wrote the prettiest arrangements of the two songs, without being too corny, and Rob picked "I Have Dreamed."

Aside from the fact that Marc wrote a beautiful main title, orchestrated by Jeff Atmajian, and it was a lovely movie, I got a lot of recognition for this little moment in the film, which was so sexy and warm. It was so successful in the shoot, that Rob decided to go back into the studio and replace the band with the Hollywood musicians. This was mostly for reasons of proper audio and mixing. In any case, it was a highlight and I'm happy to have been part of that.

Meanwhile, my benefactor Don Pippin came up with another one. TV and movie celebrity Paul Sorvino was planning to do a concert. Paul had originally been a singer in a few Broadway musicals, and then had become popular on *Law and Order*. He was playing nice roles in a few films and some heavies in others, like *Goodfellas,* where he played the don. Right then, The Three Tenors were popular: Luciano Pavarotti, Placido Domingo, and Jose Carreras. Paul was apparently thinking *What three tenors? There is only one!!!*

Don was to do the conducting, and I was hired to do the arrangements for much Italian literature and some light classics. I was looking forward to it. I did farm out one song, "Mama" to Nick Perito, who was playing accordion. Nick was a talented arranger, and had been Perry Como's conductor/arranger for many years. He also did the Kennedy Center Honors. I asked him to do "Mama," as it was traditional, and I didn't want to be bumped off by the Italiano music police for writing an inauthentic arrangement.

I was called to a meeting with Paul, Don, and the young gents in the waste removal and sanitation business in Philadelphia, who were financing this extravaganza. When I told Paul that the music would cost 100K, he said, "Don't worry, they have it on them." I liked him very much. He was quite charming, and you could understand his success. His singing, in a word, was operatic.

I have changed some of the names below for my own safety …

At the recording session, with an orchestra in Seattle contracted by David Sabee (mostly the Seattle Symphony), I got in the recording truck behind the Fifth Avenue Theatre, where the concert was being filmed. Just before the concert began, the door swung open and "Johnny Boombatz" (my name for this rather large gent in a pin-striped suit) appeared. This was a very big man, with fingers that looked like ripe bananas with rings on them. He swooshed down in a big canvas chair next to the director, Clark Santee.

The concert opened with my instrumental composition "Americana Out West," which was well received. Then the music began again, and it was announced: "Ladies and gentlemen, Paul Sorvino!"

Paul sang "Without a Song" and as he got through the second sentence, Johnny Boombatz said out loud, "Nobody told me he couldn't fuckin sing!"

Now, that's not true. Paul could sing, it was just a little raucous, and he could've used a bit more training. Mr. Boombatz turned to me, standing in the corner, and said, "Who the fuck are you?"

I edged towards the door, swung it open, and said "Nobody," making it out the door and up the alley before I caught any responsibility, or any warning shots. I have never moved so quickly in my life.

This concert was released on audio and video recordings. I actually found two CDs in the bins at the old Tower Records on Sunset Blvd. Going through the S's in male vocalists, right after the many recordings of Sinatra, was a little marker for Sorvino with two CDs. I still have them. But after I purchased them, there was no longer a Sorvino folder in the S's at Tower Records.

I did make a pile of dough for these orchestrations, thanks to Pippin. And Paul hired me a bit later to write the score for *That Championship Season*, which he directed for Showtime.

The last time I saw Paul was at a well-known Italian restaurant on Beverly Blvd. He saw me and said, "Larry Blank, I heard that you were dead."

I said, "Obviously, you were talking to one of my competitors."

He introduced me to his dinner companions, "Philly No Ears" and "Jimmy Baretta." Paul had a lot of friends who obviously invested heavily in show business. I disappeared to my own table and companions.

(As of this writing, July 2022, I have only just heard that Paul Sorvino passed at age eighty-three. RIP Paul. There was more than one tenor but only one Paul Sorvino.)

Chapter Eight

A s the year progressed, Michael Feinstein hired me to conduct some fun gigs. One was with David Raksin and one was with Carol Channing. David was one of the most respected of Hollywood composers, and really on top of his game into his 90's. Carol was super intelligent and not at all the character she portrayed so frequently on stage and film. A character yes, but it was a persona she presented to the public. Along the way, she asked me to conduct for her. I turned her down because my desire was to be writing. I didn't want to commit to a more or less regular conducting job with limited musical variation.

Composer/saxophonist Tom Scott hired me to write some charts for the Academy Awards. He was conducting, but Quincy Jones was technically the MD. I wrote a chart for "Luck Be a Lady" using the underlying figure from Quincy's "Killer Joe." "Killer Joe" was a Benny Golson jazz piece that was quintessential of its time. Quincy asked who had written "Luck Be a Lady", and I said, "I'm the white guy who wrote that." Hubert Laws was playing flute, Greg Phillinganes was playing piano, and Harvey Mason was on drums—it was very difficult to sound bad. These guys were famous players and gave me a great deal of credibility. I was slowly moving away from being just a "Broadway" guy.

I was engaged to be the music director for the "Share Show." Ian Fraser, who usually did it was not available. This was a big deal, yearly gala, produced by all the "Hollywood" wives. There were great performers. I got to conduct for Bob and Dolores Hope, and it was a very high-profile job for me. It was nice to be part of the Hollywood community, and I appreciated the opportunities coming my way.

Through composer Mark Watters, I was asked to do a chart for country/western singer Trisha Yearwood, and I was still doing lots of arrangements for Michael Feinstein. And then, once again through the auspices of Don Pippin and Jerry Herman, I was asked to orchestrate and supervise the music for *Mrs. Santa Claus*, an original TV musical written by Jerry Herman.

Terry Hughes was the director—the nicest and most talented man. He knew the genre and had directed most of the videos of the Sondheim musicals for television. Terry was very respectful of the idiom and a great collaborator. Rob Marshall was given his first opportunity choreographing for film, and did a marvelous job. Rob brought in his dance arranger, David Krane. David was very facile and perfect for this project. Pippin was in charge, but because I was a "Hollywood guy," everyone thought it best that I supervise and get the elements in place. The producer was Boyce Harman for Hallmark, and he certainly knew his business and was a joy to work with.

Jerry had decided that he didn't want to do any more stage shows, except for revivals of his existing and successful musicals, *Mame, Dolly,* and most obviously, *La Cage.* He mentioned to me that after *Gypsy* and *Funny Girl,* Jule Styne had been very prolific, working on many not-so successful musicals, and it had diminished his earlier success. Jerry thought that TV was the perfect idiom and was ecstatic to have Angela Lansbury and Charles Durning doing *Mrs. Santa Claus*. What's not to like? Angie was one of the nicest people in the business and delightful to work with. She was warm and most knowledgeable, knowing exactly what she was doing and how to get it across.

Jerry, sometimes with Don, would go through the music, and I would learn what he wanted to hear and the context of the songs. Terry Hughes was waiting for us to dictate the style and he would work around it. Not that he didn't have his own opinions, but with people like Jerry and Don around, he just knew to defer to these experts of the musical genre. Jerry would play a song for me and indicate the style. I would go home and come up with a background, sometimes with indications from Pippin, and sometimes not. I'd play it for Jerry over the phone, and he'd say "perfect", or "change this", or "please don't change my harmony," etc. I'd grown up listening to all of the Phil Lang orchestrations for *Mame, Dolly, Mack and Mabel,* and I knew what Jerry liked. I had already worked with him on *La Cage* and *Mack and Mabel,* but as conductor—although I had done orchestration fixes on *Mack and Mabel.*

Don had convinced Jerry that I was the perfect guy for this, and Jerry was very secure in Don's choice. We got along famously. In one instance, *"The Best Christmas Of All,"* Jerry asked for reindeer hooves in the accompaniment. This was a tough assignment. I studied the music of LeRoy Anderson and *"Sleigh Ride,"* and decided that I wouldn't use any sleigh bells in the accompaniment of the songs until this finale, "Best Christmas." I came up with a figure for the clarinets and violas that I knew was spot on and played it over the phone for Jerry.

"Perfect," he said. "If you play it in every measure, I'll kill you."

Of course, I did play it in virtually every measure, and he loved it. I was able to use the figure in underscore in several other spots of the film, as well.

With Joe Soldo as contractor, we assembled the best orchestra in LA and recorded the tracks with the artists. I summoned all of my best "Kostal" tricks and devices as we played. It was a very happy experience. When we got to "Best Christmas," Jerry turned to me, his jaw dropped, and he started crying. He said, "Where did that come from?"

I walked into the room to talk to Don, walking past Angie in the vocal booth, who said "How can I help but sound terrific with an orchestration like that?"

And Don in his deep booming voice said, "Good boy."

I have to admit, that I'm most proud of that arrangement and orchestration, and it came from everything that had preceded it and all that I had been trained to do. It came from my affection for the genre and the music of Jerry Herman, and from everything Don Pippin and Irv Kostal had instilled in me. Of anything I've ever done or will do, that was in the best spirit of what I wanted to achieve. It came from somewhere beyond my skill level at the time. Listening to it now, I might say, "Of course, what else would I have written?", but it was the culmination of my skills at that time. I could feel Irv smiling over my shoulder.

Mrs. Santa Claus was a labor of love, and the rest of the year went smoothly with various conducting and arranging jobs, knowing that *Mrs. Santa Claus* would air on Hallmark at Christmas. I had orchestrated a Jerry Herman musical with Angela Lansbury cover to cover. Happy me!

Don Pippin summoned me to London to help with an Ira Gershwin tribute, produced by Jo Benjamin at the Royal Albert Hall. It had a lot of very fine moments, and I enjoyed conducting and becoming friends with British conductor/arranger/pianist David Firman. He was another Pippin protégé, but very accomplished in his own right, and we became fast friends. The show was fun and well-directed by Hugh Wooldridge. There were lots of very good moments, and an opportunity to arrange some nice music and to conduct for some fine artists.

Through Ray Charles (of the Ray Charles Singers), I made a connection with Wayne Baruch, who was working with Tibor Rudas, producer of *The Three Tenors*. They were now working on *The Three Sopranos*. The ladies were not of the status as *The Three Tenors,* and it was difficult to select material for them. In fact, when you start taking songs like "Al Di La," "Three Coins in the Fountain," and "Arrivederci Roma," it begins to sound like a collection of Connie Francis's greatest hits. At any rate, that occupied quite a bit of my time.

Eventually, Rudas and Baruch changed their minds about doing a recording and tried to get away without paying me—more Rudas than Baruch, who was simply an agent of Rudas. I eventually collected my full fee, but that left me with a very bad feeling about both Rudas and Baruch. I have discovered that when I feel mistreated or develop a sense of dread early on when working with people, it's time to leave ASAP. I did do a lot of good work for the project, making quite few demos for them. I learned a lot about the process but was delighted that it didn't go further.

The year 1997 began very well. Through my drummer friend, Albie Berk, I was introduced to Steve (Goldy) Goldstein. Steve was a wonderfully talented pianist/arranger, who had played a lot of contemporary acts and was Dolly Parton's music director. We both came from Long Island, not far from where I grew up, and we were contemporaries. We hit it off straightaway.

Goldy was booked to do the score for *Cats Don't Dance*, an animated feature with songs by Randy Newman. It was about a cat that goes to Hollywood to be a movie star. There were several production numbers, and Goldy hired me to be Mr. Musical Theatre, which was not his métier. He was writing the underscore cues and doing a lot of arranging. Randy Newman had written the songs, and they were recorded in "Randy Newman Time," meaning without click, a tool that keeps the drummer and band in time. Scott Bakula and others had provided the vocals. I was to add the orchestra and conduct most of the sessions, and Goldy asked Mort Lindsey and Larry Schwartz to do some song orchestrations, too.

There were several numbers that were right out of the Broadway playbook, and Goldy gave me a free hand to arrange and orchestrate as I saw fit. It was great fun with a huge orchestra. Pianist Alan Steinberger helped tremendously, working out a piano arrangement on sections of the "Animal Jam." He also played brilliantly on the recording.

Goldy was not a conductor by trade. He was more than happy to have me on the podium, and it was a very joyful experience. Because of the wandering tempi of Randy Newman on the prep, we had to "chase" the click, meaning we had to make a click track that fit the ups and downs of the tempi. Because of my extensive Broadway pit experience and my experience in the studios, it was easy fun for me, and the tracks turned out beautifully. *Cats Don't Dance* was a beautiful picture and quite under-rated. I enjoyed working with Goldy, and we developed a great friendship, as well. Goldy died prematurely in

2011 from cancer. He was a great friend and great talent and is missed by everyone who knew him. Much later, when I was introduced to Dolly Parton, the very first thing she mentioned was my friendship with Goldy. I was very moved.

Shortly thereafter, Barry Mishon reached out and asked me to help him put together a tribute to composer Jule Styne called "The Styne Way."

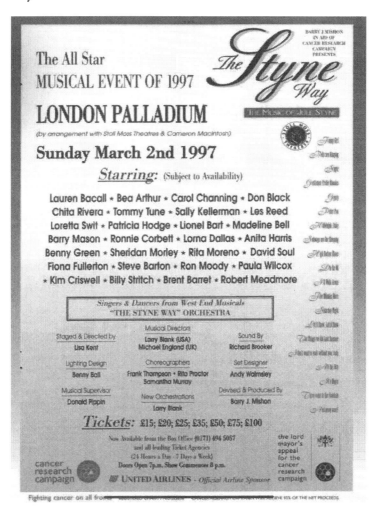

It had quite a line up. Helen Mirren presented with Sheridan Morley and spoke/sang "The Party's Over" at the finale. Bea Arthur sang "The Music That Makes Me Dance," and Sally Kellerman sang "Guess I'll Hang My Tears Out To Dry." Chita Rivera sang "Rose's Turn." Rita Moreno sang "Some People," and Tommy Tune sang "All I Need Is the Girl."

It was a fantastic program.

My greatest memory however was sitting with Bea Arthur, Chita, and Sally at Joe Allen's Restaurant. Bea and I got into a discussion about sushi. We were both great sushi fans. I mentioned to her that tuna was not plentiful in the Japanese waters, and they imported much from New England. Without missing a beat Bea said, "I suppose you are going to tell me that all the blowfish comes from Fire Island." It took me a few minutes for it to sink in, then I slowly started laughing uncontrollably at Bea's wit. After a few minutes of me trying to calm down, she said, "If you don't calm down, I'm leaving."

Of course, that made it worse and both Chita and Sally were enjoying watch me totally losing it. After a while I calmed down. A moment later, someone asked Bea what she thought of Betty White. Bea stood up, turned to the entire restaurant, and said in her loud voice, "Betty White is a c***." She sat down, stood up quickly, turned to the restaurant again, and said "For those of you who didn't hear me, Betty White is a c***." At this point, those around Bea were doing damage control. I never understood her animus and didn't pursue this any further. I know there are other similar stories, but that one's mine.

I headed back to LA and a pile of work. I said yes to everything. The more varied things I was doing, the happier I was. Don Pippin gave me some assignments for Marilyn Horne, doing crossover work. She was such a wonderful singer, she was comfortable doing operatic literature, as well as pop and traditional songs. Don did some humorous arrangements of "Ding Dong the Witch is Dead" and a beautiful routine for "Somewhere Over The Rainbow." It was always great fun to work with Marilyn and Don.

My friend Ken Kugler, a talented trombonist/orchestrator/ conductor, asked me to do some orchestrations on a film called *Kiss The Girls*. I also did something for *The Net*, both for composer Mark Isham. Mark said to me, "You don't remember me, do you?" He was right. He reminded me had been a trumpet substitute in the pit of *A Chorus Line* in San Francisco when I conducted there in 1977. It is indeed a small world.

I was doing a bunch of symphonic concerts for Michael Feinstein, when I received a curious call from Paul Blake. Paul Blake was running the St. Louis Muny. The Muny Theater has been in existence since the '30s, doing summer musicals. It's a wonderful venue, with a tree in the middle of the enormous stage. It's a national park, so it can't be touched. I think things may have changed in recent years, but it was always a lovely venue.

Paul had been a substitute drama teacher at the High School of Performing Arts in New York, when I was a fifteen-year-old student. He was planning to take the music of Jule Styne and the lyrics of Sammy Cahn and create a musical version of the film *Three Coins in the Fountain*. The very gifted Bruce Pomahac was going to do dance music, and Ralph Burns was set to do the orchestrations, with my help. Paul handed over the music, and the job turned out to be much more than just orchestrating.

Working with Paul was fun, and basically, I was to be the arranger (along with Bruce). Lynn Crigler was hired to be the music director/ conductor. Gemze de Lappe, who was famed for her dancing in

Oklahoma and *The King and I,* and for assisting Agnes De Mille and Jerome Robbins, was supervising the choreography and was great fun, too.

It was a great challenge to put together a new musical, routine the music, pick the keys, do choral work, etc. Paul brought in the famed Hugh Martin to do vocal arrangements. That was an honor, as well. Hugh is the great song writer of, "Have Yourself A Merry Little Christmas," "The Trolley Song," and the world class vocal arranger of "Sing For Your Supper." I knew him slightly from *Sugar Babies.* He had done some of the original vocals for that. So, Jule Styne, Sammy Cahn, Ralph Burns, Hugh Martin, Bruce Pomahac, and me … what a happy break for me!

After writing two arrangements including the overture, Ralph said, "I'm busy, can you handle this yourself?" Hugh wrote a vocal arrangement and did the same. They were not wanting to work so hard and left me holding the bag. I really didn't mind, and it was quite a challenge. I liked the music and I worked very hard at making it work, for the project, for Paul, and for myself. I was forced by circumstance to orchestrate almost an entire Broadway-style musical on my own, and I enjoyed the challenge. Aside from the overture and opening number, I wrote the rest. I felt very accomplished and grateful to Paul Blake for the opportunity. The show did what it did at the Muny, with no hope for much past that. However, it opened a new stream of work for me at the Muny and in the future with Paul.

Coming back from St. Louis, I was asked to music direct "Carnegie Hall Celebrates the MGM Musicals." This event was happening on my birthday, July 15, 1997. My forty-fifth birthday. Roddy McDowall and Michael Feinstein hosted the event. Clearly, it was my association with Michael that got me booked as MD.

The press release looked something like this:

> More than a dozen great stars of the MGM musicals of yesteryear will appear at NYC's Carnegie Hall, July 15-16, in a celebration concert sponsored by Turner Entertainment and Turner Classic Movies. Titled "Carnegie Hall Celebrates The Glorious MGM Musicals," the evening will feature film clips, along with songs and anecdotes. Hosted by Michael Feinstein and Roddy McDowall, the event will feature appearances by Leslie Caron, Cyd Charisse, Betty Comden & Adolph Green (*The Will Rogers Follies, On The Town*), Arlene Dahl, Gloria DeHaven, Betty Garrett, Kathryn Grayson, Skitch Henderson, Celeste Holm, Van Johnson, Tony Martin, Ann Miller (*Sugar Babies*), Donald O'Connor (*Show Boat*), Mickey Rooney and cabaret legend Julie Wilson. Larry Blank serves as musical director.
>
> Garrett will pay tribute to Frank Sinatra; Charisse will present a salute to MGM dancers; Rooney will tell of his days with Judy Garland, Miller will talk about the making of *On The Town*, and DeHaven will sing "Who's Sorry Now?" Also singing will be Holm, Grayson, Martin and Feinstein. Guest vocalists will include Stan Chandler, David Engel, Steven Freeman and Larry Raben
>
> Murray Horwitz directs the event (part of Carnegie Hall's "American Popular Song Celebration" series), which is scripted by John L. Miller.

This show was a delight to work on. It was Michael's love of MGM and the musicals, and my already established relationship with some of the people involved that made it so much fun. Betty Garrett was always a pleasure, and I would encounter her many times on many different jobs. In fact, her boyfriend had been the bass player for my San Francisco run of *La Cage*. So, we had a friendship that dated from that time. Arlene Dahl and her husband Marc Rosen were friends from many Barry Mishon concerts in London. Ann Miller became unavailable at the last minute, but Mickey appeared, doing everything at once, as usual. At rehearsals, he was playing the drums, playing the piano, and running around as the funny madman he always was. Julie Wilson always *killed* with whatever she chose to sing.

In the dressing room I shared with Roddy and Michael, I found a couple of large envelopes on the table and assumed rightly, they were birthday cards. I opened the very large card on top to find it was a birthday card from Rhoda. We had not communicated since 1986, or perhaps even 1985. Quite stunned, I sat down in a chair with an open mouth. Roddy (unknowingly and joking) looked at me and said, "You look like you got a subpoena from your ex-wife."

I couldn't figure out why/where/how, and then realized that there had been a half-page ad in the Sunday *New York Times*. It had my name, the date, and Carnegie Hall. In those days, New Yorkers and ex-New Yorkers would pick up the Sunday *Times* to see Section Two: Arts and Leisure and check out what was happening in show biz in New York City. Rhoda and I had parted amicably, but I decided it was in my best interest not to respond.

John Schreiber, the producer for the Carnegie Hall show, did another MGM Tribute a couple of years later. It was also quite excellent, with lots of MGM stars including Marge Champion. Marge came in at the rehearsal with pianist Peter Howard, who had been so helpful to me earlier in my career. Peter was a lovable and most talented man, and I was very grateful for his friendship. He was the best of the best of dance arrangers. So much familiar theatre music in the '60s and beyond was because of his great invention, such as the wonderful dance music in *Hello Dolly, Carnival,* and so many other shows. I asked John if he would engage Peter to appear on stage at the concert as Marge's accompanist. It was a gesture on my part to include him as a thanks for his past help. Peter was happy to participate and was a great asset to the proceedings.

More little film bits and concerts followed. There was the potential for a big new original musical called *Ginger*, about the life of Ginger Rogers. This was being sponsored by Dallas Summer Musicals and would use original songs and some standards by Gershwin, Jerome Kern, and others. They wanted to get Michael Feinstein to play George Gershwin, who apparently had dated Ginger for a minute.

The authors of *Ginger* had written young George romancing young Ginger with the song "A Fine Romance." I pointed out that the script should read, "Ginger, I love you so much that I'm going to sing a Jerome Kern song." *A Fine Romance* is by Dorothy Fields and Jerome Kern.

The director/choreographer was Randy Skinner, an extremely gifted dancer and tap choreographer. Later, we were both Tony-nominated for our work on the stage musical *White Christmas. Ginger* had potential to be fun and have some nice music. However, this kind of stuff is a bit misguided. After casting the show and getting ready for production, Michael Jenkins, the producer, pulled the plug … rightfully, I thought. Still, Randy and I had had great fun getting it going and assembling an exceptional cast. Too bad it never came to fruition.

Tom Scott called me to do an arrangement of "Mack The Knife" for a Celebration of American Music at the Kennedy Center with George Benson and Diana Krall. It was an honor to be asked to do this jazz standard for this event. I asked Bill Hughes, contractor/copyist for the event, how my chart had gone at rehearsal. His response: "I don't know if the chart was any good, but there were a lot of people jumping up and down and singing on stage, so it must've been ok."

215

The calls kept coming, and I did charts for this one and that one. Jerry Herman asked if I would do an orchestration/arrangement for a new film, *Barney's Great Adventure*. Yes Barney, the purple dinosaur that kids seemed to love. Although my kids were eleven, nine, and seven at the time, and said, "Oh Daddy, that's for *little* kids, not us."

Jerry wrote the theme song called *Barney*, Bernadette Peters was going to sing it, and I was going to orchestrate and conduct. It was a Canadian film, and we had to go to Vancouver to record the song with Bernadette. We would record the track in LA, meet Bernadette in Vancouver, and go into the studio where she would pop in the vocal.

I wrote a Nelson Riddle-type chart for children (and young adults) with a rather large orchestra contracted by Joe Soldo. John Richards (recording engineer extraordinaire), Jerry, and I, flew to Vancouver. At Jerry's insistence, we dined at a local Chinese seafood restaurant and had fresh, giant lobsters cooked to perfection, along with some other delicacies. There are perks to traveling for work sometimes.

Into the studio the next day to record with Bernadette. I had not worked with her before and was so impressed with her natural rhythm and interpretation. People like Bernadette, who are so loved and successful, always have some talent beyond the norm. She was no exception. I told her that she sang as if there was a high hat under her foot. Her time was exceptional. We got a beautiful track and happily departed back to LA.

I was music director for *Gypsy* at the Alzheimer's Association yearly gala. Donna Murphy sang *Some People*. Bea Arthur, Joely Fisher, and Charley Durning did other songs. These events were usually lots of fun. I recommended my old friend Larry Fuller to stage it. Larry told me that he had a surprise for me—someone I had worked with many years before. I couldn't imagine who it was.

Back in 1973, I had been rehearsal pianist and assistant conductor to Bill Cox for *No, No, Nanette* with Ruby Keeler and Cyril Ritchard. The director was Christopher Hewett. Chris Hewett had played Roger de Bris (the very gay director) in the original film of *The Producers.* He had also played Captain Hook in the Sandy Duncan *Peter Pan.* Cyril Ritchard had been Hook in the original with Mary Martin. Chris and Cyril used to camp it up, out-Captain Hook(ing) one another at rehearsals for *Nanette.* For some reason, known only to Chris, he called me Betty Blank in his haughty Brit accent. I think he loved the alliteration of Betty followed by Blank. He would say, "Betty Blank, please go to the piano. Play something Betty," and so on. It was quite funny, and I found it charming that I was noticed and called out to the piano all the time, just to amuse Chris.

At the performance for *Gypsy,* I went over to the table at the event where Larry was seated. Sitting next to him was a huge figure, Christopher Hewett, now Mr. Belvedere from the television show.

I looked at him, he looked at me, and said, "Betty, you've come a long way."

It was a nice reunion and lovely to see Chris again. He died not too long after that.

It had become traditional for a few years, for Billy Crystal to do special material for the opening of the Academy Awards. Marc Shaiman and Scott Wittman wrote the material. Marc called and I orchestrated some of that opening number. It was usually a lot of material, and it took an army to turn it out in time.

Michael Feinstein called and said we were going to do the first pops concert ever with the Chicago Symphony. It was a big deal, because they didn't do pops concerts. They were a bit fussy and not particularly friendly towards a "pops" conductor. The first half was done by another conductor, and they did the three dances—from *On the Town*—very difficult for the orchestra and the conductor.

We then had our rehearsal and a bit of good fortune. I saw two players who recognized me. One was a violinist named Fred Specter, who had been in the pit of *A Little Night Music* in 1974 at the Shubert on Monroe Street. The first horn was Dale Clevenger, a world-famous horn player for his fearless and strong playing. He said very loudly, "Nice to see you, Larry."

I was now "in" with the orchestra. I was thrilled, as there had been an air of "make my day" coming from the orchestra. Everything went rather smoothly, although the orchestra had played a year and a half behind the stick, and they hated the drummer (who is always too loud for a symphony orchestra).

Backstage, Dale shook my hand and said, "Larry, please remind me where we met."

I said, "Dale, when I came to Chicago to join *A Little Night Music* at the Shubert in 1974, I sat in front of you at the piano and celesta in the pit."

"I have never played in a theatre pit," he said.

"No Dale, I remember very clearly, you sat behind me in the pit at the Shubert."

"I have never played in a theatre pit."

Well, I could swear that the horn player who sat behind me at the Shubert in 1974 was Dale Clevenger. He had been a member of the Chicago Symphony even then. He must've wanted to play the show out of interest, or perhaps he was substituting for a colleague. Violinist, Fred Specter recalled completely and said hello. In any case, Fred and Dale were great players, whether in the pit or on the stage for the Chicago Symphony. The concert went well and it was a nice feather in my cap.

Little Girl Fly Away, was a TV film I did for composer David Michael Frank. I knew David from circa 1970 when he was substitute MD on Broadway when I had conducted a tour of *The Me Nobody Knows*. We re-met in LA, and he hired me to orchestrate a Disney Channel film called *Under Wraps*.

I got a very last-minute call from David. He said he was on the way to the Czech Republic to record a TV film but didn't have a main title. Would I do it for $500.00? And it had to be ready to go the next morning for him to have the parts and board his flight to Prague. He would send me a two-line piano sketch and I had a big orchestra ... in fact, a huge orchestra.

I love a challenge, was working freelance, and I loved working all night to orchestrate a main title. It was a good challenge and 500 overnight, while really not enough, was 500 more than I had the day before.

He sent the piano part by fax, and I spent several hours orchestrating and then called the copyist. The copyist delivered the parts and score to David at LAX as he went to the plane. David called and said thank you, and that he would send me a check on his return in a week. (He hadn't told me that part ahead of time, but I could wait). When you are living freelance and dependent on payments, delays are inevitable, just not fun. Usually, when you do this kind of work, it's immediate payment – especially for an overnight delivery of a main title for a film.

One week later, I called David. No answer. I waited a day ... no answer, and so on. Finally, the phone rang. "Oh, I'm so sorry, I got back and I'm in Las Vegas with my wife and kids."

"Well David, I could really use the money."

"Vegas is really expensive y'know."

"I'm sorry to hear that, but I need the dough and it was about two weeks ago."

"I'll be back in a couple of days and will send the check."

A couple of days later a check arrived in the mail. I opened it up and it was for $250.00.

I phoned David. "What's up with this check?"

He said, "Well, you know it was really expensive taking the kids to Las Vegas."

There was silence on my end.

Then he said, "The orchestration wasn't that good anyway."

I bit my tongue so that I wouldn't explode, and said, "Did you use it as I wrote it?"

He said, "Yes."

"Well then it was good enough! Please send me the balance and don't ever call me again."

Truly, I don't remember if he paid me the balance. I seem to recall he called again about something else, and I was fortunately too busy.

The most important thing I learned was that if you work for free or for a low fee, that is your price forevermore. If you undercharge, it's never a favor, it's your new price scale. If you charge a fair price and your work is good, you'll get called again and again. If you undercharge, you will get called when they don't have the money to pay properly.

There was a redux of the MGM Tribute from Carnegie Hall in London at the London Palladium with me as conductor. We had Van Johnson, Rita Gam, Cyd Charisse, Lilliane Montevecchi, Tony Martin, Marge Champion, and all the others. Another real treat for me and another chance with all of these wonderful artists. I had the fabulously gifted Mike Renzi on piano with the equally talented Michael Berkowitz on drums. Great stuff. This was directed by the very talented Lisa Kent. Another Barry Mishon extravaganza we called affectionately, "Mishon Impossible."

I was asked to be MD for a Judy Garland Tribute at Carnegie Hall, in June 1998.

This was quite an honor as Judy Garland's 1961 concert was iconic. Anyone who was anyone in New York insisted they had been present and everyone who hadn't been, wished they had.

John Schreiber, the producer of the tribute was assembling an amazing cast of characters for the event. The song list was also iconic and we had to find some arrangements. Sid Luft, Judy's husband at the time, had been the producer of the original concert in 1961. Sid was the father of Lorna and Joey Luft. I had become friendly with Lorna over the years. She is a few months younger than I am, and in fact, her first husband, Jake, had been my agent for a short while. I had been music director for Lorna on several occasions as had Don Pippin and others.

Lorna's relationship with her father was somewhat strained. He was a tough character. Being Judy's daughter and Liza's half-sister carries some burdens. I reached out to Sid, who was very friendly on the phone and invited me to come to his apartment in Brentwood to have a chat. For some reason, we hit it off instantly. He was about the same age as my parents and, coming from that New York Jewish background, I was very much at ease talking with him. After a few minutes he said, "Larry, y'know I have all of the arrangements from the Carnegie Hall concert on microfiche." (Microfiche and microfilm are similar. One is on card stock and microfilm on film.)

Finding the arrangements for Judy's Carnegie Hall concert was like finding The Holy Grail of Garland memorabilia. Sid was a clever man and had been hoarding this stash since the concerts. Some of the material had been used while Garland was still alive, and he'd stored it since her death. His only stipulation was "Please don't share this with Lorna."

I immediately nodded in agreement. (Of course, I made sure that Lorna had access and, through Michael Feinstein, made sure that Liza had it, as well.) It is forever preserved, and it was I who passed on the materials to Rufus Wainwright at a later date.

Sid's reticence to pass on the materials to Lorna was due to her recently published book *Me And My Shadows,* which were Lorna's memories of growing up as the daughter of Judy Garland. It seemed to me at the time that he was rather jealous that Lorna had beaten him to it.

The concert was truly amazing for the talent on the stage. Great ladies knocked out the familiar songs with the original arrangements. Drummer Michael Berkowitz contracted a stellar orchestra and played drums. It was legendary stuff. Berkowitz knew every drum fill and the music fit like a comfortable glove.

There was an arrangement of "But Not for Me/If Love Were All," put together for Elaine Stritch by Larry Grossman. It was my job to orchestrate and conduct. Jonathan Tunick admitted that he had adapted my orchestration for Stritch's act/concert later on. Regardless, it was Stritch and Grossman's arrangement that shone.

I fondly remember getting a call from Stritch the night after the concert. She asked if I would like to work with her further on some other material, and perhaps some concerts. I was extremely flattered but told her I had to pass because I was based on the west coast. A

couple of years later, Elaine hooked up with the most talented pianist/
arranger/conductor, Rob Bowman. That was a match made in heaven.

Vikki Carr was amazing in the concert, as well. Dee Hoty knocked
"As Long as He Needs Me" out of the park! Mort Lindsey (Garland's
conductor) conducted the famous "Overture from Carnegie Hall."

Jerry Herman wrote a tribute based on "That's Entertainment"
and performed it with my arrangement and me conducting for him. A
little-known fact was that Jerry had desperately wanted Judy Garland
for *Mame*. He told me that he had played her audition. But because
of her troubles at the time, the producers wouldn't go for it, unable
to insure the show if she didn't appear.

Pam Myers did the iconic "Happy Days/Get Happy" medley with
Dee, as well as the "You Made Me Love You" medley, and Nancy
Dussault sang "Any Place I Hang My Hat Is Home."

We had Gogi Grant singing "Stormy Weather." She was a really
fine singer, who had a hit with "The Wayward Wind," written by
Broadway conductor Stan Lebowsky. I sent her the recording and
asked if she could do it. She said, of course, but that it would be better
a tone down. I told her that we didn't have the wherewithal or budget
for that, and nobody else had really requested a transposition. Truthfully, it wasn't an unreasonable request, but these galas and events are
usually for charity and couldn't afford transpositions unless necessary.
At the rehearsal, the day of the show, she sang it in the original key
and sounded smashing. She then threw quite a fit, saying that I had
promised to transpose it and got quite ugly. This was a real shock
because she had been so docile before. I was really at a loss at that
point, with the concert starting in a few hours. In today's world, the
music would be in Finale/Sibelius or some other music program, and
the copyists could turn it out in a few minutes, print it, and hand it

out. At that time, it meant a crew of copyists would have to sit down, use their brains, and transpose it. It was a big deal.

Harvey Estrin who was playing lead alto said, "We can transpose it a tone." I looked around and all the "blowers" brass and reeds said sure. We had a bunch of all-stars. Our concert master said," What about us?" After a few words of fuss and all, we played it in her key and it was indeed better. Don Pippin had told me that he and Goulet were old friends from summer stock days at the Lambertville Music Circus in New Jersey. I invited Don to the rehearsal, and he showed up onstage while Robert was rehearsing "Smile." When they saw each other, they ran towards each other for a big embrace. I was standing a few feet away and I heard Goulet say, "Don, old friend, I'm so happy to see you, you look great. I am just getting over prostate surgery."

Don, without missing a beat, said, "I thought you looked shorter."

You can't make this stuff up. Robert and his wife Vera later asked me to be MD for Robert's act. I was unable to do it, but I worked with Robert again when he was a replacement for a revival of *La Cage Aux Folles* on Broadway opposite Gary Beach. He was a major talent and force during his career. In 1968 he won a Tony for the lead role in the Kander/Ebb musical *The Happy Time.* If you take a look on YouTube, it is exceedingly clear why. He was an amazing talent.

With so much talent on one stage, A Celebration of the Music of Judy Garland was a huge success. Lorna and actor Robert Stack hosted, and it was a very memorable two evenings.

A Celebration of the Music of Judy Garland
(Carnegie Hall; 2,804 seats; $ 75 top)

Production: Presented by Carnegie Hall. Orchestra conducted by Larry Blank. Hosted by Lorna Luft and Robert Stack. Reviewed June 16, 17, 1998.

With: With: Shana Alexander, Lionel Bart, Vikki Carr, Betty Comden, Lea DeLaria, Nancy Dussault, Robert Goulet, Gogi Grant, Adolph Green, Skitch Henderson, Jerry Herman, Dee Hoty, Jack Jones, Alan King, Mort Lindsey, Jerry Maren, Robert Morse, Pamela Myers, Bebe Neuwirth, Elaine Stritch, Weslia Whitfield.

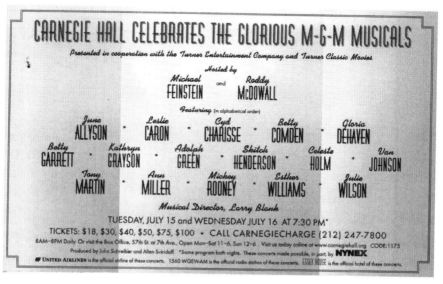

Chapter Nine

In my days as president of ASMAC, we would have yearly events, one of which was The Golden Score Award. It was usually given to a big name in the Hollywood composer genre: John Williams, Jerry Goldsmith, David Raksin, Irwin Kostal, Walter Scharf. After Irv's passing, there was also an Irwin Kostal Award. I would give a big speech about ASMAC and so on, and we would have some distinguished guest speakers.

One year, Van Alexander won the President's Award, Billy Byers (posthumously) won the Irwin Kostal Award, and I spoke. At the end of one event, a tiny older woman approached me from what seemed out of nowhere. I recognized her instantly from a favorite childhood TV show called *Bewitched*. She was the busybody, next-door neighbor Mrs. Kravitz. The woman approached and introduced herself as Sandra Gould. She complimented me on my speech and on speaking to the group, and told me that her brother, Danny, ran the music library at Warner Brothers Studios. I knew Danny slightly from some of my work around town. She then said, "Larry, I don't know why, but you seem so familiar to me and that is why I wanted to say hello. I feel like we've met before, and I just wanted to compliment you." I said thank you, and we went off on our different ways.

The next day, I called my mom to tell her of the evening's events. Both Cy Coleman and Sally Kellerman had spoken and entertained, and I was on a high from my position as president of ASMAC. I told my mother about Sandra Gould saying hello to me and asked if she knew who Sandra was. After a short pause she said, "Larry darling, my best friend at Erasmus High School in Brooklyn was Sandy Gould." They'd sat next to one another in class and were very good friends. Time gets out of hand sometimes. When I finally tried to track Sandy Gould down, I found that she had passed away.

I was asked to go to Toronto to write some new orchestrations for a musical called *Hot Shoe Shuffle*. It had begun as a very successful Aussie musical, directed/choreographed by David Adkins. It had a successful run in the UK and now was being "tormented" for a run in the states. They hired David Goldsmith and Megan Cavallari to do new songs. I was asked to do arrangements for it and I suggested they hire Bill Cox as music director, and I would do whatever I was asked to do.

It was trying out in Toronto the same time as the musical *Fosse* was having its Broadway break-in. Ralph Burns was the orchestrator, along with Gordon Harrell as dance arranger, and Gordon arranged a dinner for the three of us. Ralph informed me that he wanted me to meet his co-orchestrator, the very young and talented Doug Besterman. I was excited to see the new show, which was to be the next *Dancin'*, and I was so happy to be their guest for dinner and the show.

Ralph had talked me up to Doug and jokingly said, "Larry was so young on 'They're Playing Our Song,' he had a chorus girl hanging from each arm." Doug smirked like … *sure* … *sure* … and as fate would have it, just at that moment, two young dancers showed up at the stage door, returning from dinner and came running up to me.

They embraced me like a long-lost brother with a smother of kisses and wrapped themselves up on me. I couldn't have staged this any better. They were Dana Moore and Jane Lanier, who had both been on *Colette* and *Sugar Babies* (along with Kaylyn). Dana had been in *Copperfield,* as well. Ralph was so pleased with himself and said to Doug, "See what I mean?"

I sat with Doug and Ralph for the show and enjoyed it very much, knowing so many in the cast and being surrounded by the current musical royalty on Broadway.

A short time later, Ralph called and asked if I were available to do an additional orchestration of "Who's Got The Pain?" for *Fosse.* He said that he and Doug were up to their ears and could use some help. Gordon was laying it out for me. Ultimately, they changed their minds and the number didn't go into the show, so no arrangement from me. It was very flattering to be asked though. And meeting Doug was a good thing, as it prompted him to ask me to join him on various projects later down the road.

I received a call from Danny Guerrero (who knew Kaylyn from work at Disney). Vikki Carr was doing a TV show/concert called *Memories/Memorias* for KCET in September 1998. Danny was the producer. Vikki knew me from the Garland concert at Carnegie Hall. Bob Florence was her arranger and music director, but he was having some vision issues and had suggested that I conduct the concert/TV recording. He would play piano for Vikki. Vikki was amenable along with guest artists, Jack Jones, Pepe Aguilar, and Arturo Sandoval.

Joe Soldo hired the band, which was truly excellent. I was exposed to some really great Latin music with some wonderful players. Bob Florence was a tremendous talent at the piano and as an arranger. Vikki was delightful. It also brought me together with Jack Jones.

I had been MD for *Man Of La Mancha* with his father Allan Jones in 1972. Jack was thrilled to hear that, and I was honored to get to work with him.

Since it was a TV show, I was wearing headset in communication with the director Paul Miller and could speak to every member of the band, who were all on earpieces. This was done on the stage of the Beverly Hilton Hotel in Beverly Hills. This hotel was owned by Merv Griffin at the time. It was a very popular venue, and Merv was happy to have these shows done there.

On one of the numbers during the taping, Bob Florence was noodling at the piano, playing soft little nothings in the background as Vikki talked about her humble beginnings, and opening for Nat King Cole when she was very young. Vikki said, "I was so young, and Nat tapped me on the shoulder, and do you know what he said to me?"

At this moment, *bad* Larry stepped on the microphone pedal to the band and said something totally rude and inappropriate. The entire band broke into hysterical, embarrassed laughter, and you heard through the speaker, "Cut! Cut! Cut!" Paul Miller came down to the stage and started screaming at the band, reminding them it was a taping for a TV special and to control themselves. Not wanting to get me in trouble, the members of the band had their heads down. I was quietly smirking as "bad boy of the orchestra." Bob Florence was suffering tears of laughter at what I had done. I didn't need any encouragement.

We were now going back to the lead-in, and started in with Bob playing and Vikki talking, with the band looking at me and Bob still wiping some tears from his eyes. The tape was rolling and it came up to the same moment: Vikki said, "I was so young, and Nat tapped me on the shoulder, and do you know what he said to me?"

At that moment I stepped on the mic switch with my foot, an audible click was heard in the headsets, and the entire band, especially Bob Florence, started laughing again.

"Cut! Cut! Cut!"

I hadn't said a word, I had just stepped on the mic switch. The tension of the moment and absurdity of the situation had just tickled everyone, and it became a moment of chaos. Paul Miller was furious and was shouting at the orchestra, who were holding their heads down in shame. Of course, I couldn't be blamed, because I hadn't done anything (this time). Bob was shaking his head at me, still laughing. We were coming down.

Vikki, who is a lovely person, wandered across the stage looking at me and said, "Honey, what did you say?" with a very knowing smile on her face.

I said, "I didn't say anything."

She smiled at me and we finally went through the show without a hitch. As badly as I had behaved, I thought that making everyone crack up helped us to breeze through the rest of the show. That's my story and I'm sticking to it.

All of a sudden, I received a call and invite from Mort Viner, Michael Crawford's manager, to come and see Michael's act at the Hollywood Bowl. Ian Fraser was conducting and had put it together. It was also done as a TV special with Dale Kristien singing the *Phantom* numbers with Michael. It was quite well-done and directed by Gary Smith.

Mort was Gene Kelly's, Jimmy Stewart's, and Shirley MacLaine's manager. He was especially known for being Dean Martin's manager, as well. He had masterminded Michael's *Phantom* image and helped Michael to make superstar money. It was a good fit.

A typical Mort conversation went like this: "Larry, it's Mort Viner, are you available Sept 23 to Nov 1?"

"Well, let me look. Ok I'm available."

Click

"… Hello, Mort? Hello!!!!"

He had the answer he needed and that was the end of the conversation. Another time, I did a one-off gig with Michael and conducted one song in Palm Springs. At the end of the gig, I was handed an envelope that had forty crisp 100 bills in it. I said, "Mort, what's this?"

"Sometimes I can make it happen."

Several months later when I complained that I had not enough per diem while working in the UK, I was handed an envelope with £37, worth about $50 US. I asked Mort, "What's this?"

He said, "Sometimes I can't," and walked away.

However, if I needed something truly important, his warmth would come through all of his Big Agent stuff and he would come through. He was quite a character.

Crawford was asking for me to be his conductor/music director for his tour of Australia and New Zealand. I don't know what happened with Ian Fraser, who was a major talent and a very fine conductor. Julie Andrews wouldn't make a move without him, and he had been partnered with Anthony Newley and Leslie Bricusse from the beginning. Perhaps it was about money.

In any event, Ian was very helpful in preparing me for the tour and, if there were any hard feelings, he never showed them. I remained with Michael for some time. I was very happy because Michael and I were a good fit musically, and I knew how to accompany him. He was happy, too.

I spent time hanging with Dale Kristien and Lucas Corrubia (the sound engineer), and it was great fun. We traveled with the same band through most of Australia and NZ, and they were quite wonderful. Ken Laing was percussionist and fixer/orchestra contractor.

I made good friends with many in the band. It was a new and exciting place to travel, and I saw most of the major cities in Australia, especially loving Brisbane and Perth. In Perth, we were playing the Leeuwin Vineyards. Denis, the owner, would fill huge metal containers with bottles of their very best wines to take back to the room. He said if the container got empty the next night, he'd refill it. It was a fun time, and we enjoyed making music with Michael on a daily basis.

When we went to Perth, we had a different orchestra. It was the Western Australia Symphony Orchestra. We carried our main rhythm section, but the rest were the new orchestra. I had almost a full week scheduled to rehearse the orchestra, which was full of Brits, Americans, and Australians, as well as many Asian players. They were an excellent group and had sight-read the entire show at the first three-hour rehearsal. I had several days scheduled, but I really didn't need them, so I took to dismissing the orchestra early. Being a "Yank," growing up in New York City and working in the big music cities, I was accustomed to this kind of speed.

Michael took issue with my dismissing the orchestra and not using all the allotted time. He felt that I was treating the music lightly and was dismissive of it. On the contrary, I felt that by dismissing the band and being a bit light-hearted with them, they would play their hearts out for both me and Michael. I asked him if it sounded bad, and he admitted that it sounded wonderful. My logic was—ok then. But he assumed that I thought it was not very good and not worth the effort. These were not my feelings at all. I liked the music, and

I thought that Michael was one of the most dedicated performers I had ever worked with. Even though he had done *Music of the Night* a thousand times, every time was the first time. I seriously enjoyed our collaboration on stage. But Michael really took issue with what he thought was my bad attitude, and we had some very harsh words in the privacy of his hotel room. I left his room fully expecting to be going back to the States the next day.

The rhythm section invited me to go see the "Yank" film *American Beauty* with them, but the Aussies didn't get it at all. I was very depressed after the film and was really ruminating over my SNAFU with Michael. I went to his hotel and asked if I could speak with him, and he invited me up. I told him that we'd obviously had a disagreement about how I worked with the orchestra and asked him if he was happy with me as conductor. He said he was.

Was he happy with how the orchestras sounded under my baton? He said yes.

And I said, "It's your show, you are the boss, and you hired me. If you want me to spend more time rehearsing the orchestra, then I will do as you wish, unbegrudgingly. I will do exactly as you wish because you are the boss."

We shook hands and that really helped us bond for the rest of the tour. I think he realized that I really did have his back and was supportive. I was never a "company" man and was used to being the maestro. In this case, I was maestro for Michael Crawford, and I took the job seriously. I never sensed the slightest doubt from him when I was conducting. I don't remember him ever giving me a note, and we made some beautiful music together in concert.

His hiring me as his MD had totally eradicated any bad feelings that I had from being released from *Phantom* a few years before. I have always been grateful to Michael for bringing me on board. We did a lot of concerts together.

Shortly after this tour ended, Calvin Remsberg (a brilliantly talented singer, who played one of the opera producers in *POTO*) asked if I'd like to do *Sweeney Todd* for Reprise, the west coast version of New York's Encore series. This was a dream come true for me. Peter Matz, who was their regular MD, phoned as well, to explain that he thought this was more my cuppa tea than his and that he had recommended me.

I thought *Sweeney* was Sondheim's masterpiece. We had Kelsey Grammer as Sweeney, Christine Baranski as Mrs. Lovett, Davis Gaines, Ken Howard, Dale Kristien, Melissa Manchester, and Neil Patrick Harris. What's not to like? We'd use the full orchestration with the orchestra contracted by Joe Soldo. Some very good singers had been hired by Calvin, and it was really a bit of a dream team.

Kelsey was very successful with his TV show, very wealthy, and a bit cavalier about the whole thing. I went over to the Paramount lot (actually the old Desilu lot), where he was shooting his show *Frasier*, and I worked with him an hour every day. He really didn't put a lot of effort into it. He was a lovely guy, very musical, but was singing really flat. He needed a voice teacher. There weren't enough hours in the day. Christine, however, was taking it very seriously and working with a vocal coach daily to prepare.

Jerry Sternbach was rehearsal pianist and my very capable assistant. Jerry used to embellish the piano part a bit, as he has great chops. I convinced him to not improve on the Sondheim parts. At one run-through, Jerry played a tremendous flourish at the end of "Poor Thing" in the presence of Sondheim, who promptly screamed, "What the fuck was that?" Jerry's enthusiasm was welcome otherwise. I had known

Steve Sondheim from my earlier days on the tour of *A Little Night Music,* and he certainly knew my career conducting on Broadway.

Steve was from the old world of Broadway and was very supportive of the people that were summoned to work for him. Calvin knew the show backwards and forwards, having played the Beadle later in the Broadway run and on tour. He was very helpful with Christine on bits of business for *Little Priest* and *Worst Pies.* Dale Kristien and I were friends from *POTO.* Melissa Manchester and I knew each other from high school and Hamlisch days. She had been a year ahead of me at Performing Arts. Neil Patrick Harris was the kid from *Doogie Howser,* whom everyone liked. He was terrific as Toby and has now developed into quite a musical star. Ken Howard was a very likable person. We both came from Long Island, and although he was a bit older than me, talking to Ken was like talking to one of the guys I played baseball with, in the park.

Kelsey just wasn't prepared, and he was winging it. One day, Christine, a thoroughly professional actress and singer, asked to be excused because she was becoming so frustrated with him. Marcia Seligson, the producer, suggested I go after her and have a chat. I ran after her and suggested we have a late lunch and talk about this. Christine and I were of the same vintage, and we hit it off immediately and laughed a lot. I talked her into sharing a couple of martinis, and we had a rather boozy lunch. We made jokes about Kelsey, and I talked about how perfect she was for this part and that doing the show with Sondheim around was a great feather in her cap. Then, I drove her back to her hotel in Hollywood. Before she got out of the car, she said, "Ok, I will stay if, after rehearsals every day, we go for a meal and a couple of martinis, and you drop me off at my hotel."

I thought about that for about three seconds, and we made a deal that got us through all of the rehearsals and performances of *Sweeney Todd*. We laughed ourselves silly talking about "Malibu Sweeney". At a dress rehearsal, when Sweeney (Kelsey) lifted his arm and was supposed to say the important and iconic line from the show, "At last, my right arm is complete again," Kelsey said, "At last ..." pause ... pause ... pause ... and before he could take another breath Christine shouted out, "Line please?" bringing the entire cast and crew to their knees with laughter.

At an orchestra rehearsal with Kelsey, he was all over the place. I put the stick down and said, "Please go in the back with Jerry at the piano and learn the show." The whole orchestra put their heads down, looking at the floor. Everyone was shocked that I'd put him down, including me. I realized that I had to say something quickly ... so I added, "After all, I have a reputation to maintain," which caused the whole orchestra and Christine to laugh out loud ... with Kelsey beating a quick retreat to see Jerry. I have to admit to being a bit arrogant, but this was an important production of an important Sondheim piece, and I wasn't going to let TV star Kelsey Grammer screw it up.

Steve Sondheim was very unhappy with Kelsey's flat singing, but Kelsey did have other assets as an actor. The show had its performances on the stage of the Ahmanson Theater (with the orchestra upstage), and it was very well received. Sondheim was pleased with the music and my handling of the orchestra. Calvin had put together a very fine production of *Sweeney*, Kay Cole did an excellent job staging the bigger group numbers, and a new Mrs. Lovett was found in Christine's superb performance. She received wonderful reviews and, aside from Kelsey's flat singing, the entire cast was praised, especially Neil Patrick

Harris as Tobias. We had a wonderful time during the brief run, and it was easily one of the finest moments for the Reprise series. I was grateful to Calvin and Marcia, and to work with Christine.

Sweeney Todd

Ahmanson Theater; 1,600 seats; $75 top

Production: Reprise! presents a musical in two acts with music and lyrics by Stephen Sondheim, book by Hugh Wheeler. Directed by Calvin Remsberg; produced by Marcia Seligson.

Crew: Music direction, Larry Blank, choreography, Kay Cole; scenic design, David Sackeroff; lighting, Tom Ruzika; costumes, David R. Zyla; sound design, Jon Gottlieb and Philip G. Allen. Opened and reviewed March 12, 1999. Closed March 14. Running time: 3 HRS, 10 MINS.

Cast: Sweeney Todd - Kelsey Grammer Anthony Hope - Davis Gaines Beggar Woman - Melissa Manchester Mrs. Lovett - Christine Baranski Johanna - Dale Kristien Tobias Ragg - Neil Patrick Harris Pirelli - Scott Waara The Beadle - Roland Rusinek Judge Turpin - Ken Howard The Company - Jeff Austin, Bill Carmichael, Nancy Gassner Clayton, John Ganun, Bill Hutton, Linda Kerns, Carol Kline, Norman Large, Phil Meyer, Marnie Mosiman, Jimmy Smagula, 'Nita Whitaker

---

Michael Feinstein asked me to help him score *Get Bruce*, a documentary about writer Bruce Vilanch, which was great fun. The title song was sung by Ann Margaret, who was lovely in the studio. I helped Michael do the background vocals, and it turned out very well.

I was at the producer Andy Kuehn's home in Hollywood with Michael, Bruce, Andy, and Andy's partner. I said, "Andy, may I use your bathroom?"

Of course.

Michael said, "Andy, may I use your phone?"

Of course.

Bruce said, "Andy, may I use your boyfriend?"

There was no answer to that one, but Bruce is the king of situational humor. It was a fun job.

Next, Marc Shaiman phoned and said, "I have something special for you to work on, please come over."

I said, "Can't you just fax it or send it?"

"No, it's really important that I show it to you."

I headed over …

Marc said, This is animated and it's for the upcoming *South Park* film. It's all stick figures, as they haven't finished the animation."

The music began and the characters started singing, "Shut Your Fucking Face, Uncle Fucka," etc. etc. etc. My jaw dropped and I couldn't help laughing. Marc had set me up to see my reaction. He said, "Please make it sound like Mary Poppins goes to *Oklahoma* … not the state, the musical." I had a great time doing this.

Over the years, I have had more notoriety with people (especially my children) from doing the orchestrations on "Uncle Fucka" than anything else I've ever done. I also did the Saddam Hussein number "I Can Change." It was a lot of fun.

Marc later did the same thing he'd done to me to the musicians at the session. The musicians don't hear the lyrics when they are recording the background for a song. So, he invited as many as could fit in the booth for the playback. A few of the older, more subdued string players, got the vapors when they heard the lyrics. I still use it as my calling card. Thank you, Marc.

Several US concerts came up for Michael Crawford: Atlantic City, Palm Beach, and Cerritos, CA. It was always fun doing his show. I started bringing Michael Berkowitz to play drums, and finally, Joe Thalken on piano, and we had a great time.

Princess Cruises and director Gene Castle hired me to do some shows for them as orchestrator/conductor. These were always a challenge, but Gene did a great job with the staging, and they raised the bar for cruise ship entertainment.

The phone rang and it was Jerry Herman. He had been commissioned by Steve Wynn, owner of the Hotel Bellagio in Vegas and more, to do an original musical called *Miss Spectacular*, and we were going to do a concept recording. I was going to orchestrate, and Don Pippin was going to conduct. It was a fictional story about Sarah Jane Hotchkiss, who goes to Las Vegas to be a star, and would be co-produced by Sandy Gallin. Sandy was Dolly Parton's manager, among others, and like Steve Wynn, was a big name in Las Vegas circles.

We were going to have as much of an orchestra as we wanted, recording at O'Henry Studios on Magnolia. Joe Soldo would hire the orchestra, and we could pretty much do as we wanted to make Jerry's score come to life. So, Don and I were left to do our thing. We went to town and wrote what we wanted for an orchestra of around fifty. The singers would be Debbie Gravitte, Steve Lawrence, Christine Baranski, Davis Gaines, Michael Feinstein, Karen Morrow, and Faith Prince, plus a chorus. Steve Lawrence and Eydie Gorme were at the sessions, along with others, and it was a fun time. We had Berkowitz on drums.

I had a fun reunion with Baranski, who sang, "I Want To Live." Funny, "I Want To Live" was a song cut from Jerry Herman's *The Grand Tour,* and I somehow remembered the tune. I had "ghosted" on it, meaning Don had asked me to do the vocal arrangement with his name on it. So, it was a revisit for me.

Steve Wynn was in love with this whole idea, and particularly the song "Las Vegas," which Steve Lawrence sang. They invested a lot of dough into this, but it never came to fruition. I never saw a book for it. In any case, the songs were very pleasant, and I got to write whatever Don and I felt suited. Jerry loved it.

I asked Mort Viner (Michael Crawford's manager/agent) to negotiate a deal. He said, "My pleasure," and explained that he didn't like those guys and would enjoy doing the deal. He got me an enormous amount of money. When it was all done, I was at a concert, conducting for Michael Crawford and sitting with Mort. I said, "Mort, I'd like to give you a commission for the deal."

He said, "I don't need your money. My pleasure. You've been so good to Michael."

"In that case," I said, "may I take you to dinner, anywhere you want to go?"

Mort looked me in the eye and gave me the quintessential Mort Viner reply. "How much do I have to pay you to not have to go?" He winked and walked away.

You had to love that guy. When I later spoke to Shirley Maclaine about Mort, after he passed, she said, "We never had a signed contract from the day I came to Hollywood till the day he died." He was one of the greats and a great agent/manager.

Don Pippin called to tell me he was booked to conduct for George Shearing with the Palm Beach Pops, but he had a conflict on the last day for the final performance. George Shearing had been born blind and was a jazz pianist of exceptional skill. His popularity had been tremendous for nearly his entire ninety-one years. Don wasn't going to miss conducting for him.

I jumped at this opportunity, flew down to Florida, and heard Don conduct for him. I was happy to fill in. George was as charming as charming could be. He played absolutely brilliantly, and it was a joy to do this job. I was able to invite my mother to this concert.

For some reason, one of my knees, never a problem, decided to have a problem in the middle of this concert. It just buckled on me during the concert, and I found myself in considerable pain. It swelled up out of nowhere and just hurt, but I managed to get through the concert.

After the concert, when I was speaking to George, he said, "Which knee was it? I heard it pop." He did have great ears.

That knee plagued me for ten years until I had meniscus surgery in 2010.

Chapter Ten

The talented Lee Roy Reams, whom I had known for ages, called to say he'd been asked to do a benefit in San Francisco in tribute for actor Michael Douglas. He suggested me as MD. It was called "Stars for Life," and the gala honoring Michael Douglas was to raise money for a giant hospital in San Francisco. Lee Roy's friend Deborah Strobin was producing it. Karen Morrow, Lee Roy, Davis Gaines, Nancy Dussault, and I did some material with an orchestra. Danny De Vito, Karl Malden, Sharon Stone, Sean Pean, Martin Sheen, and Kirk Douglas also participated. It was a really fun job to do. Ellen DeGeneres was the hostess for the event, and this fundraiser succeeded in raising $1.5 million for the hospital.

Michael Douglas's wife, Catherine Zeta-Jones came out of her dressing room and said, "Hi Larry. I said a rather surprised hello. "You don't remember me," she said, "But I was one of the dancers in a show you conducted for Barry Mishon in London." Catherine had been a dancer in the West End before her TV and movie career where she met Michael. The rest is history.

It was a rather starry-eyed event. Karen Morrow and I were chauffeur-driven to the event, along with Mr. and Mrs. Karl Malden.

My biggest thrill was sitting with Karen, Karl, and his wife. Mr. Malden wanted to talk about the Big Bands in Chicago in the '30s and '40s, when he was growing up.

Sometime later, Mort Viner asked if I was available to go to London to conduct for Michael Crawford singing "Music of the Night" on the *Michael Parkinson Show*. Parkinson's show was like Johnny Carson's *Tonight* show in the US. It was a very big deal, and I was thrilled to be on it with Michael.

After *Phantom* and his earlier stints in various musicals, as well as a British TV sitcom called *Some Mothers Have 'Em*, Michael was an icon. His character of Frank Spencer was well known in the British Isles, as well as in Australia and New Zealand.

I asked Mort if they really needed me just to conduct "Music of the Night," and he said that's what Michael wanted. Of course, I was flattered and happy to have a free business-class trip to the UK. When I arrived with my papers and work permit in hand, the immigration officer said, "So, you are here to conduct for *OUR* Michael Crawford?" Indeed, I was, but they let me in anyway.

Just when I thought I had nothing to do around Christmas and the first of the year, Don Pippin called with a wacky project. Danny Wise, a rabbi, was producing a musical event to compete with *A Christmas Carol*. It was the Jewish musical with other stories and was called *Miracles*.

The music was by Marvin Hamlisch, David Shire, and Stephen Schwartz with lyrics by Sheldon Harnick. Record producer Robert Sher was putting this together. Don asked me to do a bunch of the orchestrations. It sounded fun, but the writers weren't directly participating. Don was in charge.

Danny Wise was quite a character, and you really had to make sure you had the money in hand. However, his intentions and desire for good product were apparent. It turned out that Sheldon and the composers had no knowledge of this recording, had nothing to do with it, and were pretty angry about the whole thing. Don and I were lucky to not be part of their ultimate wrath, which prevented it from being issued. I do remember ten or twelve gentlemen in long black coats with black hats and beards ordering kosher meals from one of the delis. (They were Rabbi's and obviously investors in the recording) Many blessings before lunch. The recording came out well but no show, no release, nothing. Glad to, at least, have been paid.

In January of 2000, another tour followed with Michael Crawford in Australia. We visited several wineries and watched the America's Cup in Auckland, NZ. It seems that the concerts were secondary to the vineyard tours. Michael was always well received in NZ and Australia.

After this tour, I was invited to conduct for Michael all over the UK. This was a real treat for me as I really only knew London. A band was put together by a lovely character, a former drummer named Arthur Dakin. Arthur was northern and had an accent I couldn't understand at all. We spent a lot of time on the coaches (buses) between cities, drinking tons of champagne and eating more spicy Indian food than this Yank could handle. It was a bit harsh for my American digestion, and I spent the majority of several bus trips in the loo. The Brits found it very amusing.

I was so thrilled to travel through Glasgow, Edinburgh, Liverpool, Manchester, Nottingham, Sheffield, Birmingham, Bournemouth, Cardiff, Brighton and finally London. Each city had its own personality, and it was so nice to see places I only knew by name. The opening act in London for Michael Crawford was Michael Ball. It was a great time with good friends, and great musical times, as well.

Paul Blake from the Muny in St. Louis called again and asked if I'd like to be involved with his brainchild, a stage musical of the Paramount film *White Christmas.* It had great

Irving Berlin songs and some great roles for some strong singers/dancers. A reading in New York City was planned, and I was invited to attend, with music director Michael Horsley, and dance arranger/guru, Bruce Pomahac.

In the meantime, composer Jason Robert Brown asked if I'd like to do a few orchestrations for his *State Farm Industrial,* which he did every year. He was the composer and was coming up in the composing world, because of his insightful musical, *The Last Five Years.* Jason and I met when I conducted *Sweeney Todd* at the Kennedy Center. He told me he was impressed with my conducting, and I was very flattered by his compliments. It's always been a pleasure when Jason has asked me to work with him as orchestrator on several of his projects.

When I went to New York for the *White Christmas* reading, Bruce Pomahac invited me to stay in the guest room at his Manhattan Plaza apartment. It was ideal because Bruce had a piano and lots of space, and I would have room to write for Jason's industrial show. A good time was had by all. My writing for Jason was successful, and the *White Christmas* reading guaranteed a production at the Muny.

Marc Shaiman gave me an overnight assignment for *The Kid,* a Disney film with Bruce Willis. Everyone else was jammed up and I drew the short straw. The call came at three p.m. to be on the music stands the next morning to be recorded. It was going to be an all-nighter.

I was faxed a very sketchy sketch (unlike Marc to be sketchy, but he was under the gun to do a bunch of music quickly). It was a mess as faxes were in those days with no one to call and help clean it up. It was late and everyone was busy. I started writing as fast as I could and was guessing about a lot of musical choices to make. My attitude was beggars can't be choosers ... and I didn't mean me, I meant Marc.

At four a.m., my eyes became so unfocused that I couldn't work anymore. The copyists were coming at six and I was unable to see. I phoned Marc's main orchestrator, Jeff Atmajian and told him my dilemma. He said to go to sleep for an hour and then finish it.

I took his advice, and enough vision came back so that I finished. The copyists came by at six a.m. This was long before internet was usable, and there were too many pages to fax. The session was at ten a.m.

I slept. No calls, nothing until three p.m., when I got a phone call from Marc. He said that the cue sounded wonderful, and he was very thankful. He also said that my handwriting looked like that of a five-year-old, but no worries because they'd found another five-year-old to copy it. I went to the eye doctor the next day. At age forty-eight, I needed my first pair of glasses.

July 2000, I was on my way to the St. Louis Muny for *White Christmas* with Howard Keel, Lee Roy Reams, Karen Morrow, Karen Mason, Lara Teeter, and Lauren Kennedy. I was the orchestrator and Thommie Walsh was the choreographer. Bruce Pomahac did great vocals and dance music, and this was right up my alley—a big, old-fashioned musical with Irving Berlin tunes. At this point, I was very confident in the material and in my orchestration skills. I had done a great deal of research on the original arrangements.

The trouble with the Muny, is the limited rehearsal time. I really couldn't do any writing till the show was staged and, on its feet, so I had about a week to orchestrate the entire show. There were sleepless nights and, as long as I was awake, I was writing. I was quite inspired, and Bruce's sketches were great, so I just threw the kitchen sink in. I enjoyed writing the "Sisters" reprise and was very happy with myself for some wailing sax parts. The cast was great and just right for this material. Thommie did a great job with the dances.

I will never forget Thommie turning to Bruce at the piano while staging "I Love A Piano." He said, "Bruce, give me a homosexual vamp." Bruce roared with laughter and started playing something. That vamp remains in the score now and forever.

Bruce told me we had to write an overture, so he and I came up with a piano sketch for the overture. I was left to put it on paper for our rather large orchestra, a pit band of about twenty-six to thirty players, depending on the string section size. I wrote the overture and finished all the orchestrations in time for the orchestra readings and sitzprobe with the cast. It was a happy experience, and for the most part, the orchestrations were extremely successful.

Howard Keel, playing the general, was very complimentary and said it sounded like being back at MGM. He was very kind. I don't think he ever remembered that I had been rehearsal pianist twenty years before at Kenley for *Most Happy Fella*. He told me that he had been in a car accident recently, and it had affected his memory. Me, unable to resist a straight line said, "Did you have the entire cast with you, because they aren't remembering the lyrics either." … a bit salty of me, but he took it in good humor and laughed at himself. Truly he was getting old and a bit forgetful. He was eighty-one at the time and he died about four years later.

The Muny is an outdoor venue, so the heat in the summer is staggering, and it's very difficult to sit through any rehearsals. They tend to do the technical rehearsals at night when it's cooler. The Berlin sisters, or more aptly, Irving Berlin's daughters, showed up for a dress rehearsal with orchestra.

I was sitting in the middle of the seats in intense heat, and the Berlins were down front. The orchestra started the overture and finished with a bang. It was really smashing. It sounded great and the Muny band played it with great enthusiasm. Ted Chapin (head of the Rodgers and Hammerstein organization that handled the Berlin estate) started bounding up the aisle to talk to me ... and bounding up the aisle in that heat is not an easy thing to do. When he finally got to me, he said, "You just got yourself a Broadway show." They loved what you did, and we have the go-ahead." Thanks to Paul Blake, I had a new Broadway musical as orchestrator, with a score by Irving Berlin. A little further down the road this ultimately evolved to a Pre-Broadway tour, then Broadway.

During and after the summer, I was really busy with bits and pieces of other jobs. Composer Charles Fox (*Love Boat, Happy Days*, and much more) asked me to orchestrate four songs he had written for a musical based on *The Turning Point* for Hal Linden, BJ Ward, and the late and so talented Michele Nicastro. I really enjoyed working with Charley and his very good songs. The singers were Broadway pros, and I wish more had come of it.

The phone rang again, and it was Doug Besterman, who was orchestrating the stage version of *The Producers* for Mel Brooks and Susan Stroman. This was in the fall of 2000. Doug was in a bind. There was far too much music and he needed help. Ralph Burns was in failing health and had suggested I might be a good choice. Doug had heard some stuff that I had done, and he needed a "reliable" Broadway guy who knew the genre to help him get it done. I was an easy sell, having done work like *Mrs. Santa Claus* for Jerry Herman, along with my many conducting credits. I was more than happy that he asked me.

Whenever you work on a show, you have the hope that you can do it all yourself and, believe me, the producers, the writers, the choreographer, and director really want you to do it yourself. I think Doug felt I was the right guy. They brought me to New York, introduced me to the cast as someone helping Doug out. I expected to be shown a couple of numbers, and then fly home and get to work. But it turned out that Doug was so swamped with the giant production numbers like "Springtime for Hitler," that I was asked to do a substantial chunk of work and got presented with a huge stack of music.

I was really happy to see Cady Huffman playing Ulla. Cady had been in the chorus of my *La Cage,* and there were a few other familiar faces, too. Susan Stroman and I were acquainted, and it turned out that she and Mel were also friends of my brother.

My brother, a financial planner in New York City, had been a neighbor of Mel's on Fire Island. Mel and Anne's son Max was pals with my nephew Matt. But I really wasn't aware of that at the time. Stro, in fact, had been one of the extra singers on the cast recording of *Sugar Babies* that I'd conducted. So, it was a very friendly visit. Glen Kelly, the dance arranger, was very warm and had done brilliant work in realizing Mel's songs for the stage.

I was handed a huge chunk of the second act and a couple of crucial numbers in the first. I think that Doug thought that at very worst, they could open with them and he would redo or fix anything that they didn't like. That's the way it is sometimes, and I was fully cognizant and accepting that I was a "ghost." I was there to help out

250

and wasn't expecting credit. I was, however, expecting money, which was not an issue.

The material I was given to orchestrate was *"When You Got It, Flaunt It," "Der Guten Tag Hop Clop," "Haben Sie Gehort," "It's Bad Luck To Say Good Luck," "Where Did We Go Right?" "Prisoners Of Love," "'Til Him," "Goodbye,"* and a good chunk of underscoring, including bows, exit music, etc. So, this was now beyond the typical "ghosting" of a couple of songs—it was, by actual count of musical measures, about one-third of the show. However, with the limited time involved, and in all good will, I had to get to work. There were about ten days, give or take, before orchestra rehearsals in the tryout town of Chicago. I went back to LA for ten days of little sleep and round the clock writing. At that point, in 2000, we were still writing by hand with no helpful computers.

The song, "Guten Tag Hop Clop" was really very long, not the way it ended up in the final production. It felt like a number that would be cut out of town during the tryout. Nevertheless, I treated it as if it were the most important production number in the show. Dear Robin Wagner, the set designer, announced at the orchestra reading that it was the first time an orchestration had saved a number from being cut. While that was very flattering, I don't really think an orchestration could save a number from being cut. Robin and I went back to *A Chorus Line* and *Teddy and Alice*. It's nice to have friends that people listen to.

My training with Irv Kostal did me well here. Irv had been the lead orchestrator on *Your Show Of Shows,* where Mel Brooks had started out as a writer. Irv had also orchestrated *Shinbone Alley,* for which Mel had written the book. So, Mel was predisposed to like what I did, especially when he realized he was friends with my brother and his family. I never mentioned it to Mel, but he came up to me and said, "Are you related to Howard Blank?" I said yes, and he said, "Why didn't you tell me? I suspect you didn't want me to think you were part of that life insurance scam that he sold me." Of course, it was not a scam, but that was Mel's way of showing affection in that old New York, Jewish, hostile way with a putdown. He was very warm, and we had discussions about Kostal and their days doing *Your Show Of Shows.* A lot of what Mel does is that fast and furious humor that was part of *Your Show Of Shows,* and the Borscht Belt, as well. I just knew what this had to be, and Doug was happy he'd found me to help him get through it.

After writing all that music, I decided that it would be in my very best interest to appear at the orchestra reading in Chicago, and I asked Doug if that would be alright. He said "of course," but no one was forthcoming with including me in travel or housing. I made my own travel arrangements with Doug's approval. My cousin Judith lived in the center of Chicago and invited me to stay, so all I needed was an air fare and I booked it.

In Chicago, I was welcomed by all. Mel, Doug, and Stro all acknowledged me at the orchestra reading with the cast. It was the correct move for me to appear, regardless of being invited or not. My contribution to the show was significant, and Mel acknowledged it, as did conductor Patrick Brady.

The orchestrations I did were very successful, and my arrangements stayed as I had written them, aside from the customary tweaks for changes during a pre-Broadway tryout. Mel acknowledged my arrangements for "Flaunt It," and especially for "Till Him," which pleased him a great deal. He privately told me that I should be getting credit for my work, but also acknowledged that it was my job to negotiate that with Doug, not his. That would have been awkward, to say the least.

When I finally left rehearsals, I was followed up the street by the company manager, Kathy Lowe, who handed me an envelope. Kathy was Ruby Keeler's daughter, whom I knew from my days playing piano and conducting for Ruby during the tour of *Nanette*. Kathy felt it only appropriate that I be reimbursed for my travel expenses. I always thought that was the nicest gesture, and I appreciated her thoughtfulness.

I saw the show in New York, although I was not invited to anything. I had absolutely no program credit and was very disappointed for not being included. Eventually, some credit appeared in the back, but it was too little and too late.

At the Tonys, *The* Producers swept almost all the awards, including Orchestrations and Best New Musical. Both Doug and Mel Brooks thanked me in their acceptance speeches. I received an email from Paul Gemignani during the Tony's broadcast. We hadn't been in touch at all, except for an occasional passing email. He said, "You must've done a lot on the show for them to mention you—your name was dropped twice."

The lack of credit and frankly, the lack of sharing the Tony Award, was noticed by many who reached out to me. Because I had accepted the job as being called in to help, I kept quiet. I had been paid properly for the job, and it did lead to subsequent work on the tour, and ultimately the film, which brought me a good deal more money. However, the lack of credit seemed to follow with this position as Doug's "helper." I did quite a bit of work with Doug at that point, and my name somehow never seemed to appear anywhere except on a check. The problem was exacerbated when we worked on the film. My name did appear in the end credits, but on equal par with another very capable arranger who had done one cue, while I'd done twenty.

Several people let me have it, especially Phyllis Newman, who grabbed my collar and started shaking me in the manner of Manny Azenberg, saying, "I'm going to kill you! You are the schmuck who didn't get credit. The money means nothing, it's the *credit!*" She added that her husband, Adolph Green, had told her time and again that the credit was most important. My agent/lawyer at the time suggested suing, but he said I would win the case and lose a career in the process. Credit after the fact doesn't mean a lot.

However, as time goes by, my *Producers* credit has managed to appear, and my name appears in all the Broadway journals with "Orchestrations (uncredited)," so everyone knows I worked on it. My name is also on the scores and orchestra parts. Because I had Tony nominations a bit later for orchestrations on other shows, many think and/or have commented that I won for *Producers*. That wasn't the case.

At the recording sessions in New York for the film, Mel said to me, "How's your brother?"

"We're not speaking," I answered.

"Larry, whatever he did, whatever he said, you must forgive him. What did he do?"

"He was rude to our mother."

"Fuck him," said Mel.

When the show played in London, I was happy to see that my name was on the credits as co-orchestrator. Andrew Fell, the general manager of the show, had thought that my missing name was an oversight and had added it automatically. Bless the Brits for recognizing the underdog and rectifying the situation without a word. My credit remained for the entire UK run, but somehow never managed to make it to other venues.

Phyllis Newman was right. I was the schmuck who didn't ask for credit. I was actually the bad guy for not dealing with it at the time.

Doug continued recommending me for a lot of work, and I always appreciated his friendship

Chapter Eleven

Paul Blake called from the MUNY with another good idea. He wanted to make a musical out of the film *Roman Holiday*. It had worked successfully for *White Christmas*, so why not? This time we were using the songs of Cole Porter. Paul hired Thommie Walsh and me to help him put it together, and Michael Horsley was again the music director. I thought it was a good idea. Bruce Pomahac did some fun dance arrangements. There was a very good "Fellini" ballet, and between Bruce and Thommie, it really was great. Perhaps the show was a little too heavy duty for the Muny, but it was well attended.

Paul tried to resuscitate this very good idea several times after the Muny, but it never seemed to gain any momentum, despite a successful redux in Minneapolis, and then a less successful production in San Francisco later on. The Cole Porter estate kept pulling rights for certain songs, which forced us to keep reaching into the lesser-known Porter songs and didn't help the cause. It was a good idea and still is. There was an extraordinary amount of music, so for San Francisco I called in some favors, asking Doug Besterman to help me out. We somehow got it done.

On Doug's recommendation, I was hired by the Arden Theatre in Philadelphia to do the orchestrations for *Babycase*. It was a musical about the kidnapping of the Lindbergh baby, the trial, and so on. I thought *Babycase* was a terrible title, for obvious reasons of association with the song "Babyface," etc. The show was kind of interesting, and had some good music, but it was a misguided idea that eventually went away. It was right after 9/11 and the world was not in a very good place. A musical about the Lindbergh case was not the ideal entertainment for the time, but I enjoyed spending time in Philadelphia again.

Doug also asked me to orchestrate a couple of songs for a recording for Christine Andreas. They wanted songs to sort of sound like the originals, but not use the original charts. The two songs he asked me to do were "A Wonderful Guy" and "I Could Have Danced All Night." I felt I did them successfully, but this was another "ghosting" job, so I didn't put my name on them. I think, once Christine acknowledged that she liked them, Doug let it slip that I had done them. However, I didn't get credit.

Much later, these two recordings paid off. Christine did a recording of Piaf songs and told her husband, arranger/pianist Marty Silvestri, to get her the guy who'd done those two charts for Doug. We had a wonderful collaboration and a great time doing the Piaf recording in London.

This was followed by another call from Doug to help out on the film version of *Chicago*. I did a bunch of charts, all uncredited, along with Martin Erskine. Michael Starobin did a few, as well.

It was a rather unpleasant experience for me, because I was working in a vacuum, only communicating with Doug. I wasn't able to reach either the music director, or dance arranger David Krane, while they were in Toronto rehearsing and filming. So, if I had a question, it was more difficult to get an answer.

One of my charts for the "Cell Block Tango" was thrown out and replaced by Doug, but my others like "All I Care About Is Love," "Funny Honey," and "I Can't Do It Alone" remained. Later on, I was asked to do an instrumental intro to the new song, "I Move On." Doug did the song proper and I did the intro, which was an extended band feature. I think Krane and composer John Kander improved it in the recording studio, and the music director decided to put his name on it, for some inexplicable reason.

I managed, once again, not to have any credit on the film, or on the soundtrack. Had the communication been open, I might have been able to do the required fixes for "Cell Block Tango." It's not fun to have a chart replaced, though it is rather normal. Usually, you get to do it yourself.

One important lesson I've learned from this is that if I were to be on a project, even as a "ghost" I would have to have access to any and all info I needed. I decided that I wasn't going to be so silent if it meant not doing my job properly.

The truth is, Ralph Burns wasn't properly credited either for the film of *Chicago*. Almost all of the orchestrations we did were based on Ralph's brilliant orchestrations for the stage production. There were some dance hits added and definitely some new stuff. But just as much was directly influenced and lifted from Ralph's original work. People are strange about money, but they are even stranger when it comes to credit.

Doug asked me to do a little bit of work on *Thoroughly Modern Millie*. It was just some transitional stuff, and this time I truly didn't care about credit. Doug had inherited this job from Ralph Burns, who'd passed away while it was being prepared. Doug co-credited himself and Ralph on this and secured a Tony win and a posthumous award for Ralph.

Thanks to my old friend Kay Cameron (music supervisor for the Kennedy Center), who had been my assistant on *Mack and Mabel* at Papermill Playhouse, I was asked to be the MD for *Sweeney Todd* at the Sondheim Celebration planned at the Kennedy Center for the summer of 2002. Steve Sondheim approved me straightaway. Chris Ashley was hired as director. Christine Baranski and Brian Stokes Mitchell were to do the leads, along with my old friend Walter Charles from *La Cage*. The chorus was sublime, made up of local talent and very well chosen.

I was honored and flattered to be asked to do this, and it was a very special time. The orchestra was superb and the cast was wonderful top to bottom, with Hugh Panaro and Celia Keenan Bolger as the lovers. Jonathan Tunick was engaged to conduct *Company*, and we spent a lot of time hanging out, having meals, and discussing orchestration and conducting. This was closer to what I wanted to be doing—conducting some good music and making good theatre. Steve Sondheim was very accessible, and we had many discussions about Broadway and shows in general. He was a happy man when surrounded by his own shows, people that he liked, and good casts, and it was just a genial and special place to be.

In the opening number, the chorus sings, "What a perfect machine he was ..."

Steve came up to me and said, "Please ask them to sing, 'What a fucking machine he was.'"

I laughed and Steve said, "I'm serious." He wanted to mix it up a bit, and said that if it was at the right speed, the audience would ask, "What did they say?"

So, I gathered my chorus together. Half the chorus were theatre and opera singers, and the other half were church and sometimes theatre-choir singers. So, when I said they should sing, "What a fucking machine he was," there was a gasp and some giggles.

One of the choristers said, "Maestro, is it fuckin' or fucking?"

I said to Steve, "The fuckin' I'm getting is not worth the fucking I'm getting."

He didn't think I was funny. We did it, and Steve was right—it was a mini-highlight.

One time, when I was crossing the stage before a show, I ran into Steve going the other way and he said, "Larry, you are not just very good, you are superb." Naturally I was supremely flattered to have the brilliant Steve S compliment me, but I must've rolled my eyes or done something totally inappropriate.

He said, "You don't believe me."

I paused and said, "No no, I believe you, I just want to hear it again."

He laughed and said, "I really mean it," and we went on our way.

He never treated me with anything less than respect and I was honored to be so highly complimented. That whole episode was chronicled in Steven Suskin's wonderful book, *The Sound Of Broadway Music*.

At one performance, Steve sat in the pit, and David Gursky, my associate and keyboard on *Sweeney,* was so nervous to be sitting next to him.

Steve told me privately that if *Company* hadn't been a hit, he'd still be in a piano bar playing "He Was Too Good to Me" for Elaine Stritch. He enjoyed not taking himself so seriously.

Sweeney was a very satisfying production on every level with a wonderful orchestra to boot.

Company was the next show, with John Barrowman and the lovely Lynn Redgrave. On the day of the first preview, Steve ran into me and Michael Starobin leaving the premises. He insisted that we stand in the back of the house and watch the first performance with him.

The show was very good. It was well sung with Tunick conducting and it sounded great. After the show, Steve invited me, Starobin and Tunick for drinks. Tunick had just conducted and truly he wanted to be told how great his conducting was. I happily told him that it sounded great and that he'd done a beautiful job.

Steve said, "Ok fellas, what did you think?"

Michael said several complimentary things about the music and how *au courant* the show was (2002).

All eyes were on me, and as is my nature, I wanted to be irreverent and make everyone laugh. So, I took a sip of my drink and spoke very slowly. "Y'know, the first and last time I saw *Company* was the very first preview at the Alvin in New York in April of 1970. I haven't seen it since."

Steve said, "Oh that's great! You have a really fresh eye and you know the original."

I took another sip of my drink. Michael was staring at me, somehow knowing that I was going to go to that dark place with Steve. Jonathan was thrilled, because everyone had told him how great it was, and Steve reaffirmed.

I took a deep breath and said, "Well, the book really holds up."

There was total silence.

Steve broke it. "Oh, you're trying to be funny."

Jonathan said, "You are so lucky Steve loves you," and we all had a laugh and several glasses of wine.

Trying to be funny with Steve Sondheim was not the way to go. I was really grateful that he thought well of me. A few years later, he recommended me to Wolf Trap Opera to conduct their production of *Sweeney* with the National Symphony. One of the reviews said I took very slow tempi. All I will say is that it was Wolf Trap, outside in the middle of the summer, and the heat was so intense that I couldn't remove my jacket at the intermission because of the sweat. The orchestra and cast were dying on stage.

The rest of my time at the Kennedy Center was spent hanging out with the cast. Very often it would be Baranski, Walter Charles, and Mary Beth Peil, who was playing the beggar woman. On Baranski's birthday, it was me, Stokes, Walter, and two surprise visitors in the restaurant, Steve Sondheim and soprano Harolyn Blackwell. Steve regaled us with stories of meeting Leonard Bernstein, picked up the check, and was just Steve … a Broadway guy hanging out with his friends.

One night after a *Sweeney* performance, I was sitting on my terrace. (It was very hot in Washington, DC, and I was so grateful for a little balcony.) I was sipping on a glass of wine when my phone rang. It was my associate David Gursky, who said he had to come over straightaway. He said he had been in Dupont Circle and found a bookstore with a book written by Bernie Spiro, the book writer/lyricist of *Christy*, the musical I'd written with Bernie in 1975. Apparently, there was an entire chapter about *Christy*, and David insisted I read it in his presence.

When David arrived, I poured us both a glass of wine and sat down. The chapter basically chronicled Bernie's writing the show with composer Al Frisch. Al had had success with a very good popular song called "Two Different Worlds."

Al and Bernie had interviewed me to be music director. Al decided he didn't like me, and Bernie was distraught. After all, I was all of twenty-two and had already conducted a Broadway show and conducted *A Little Night Music* on the road for Steve Sondheim. I wasn't all that inexperienced to be MD for an off-Broadway musical. Bernie had decided that something was wrong with Al, fired him as his collaborator, and offered me the job of writing the score. I, not knowing any better, said yes and wrote the songs, which were not half bad. They weren't necessarily half good either, but I had some success. Bob Billig was the music director, by my choice, and the show had its run and closure, and that was that. I'd received one very good review, and another in one of the major papers declaring the score, like my name, was Blank, being wholly without distinction.

David's bookstore find chronicled Bernie's life and his later life as a playwright, which had culminated in the less than successful *Christy*. Though Bernie complimented me very favorably as being facile and agreeable, he finally said, in essence, that while Larry did a fine job, he was ultimately *no Al Frisch*.

David had waited for me to read the entire chapter just to see the expression on my face.

I wish I'd had t-shirts made: LARRY IS NO AL FRISCH.

We had a few good laughs and finished the bottle. Sometime later, David Charles Abell wrote and asked if I would show up at the Chatelet in Paris, where he was conducting *Sweeney* with Rod Gilfry and Caroline O'Connor. Steve Sondheim had told him I was in town (teaching an Orchestration master class), and to confer with me about tempi.

David, always the gent and a superb conductor and colleague, invited me to rehearsal and to take notes. I suggested that he take everything faster and not treat it so seriously. He was a little shocked, but this is what I had learned from Steve. He'd told me it was meant to be quick and a bit shocking, more than a tragedy. David took it on board and it was a very good production.

At the opening, I was chatting with director/composer Jeremy Sams, who told me that Steve rated me very highly. It was really flattering to hear and helped me to keep my career going in my heart and head. It was so nice to know Sondheim had complimented me to others, and I carry that with me.

I received the strangest call from a music supervisor on *Stuart Little 2*, a 2002 film that mixed live action with computer animation. Nathan Lane was going to sing a song, and they needed an arrangement of Harry Nilsson's "One Is The Loneliest Number." I knew Nathan from *Producers* and phoned him. He said he wanted a slightly different take on it and to "do something."

I said I had an idea, and would he mind? He said basically, go for it. So, I wrote "One is the Loneliest Number" as a Big Band chart, in the manner of "One" from *A Chorus Line*. I asked Mike Berkowitz to put together a band in New York City, and we scheduled a date. I showed up, played the chart, and everyone loved it. Nathan announced that I was crazy and recorded it in a couple of takes. Everyone is always amused when they hear it, and I have no idea where that idea came from.

There seemed to be a flurry of work for me. Don Pippin, my guardian angel, was always throwing stuff at me and Doug Besterman was always sending some overflow to me, for which I was grateful.

Don had a lovely relationship with opera singer Marilyn Horne. She was a delight to work with and so very musical but she was also great fun and supportive of young singers. Like Marni Nixon and others of her generation, she'd started out in pop music, but crossed over to both legit and pop. She was capable of singing anything.

She was doing a Stephen Foster medley. Don was arranging it with her at the piano, doing it in a symphonic legit/pop style, and I was to orchestrate. Like always, when Don recommended me, I was just accepted. Don gave me a very good layout that was difficult, as it really had to be orchestrated in a legit style, but with fun. I listened to some LeRoy Anderson, who was always a master at that sort of thing, as well as Morton Gould—real masters of this genre. Jonathan Tunick had also done a chart for Marilyn, for *Beautiful Dreamer,* which was to be included. Her medley included things like *Camptown Races.* While not necessarily politically correct, this music was the popular music of its time, and Stephen Foster was an important composer. I had great fun doing it.

On one song, a big section was indicated to be exclusively harp, with "Jackie," as Marilyn was called. That was her real name! I said to Jackie that I would like to cover it with some woodwinds and strings. She politely and adamantly told me that she wanted it to be harp solo with voice. I argued gently that if the harpist missed one pedal change (the way harpists change from flats to sharps to natural is with a series of seven pedals), then the whole number would go out the window. But she was firm! So, I orchestrated this one rather long ballad section for solo harp.

I was invited to attend the rehearsal and performance in Brevard, NC at the summer arts festival. There was a wonderful orchestra from around the country with some very good players that I knew from New York. Everything went swimmingly at the rehearsal with Don conducting. Jackie was very happy with my work, and Don was pleased with his own contribution, which was really something special. Don was a superb pianist, and he was reveling in going back to his legitimate piano roots. He and Jackie clearly loved working together. Everything was beautiful.

At the performance we got to the harp solo with voice. The harpist suddenly hit a bad note, got lost in the pedals, and the harp went silent. It was just Jackie singing by herself, with a harpist struggling to find a way back in, and Don helping with measure numbers and many bars of silence. I was in the wings saying *I told you so* to himself, but not happy about being right. Finally, the orchestra came in, after an interminable silence, and they got to the big finish and out.

Jackie went to her dressing room, and Don came off stage flustered and telling me I was right. He wanted to have a few words with the harpist, but it was too late to help. I decided to go back to see Jackie and assess the damage. When I got to her dressing room, she was sitting rather like Buddha in a kaftan with a big smile on her face, and she said, "Honey, do you know how many times I've been screwed by harpists?"

Unable to come up with a number I said, "You too?"

And she laughed herself silly. She was always of good humor and fun to work with. Looking back, I see that I did quite a few orchestrations for her under Don's auspices. One was a gorgeous arrangement laid out by Dick Hyman (world class pianist/arranger) that I was very proud of. But a lot of credit goes to Dick's great work.

I received a call to do a couple of arrangements for the Boston Pops for a Rodgers and Hart tribute and was very happy to hear it on TV. One was "With A Song In My Heart", and I don't know if the arrangement was bombastic, or if everything about it was over the top. Let's just say there was nothing subtle about it. Still, it was somehow ok with the Pops, and with Ron Raines, Doug Sills, Audra McDonald, Mary Testa, and Marin Mazzie singing.

Don Pippin called. Jo Benjamin, who had produced the Ira Gershwin Tribute we'd done at the Royal Albert Hall, was opening a new theatre in Cardiff, Wales. It was, in fact, called the New Theatre. Don asked if I would share the podium with him for their opening show.

He was planning to write a new overture of overtures, one of those pieces (before Barry Manilow and some others did it) where we played snippets from a lot of shows. Don was brilliant at arranging overtures. For example, he'd done them for *Mame, Mack And Mabel, Dear World, Applause,* and many others. He arranged it, I orchestrated, and it was a big hit. I, and others, use this overture all the time, and it's still quite effective as an opener for concerts. We had a nice trip to Cardiff, as well.

From Cardiff, it was back to New York to do the Sondheim Reunion at Lincoln Center. It was a concert celebrating the success of the Sondheim Celebration at the Kennedy Center from the summer. I was asked to do the selections from *Sweeney.* Eric Stern was doing *Merrily,* Nick Archer was doing *A Little Night Music,* Tunick was doing *Company,* and Barbara Cook and Wally Harper were performing, as well. Patrick Vaccariello had done *Passion* during the summer, but was not available, and I was very flattered when Steve Sondheim chose me to conduct the *Passion* segment, with Judy Kuhn, Michael Cerveris, and the very lovely and deeply missed Rebecca Luker. Baranski, Hugh Panaro, and Mark Price (Tobias) did the numbers from *Sweeney.*

At the rehearsal for *Passion,* Judy Kuhn said to Steve, "I think the tempi are a bit slow."

Steve said very loudly from the first row, "Larry likes the tempi on the back side and, truthfully Judy, so do I. Trust him, you sound fantastic."

I was flattered again by his trust and appreciated his dismissing any further discussion. Guys like Steve Sondheim, Hal Prince, Michael Bennett, and a few others of that nature knew what they wanted and were able to stop further ups and downs from the varying tempera-ments. That was a very valuable asset, and always much appreciated.

The Sondheim Reunion was a lovely concert with a lot of great people, and I was honored to be part of that event.

I heard from David Griffiths, who had become the producer for the yearly Alzheimer's Association Shows. I had done quite a few of those earlier with Laurie Burrows Grad (Abe Burrows's daughter). David told me that TV journalist Katie Couric was doing a fundraiser for colorectal cancer through the Entertainment Industry Foundation. It would be a one-night event at the Waldorf in New York City and would use the music for *West Side Story.*

Katie was a major player in TV interviewing, and everyone was her pal. So, the names involved were top-of-line film industry stars. Susan Sarandon and Meryl Streep introduced Robin Williams, along with host Kevin Spacey. Bette Midler, Rita Moreno, and Chita Rivera did "America." Robert De Niro and Kevin Kline sang "Jet Song," along with Jimmy Fallon and Chris Cattan. Tony Danza did "Gee, Officer Krupke" with Rudy Giuliani as Krupke, and the actors from *The Sopranos* as the Jets gang. Country music stars Vince Gill and Amy Grant sang "One Hand, One Heart." We had Heather Headley, Whoopi Goldberg, Davis Gaines, Rebecca Luker, Josh Groban, Kelsey Grammer, and to top it off, Beyonce sang *Somewhere.* She had not yet achieved her full super-star status, but she was coming up fast.

I invited Thommie Walsh to do the staging. He brought in some wonderful people to sing backup and it was a stage of all-stars. Mike Berkowitz contracted the band, also all-stars from the New York music scene. Don Oliver helped coordinate the music, and I had David Gursky assisting me on piano.

My greatest treats were working with Chita, and private rehearsals with Bob DeNiro. He was a lovely man, and having grown up in New York, he knew the music for *WSS*. However, he was totally unmusical, and it really was like teaching Don Corleone to sing. He was the most shy and sweet guy. He would navigate walking the streets of New York dressed in a pea coat with a scarf and fedora, and no one recognized him with the scarf wrapped around his face like any other New Yorker. In this particular circumstance, he was out of his element, but was diligent in learning "Jet Song." Kevin Kline (whom I knew from earlier galas, and who had been my neighbor on the West Side) was charming. He had been a piano student from Indiana U in Bloomington, and he conducted the prologue before "Jet Song." It was a heady event.

At the after party, Bette Midler grabbed my arm and said, "Who's your new best friend?" Bette knew I was friends with Marc Shaiman, and I had done some arrangements for her via Marc.

Bob DeNiro was lounging nearby and summoned me over. I leaned over and he said to me (in his distinct New York voice/accent), "Larry, you're a fuckin' New Yorker, what are you doing living in fuckin' California?" I ran into him at the Mark Twain Awards one year later (I was conducting for Martin Short), and he said, "Larry, right? Nice to see you. You taught me to sing." His success as an actor is enhanced by his altogether charming manner privately.

I enjoyed working with Ken Ehrlich, who was the producer for the Grammys. He helped line up the talent, like Josh Groban and Beyonce. A bit later, he asked me to help out on the Grammys.

Out of the blue, I got a call from Leonard Soloway, a legendary Broadway producer and general manager who'd been around Broadway since 1947, and only passed away in the last part of 2021 at the age of ninety-three. He was producing Tommy Tune's *White Tie and Tails* at the Little Shubert in New York City, part of a string of new theatres on 42nd Street in Times Square. It was a one-man show, just Tommy Tune with a band. Michael Biagi was conducting, and Wally Harper was doing the arrangements.

I knew Tommy from *My One And Only and* had met and known Wally through mutual friends Jack Lee and Jane Summerhays. Pete Matz had been their go-to guy, but sadly Peter had died during the summer. I seemed to be their substitute for him, and I was flattered to be thought of that way.

Tommy was happy to see me. He said we needed an overture, the opening number, and a few other bits and pieces virtually overnight. He wanted me to go visit Wally, get the layouts, and get to work … and he asked if I could get it done. I had two days to make an orchestra rehearsal for the overture, opening number, and a closing number. I told him, that if that was the deadline, it would be on the stands. He was happy if a bit suspicious that I could do it.

I went to visit Wally. Wally Harper was an amazingly talented pianist, composer, conductor, and raconteur. Wally was also known to drink a bit. But his talent was so amazing, and he was so lovable, that people accepted the whole package.

We sat and he showed me his very sketchy ideas for the overture—sketchy in that he had barely notated anything. He told me about the opening song and also about the end credits, which they wanted to feel like the end credits for *The Carol Burnett Show*, with a screen rolling, behind and upstage, after Tommy finished singing.

Wally handed me two or three pages with some of the ideas written down. I had my work cut out for me. There was really no sketch to work from, and I had to do some serious arranging in a hurry. I was used to orchestrating in hotel rooms on the road, without a piano or keyboard, but I really needed to arrange before orchestrating.

Tommy summoned me back to the theatre to find out what Wally had given me. I was holding an envelope that held the three pages. Tommy literally snatched it from my hands and opened it. He looked at me in astonishment, because of the limited offering.

I looked him in the eye and said, "Don't worry about it."

He said ok and stared with fear and prayer in his eyes. Both Jack and Jane phoned me and asked how Wally was. They were both familiar with his unpredictable behavior.

I pointed out my dilemma, and Jane immediately offered me the use of her piano. I spent a few hours at her piano arranging and sketching out something I could orchestrate. Then I sat down to write and didn't stop till I finished. Irv Kostal had taught me well, and I could write quickly. The trick was to have ideas and just keep going. Irv had been known for his incredible speed and creativity, and I was really trying to emulate his methods. I often say that Irv taught me everything I know. Unfortunately, he didn't teach me everything *he* knew.

However, ideas were rolling, and I finished all three numbers and got them to the copyist. At that time, most of us were still writing by hand, and I couldn't believe I'd turned it all out. Tommy and Biagi were both flabbergasted since they hadn't really expected it to be done. It went over very well and all were happy. The show was not bad, but it didn't run as long as it might have. Tommy is really talented and could sustain a show by himself.

I invited Thommie Walsh to see a performance. Walsh was a major talent and had a long working relationship with Tune, but they'd had a falling out. At one point in the show, Tune was sitting down at the edge of the stage à la Judy Garland (with much longer legs). Walsh turned to me and said, "Why is he sitting down? What, is he tired?" You had to love Thommie Walsh. Tune was pretty good, too.

Nigel Wright, a well-known arranger and ally of Andrew Lloyd Webber in the UK, contacted me to write a couple of arrangements for *American Idol*. I did a couple, but truly, to me it's the worst kind of work to do musically, since it's mostly soundalikes of existing music for a talent contest. I knocked them out as quickly as possible but made it clear that I had no interest in doing more. Apparently, they felt the same about me. Nigel is a good guy, but that isn't what I do. I find that kind of work soul-less and lacking creativity. However, it is very lucrative if you want to put in the time.

Jerry Herman asked me to do some orchestrations of his music for the Boston Pops. Working with the Pops was always a treat, and Keith Lockhart was conducting a very large orchestra. I always enjoyed working with Jerry, and he was most appreciative of our collaboration. He is missed. He and Steve Sondheim were among the last of a dying breed. John Kander and Charles Strouse are still with us, at least. All are great composers of an era that is passing too quickly.

Tommy Tune and Michael Biagi got in touch because Michael needed someone to sub for him conducting for Tommy, and I was the lucky guest. It's always fun to work with Tommy. At one point, I was apologizing for being slightly off tempo for something, and he said, "If you don't get the tempo you love, you'd better love the tempo you get." It's a great line, something to keep in mind.

Composer Les Reed ("It's Not Unusual") and Lyricist Roger Cook ("I'd Like To Teach the World to Sing") asked me to orchestrate their musical *Beautiful And Damned*. Les and I had met on some of the Barry Mishon galas in London, and his ambition was to write a

Broadway/West End musical. *Beautiful And Damned* was based on the story of Zelda and F. Scott Fitzgerald's romance. It was nice to be asked. Les and Roger wrote a beautiful score, and I had high hopes for the show. The book was by Kit Hesketh Harvey. John Barrowman and Helen Anker were set to be the leads. We were to open at the Yvonne Arnaud Theatre in Guildford, England—a beautiful theatre and setting. Craig Revel Horwood was the choreographer, and ultimately took over as director. Craig is rather well-known on TV in the UK.

The show opened with a fantastic orchestra in the pit, conducted by my pal, David Firman. David is so solid, and the band included Derek Watkins on lead trumpet. Derek was most well-known for the iconic trumpet solos on "Goldfinger" and "It's Not Unusual."

There were problems getting the show on its feet, and it needed some re-writes and work. However, it did sound great. Producer, Laurence Myers informed me that we would have to cut down the orchestra a bit to make it viable in the West End. We were going to the Lyric Theatre on Shaftesbury Ave. I was then informed that there would be no orchestra pit and a booth was being built under the stage to accommodate the undersized and now totally unseen orchestra. I reported this to Les and Roger, and said that their show was being sabotaged. They were eager to get their show on, so were willing to compromise with "experienced" producer, Laurence Myers.

I disagreed wholeheartedly and pointed out that the reviews had singled out the visible orchestra in the pit. I felt the success of the show depended on this. It was a musical about the '20s, and the presence of a live orchestra was a major part of the excitement of that era.

Cutting the orchestra and eliminating the pit damaged the show irreparably. Charlie Dobson, (co-producer and major backer) with all good intentions and some bad advice, kept the show open at a loss. Still, the show had so much potential. I advised that if we did a very good cast recording, it would demonstrate the excellent score and potentially inspire future productions. Laurence Myers suggested that it would be better to do a video of the show, which I argued was a poor and expensive decision. My logic was that people would buy the audio recording, because of the great music and lyrics. The ill-advised, *pitless* musical did not ignite the imagination, and making a much more expensive video of the show would only point out the flaws even more. But a video was made, and when it was finished, my credit and the credit for David Krane (the dance arranger) were totally absent. Regardless of all explanation, I was and am convinced that it was deliberate pettiness over my being very outspoken.

A while later, Les Reed phoned me in the States and asked if I would give my permission to release the video for sales, though it had only been created for promotion. I was very fond of Les and had no desire to hold this for ransom. I told him my feelings about the credit and the bad handling of the entire matter, but I agreed to the video and charged absolutely nothing, even though I was entitled to a re-use fee. He said there was nothing to be done about the credit.

The video is now a collectors' item. Twenty years after the recording, Charlie Dobson reached out to me, and the first thing he told me was that he had corrected my credit omission. That indicated to me that it had indeed been deliberate. However, I have fond memories of the late Les and his lovely wife June. They were wonderful people and deserved better. Perhaps the show will surface again.

Chapter Twelve

Donna McKechnie asked me to play piano for her act at Pizza in the Park in London. I was already there and I was happy to spend time making music and enjoying Donna's company. We had been friends for a long time, and it was great to hang out to hear her stories and accompany her.

On my return to the states, Don Pippin asked if I would orchestrate an *Oliver* medley. It had been his first big Broadway show, and he wanted to include it in his concerts. I was happy to do it for him and he played the medley frequently. It required a bunch of singers and was a great showcase for him.

The phone rang … Wally Harper!

Barbara Cook was going to do a Christmas CD. She had never done any of that stuff, and Wally and the record producer, Hugh Fordin thought it would be a big seller.

Wally said to me, "Peter Matz is gone and I think you are going to do this with me."

I realized how lucky I was. I had become the heir to the Irv Kostal and Pete Matz mantle. I always marveled that I had become what my mentors wished for me to be. I had been so used to being a conductor and conducting the work of orchestrators, composers, arrangers that I really respected. I was happy to be on the other side of the conductors stand for this project.

Wally was going to conduct a hand-selected band. Red Press was going to contract the orchestra. Red had been in the pit with me for two of my shows, *Goodtime Charley* and *Onward Victoria*. He had also contracted the orchestra for the Sondheim Reunion at Lincoln Center.

I got up in front of the orchestra and said, "In 1975, I was the youngest guy in the room, and here it is 2003 and I'm still the youngest guy in the room."

Red said to me under his breath, "You haven't changed, you're still a prick." (Of course, he meant that with affection.) My sense of humor often dampened the sharp tongue that I had developed over the years. I never really meant to be mean. It was just a bit of the Larry David/Jerry Seinfeld perception of things. It's a real New York attitude transplanted to LA, so it's a little gentler now. Don Pippin and Irv Kostal both commented that if my skills hadn't been so evident on the podium, my pointed humor would've led me straight to the unemployment line. I've managed to mellow with age. (I hope.)

Wally did some nice layouts for the material, and I was able to realize them easily. I knew Barbara's voice from my childhood listening to cast albums and seeing Broadway shows. She was a superb musician and really knew how to put a song over. Wally wrote beautifully fitting backgrounds, and I custom fit them to Barbara's voice.

We got into the studio and Wally conducted the first number, "Count Your Blessings." Michael McElroy and the Inspirational Voices did the back on some. Norm Lewis was a member of that group. When we got to the second number, "O Holy Night," things were getting very slow in the studio. We were on a budget and needed to move along. I suggested that while they were listening in the booth, I would rehearse the next number with the orchestra to get out any wrong notes. Wally agreed and he lay down in the control room while they listened. When it came time to record, from the booth Wally said, "You do this, I'll listen."

Barbara came into the studio a bit grumpy and went into the vocal booth across the room. We made a beautiful take or two with me conducting, but Barbara had a really foul look on her face. When she came back to the booth to listen, I asked her if I had disappointed her.

She said, "No honey, I'm just pissed off at Wally."

Wally had put some vodka in his Coca Cola bottle and was napping it off in the booth.

Wally was a brilliant musician, a fantastic pianist, and a very skilled conductor, but he drank too much and everyone knew it. He had rescued Barbara from alcoholism and brought her back from a very bad place. She, unfortunately, couldn't do the same for him.

So, the sessions went like this. Sometimes Wally conducted, sometimes I did. Wally played piano on a few cues. On one, "Breath of Heaven," Wally played like Horowitz. Though he was more than mildly inebriated, his piano playing was impeccable. I brought in the strings on the orchestration I wrote, and Barbara turned to me and said, "This is gorgeous." Well with Wally playing, and Barbara singing, and some beautiful strings on top, what's not to like? We finished the recording, did some mixing, and it indeed was a beautiful recording.

Barbara was shocked sometime later when she told me that it had been the biggest selling recording of all that she had done. Christmas was a big seller. Barbara Cook was a big draw. Put them together and you have a very much in-demand recording. *Count Your Blessings* is an excellent recording and very much worth having. Barbara was a very talented woman, a bit moody at times to work with, but really so talented. The best of Barbara was her loyalty to friends and to Wally.

Between Jerry Herman's *Mrs. Santa Claus,* Irving Berlin's *White Christmas,* and Barbara Cook's *Count Your Blessings,* I had become the Christmas Jew. I followed up some years later with Irving Berlin's *Holiday Inn.*

A few years later, I was nominated for a Tony for my orchestrations for *Drowsy Chaperone,* and I was invited to the nominees' party in New York City. Now to be honest, an orchestrator at the Tony nomination party is somewhere beneath the catering and far below the hairstylist. No one could care less. I walked into the party and no one noticed. The press core that was there to do promos looked and said, "Oh, who is that?"

"An orchestrator."

"What is an orchestrator?" They were far more interested in the shrimp cocktail being served.

As I walked in, I saw old pal Donna Murphy being interviewed on the left, and Barbara Cook being interviewed on the right. A moment later, my left arm was grabbed by Donna Murphy and my right by Barbara Cook, and they walked me into the party. Barbara said, "We want to make sure you get your picture taken." That was the real Barbara Cook, that you could see and hear in the warmth of her voice, and in her way with lyrics when she sang. Donna Murphy ain't too bad either. Donna had been the first replacement in the ensemble for *Playing Our Song.* Together, they made me feel like a million bucks. I was so happy to be on the arms of these two very great dames.

I did a few more charts for Barbara at Wally's behest. They don't make 'em like that anymore. Barbara, I mean … not the charts.

On September 9, 2003, Marissa Benetsky called to inform me that my conducting teacher/friend/mentor Rudi Bennett (Rudolph Benetsky) had passed. Marissa was his daughter and only child, and a great friend to me. Rudi had retired near Cape Cod with his wife Barbara. After *La Cage Aux Folles* closed on Broadway, he was the person who really taught me to conduct, and most importantly, not to "goose butterflies" when I was conducting. He had been a good friend and an important teacher to me. He was always there for me if I needed something—advice, a place to stay, loan of a car, money, a meal—always my go-to person when in need.

Between Rudi, my piano teacher Leslie Harnley, Irv Kostal, Don Pippin, and a few others, it was hard for me to go wrong professionally or personally. I always had someone to call for a good word. I think the most important thing to have in any profession, is that wise person to look over your shoulder. I miss having Rudi in my life and am so grateful for the time we spent together.

Next, my dear friend Jim May required serious surgery. Doctors had discovered a rare and freakish tumor in the naso-pharyngeal space above his hard palate! It was life threatening, even if not malignant, and had to be removed. The surgery was so difficult, that many doctors refused to even attempt it. Jim had no choice but to have this extremely difficult, but life-saving surgery. The good news was that Jim became the poster boy for recovering from this surgery. When it was over, you couldn't tell it had been done, and he made a full recovery.

A huge party was scheduled, and Jim asked me to be the music director for the event. Many friends sang and I played the piano. Peter Marshall and Nancy Dussault performed, among many others. The highlight was John Raitt coming out and, instead of having me play for him, he asked for *his* music director, and Jim came to the piano and played for him. The evening was a triumph, and it was nice to have Jim back.

Jim had been my associate on Broadway for *Teddy and Alice,* and we worked together all the time. When we'd first met, during the run of *La Cage* in LA, he had looked so familiar to me. After much guessing about how and when we might have met, I realized that Clifford May, my best buddy at the High School of Performing Arts in New York, was Jim's first cousin. Small world, isn't it?

In 2003, Katie Couric came up with another event, once again to raise money for colorectal cancer. This time it was on the *Queen Mary 2*, which was docked in New York Harbor. We'd be using the music of Rodgers and Hammerstein in an event hosted by John Lithgow. The show featured Christine Ebersole, Nathan Lane, Brian Stokes Mitchell, Anne Hathaway, Antonio Banderas, Beyoncé, the guys from *The Sopranos*, Marc Shaiman, a very young Dakota Fanning, The Muppets, Whoopi Goldberg, Jon Bon Jovi, and Harry Connick Jr, with a realtor/playboy from New York City named Donald Trump, who would be singing "I Own Manhattan." I asked Annie Skates in London to bring over some singers to sing backup for the event.

Backstage in the ship's green room (the green room is a waiting area where artists can gather when they're not on stage performing—it's not necessarily green, that's just the name of the designated area), Donald Trump was sitting flirting endlessly with Annie Skates. When asked who she was, he said, "Hopefully the next ex Mrs. Trump." Percussionist Ed Shea, my old friend from Philly asked "The Donald" if he used Dippity-Do in his hair. Sitting next to Trump, or rather a few feet away, was Hilary Clinton, who was a guest seeing the show, but was hanging there with us to stay away from the crowds in the audience. Trump rehearsed with us and was as friendly as one could be to an MD on a cruise ship in New York harbor. When he sang on stage with Harry Connick, Harry said to the audience, "This is the most surreal experience." Then, Little Dakota Fanning sang with The Muppets.

Nathan sang "My Favorite Things" with special lyrics by Marc Shaiman. I asked Pete Myers to do some of the charts, as I had no time at all. He did some beautiful arrangements for Christine Ebersole and Beyonce, and a beautiful chart for Heather Headley, as well.

I have to say, it was indeed a *surreal* experience, and I could now say I've conducted for Donald Trump. However, I've managed to leave that off my resume. It was fun to be on the *Queen Mary* 2, fun performing the music of R and H, and fun doing this show for Katie. She was always as sweet as could be and grateful for everyone's participation.

I was invited to teach film orchestration and conducting in Matera, Italy. Nicola Ventrella had discovered my "Best Christmas of All" arrangement on the internet and persuaded the mayor of the district to get the city to fund my visit. Kaylyn and I took off for Matera and became great friends with Nicola, his wife Nuccia, and their children, Sara and Domenico. We return to Matera whenever our travels allow. Matera is a beautiful spot in Southern Italy, with an amazing history of homes carved into hillside caves, called "the Sassi". It's very much worth exploring.

After our return, I heard from Michael Gibson, a very talented arranger/orchestrator. We had become friends over the years, and I feel that I was helpful in pushing his career forward by hiring him for *Onward Victoria*. I'd suggested him to Ralph Burns, who recommended him to John Kander for *Woman Of The Year*. Michael continued with John for many shows, and worked with many other composers, as well. Sadly, Michael had been diagnosed with lung cancer. He was scheduled to attend orchestra rehearsals near San Jose for *The Little Princess,* with a score by Andrew Lippa and conducted by Joel Fram. He asked me to cover for him.

I really was just sitting in for Michael and doing whatever fixes were needed, but I ended up doing one chart for a number called "Another World." I tried to emulate Michael's style, and it was very successful in blending with the rest of his score. When I returned home, there was a case of fine wines from Michael waiting for me. I was sorry to hear he died a short while later. We had flown together in my airplane, and worked together, and enjoyed each other's company. He was gone far too soon and is sadly missed by all.

There was a flurry of work for me, including orchestrations for the UK production of *The Producers* at Drury Lane, with Nathan Lane and Lee Evans. There had been a slight change in the size of the orchestra and Doug asked me to help him make the adjustments. It was almost like having to do the whole show again.

Andrew Fell, the GM, put my name on the adverts, and I was happy to be included. The orchestra was excellent, and in many ways the show was stronger in London than originally. Lee Evans and Nathan were very good together. Leigh Zimmerman was playing Ulla and was excellent, just as Cady Huffman had been originally. I attended the opening and was happy to see the show's success continue.

Jerry Herman asked me to do some new orchestrations for a revival of *La Cage Aux Folles* at the Marquis Theatre. Gary Beach was to play Zaza, and it was choreographed by Jerry Mitchell and directed by Jerry Zaks. David Krane was doing new dance arrangements. There was nothing wrong with the originals, but choreographers like to have the music tailored to their needs. Patrick Vaccariello was the MD. Jim Tyler was no longer with us, and I enjoyed doing the adjustments to his original charts. There were also some new tweaks, plus the new dance music, which was formidable.

The pit at the Marquis is very oddly shaped and requires careful seating. Usually in a pit, the strings are on the left, the reeds in front, and the brass to the right. Because Patrick is a left-handed conductor, and because of the odd shape of the pit, he had a strange setup. It worked fine in the pit because of miking, but it didn't work in an acoustic way.

We set up at Carroll's rehearsal studios, for the orchestra reading with Patrick's pit setup. The brass were on the left, the strings were far left and, in the back, with reeds sort of to the left, and the rhythm section to the right. When they started playing, it was totally unbalanced. It sounded terrible and my heart sank to the floor.

Jerry Herman turned to me in despair and said, "What have you done to my orchestrations?" He was seriously and rightfully upset. I knew what was wrong, but how do you explain this away and blame it on the setup? Then, Jerry started taking David Krane to task, saying, "I hear a lot of David Krane and not enough of Jerry Herman." David became defensive, and Jerry was getting even more upset. I discussed all of this with Michael Keller (my old friend and drummer from *Playing Our Song*), who was the contractor. Michael had also subbed as drummer on the original show, and knew the setup wasn't working.

At lunch time, I promised Jerry that we would set it up properly and it would sound fine. Patrick was agreeable, as long as he could set up as he liked in the pit. Keller and I personally moved the stands and instruments into a traditional set up in the room. Jerry came back from lunch and we began with the Entr'acte, which is a second act overture. In the case of *La Cage,* it's really the overture, as the beginning of the show has a short prelude. It sounded as it should, and Jerry was beaming. He turned to me with a smirk and said, "So you re-wrote *all* the orchestrations over lunch?" I had restored his faith and trust in me.

The sitzprobe with the cast was the next day, but I unfortunately had to fly to London. Word got back to me that it was a success and my career was still happening. Everything else had been great, and the dress rehearsals in the theatre were excellent.

I came back for the first preview and was at the sound board with Peter Fitzgerald, whom I had worked with on several shows, including *Teddy and Alice.* The sound board went awry, and the orchestrations and cast sounded terrible. There was a production meeting with all the department heads, me, and Jerry Zaks. Jerry turned to me and said, "What happened to the orchestrations?"

I said, "There was a SNAFU with the sound, but it will be up tomorrow."

He said, "Oh … you're one of those people that blames someone else."

"No," I said. "There was an issue."

He said, "Next," and turned away from me.

Peter Fitzgerald piped up and said, "No Jerry, Larry is right. We had an outage and it was my fault."

Again, Zaks said, "Next."

Jerry Mitchell chimed in and said "No Jerry, Larry is right. I was sitting down front and everything was fine—it was a sound issue."

Jerry Zaks wouldn't have any of it and was moving on until I said, "Hang on, you cannot speak to me that way."

Jerry Herman pulled on my sleeve to sit down and shut up, and I looked at him and shook my head. "I've done far too much to be spoken to in that manner. I'll sit with sound tomorrow, and we'll have it fixed."

At that moment, I had clearly severed my relationship with Jerry Zaks for all time. He was used to having people back off and let him have his moments. Unfortunately, I couldn't have cared less. I've never wanted to work with or for people like that, and I was there at the request of the composer.

The next day I was at the soundboard, and Zaks came over and said, "It sounds great, thank you for fixing it." But I knew it was lip service, and I had done the damage. The music did sound great. The orchestrations and dance music for the Cancan sounded fabulous, and Jerry Mitchell won a Tony for his choreography.

In my opinion though, Jerry Zaks's direction didn't have a patch on the original … and that's not just sour grapes from me. Nothing succeeds like excess, but the show didn't run as long as it might have. Robert Goulet came in for the last months as Georges. He was excellent as always, but sadly, through no fault of his, didn't help it to run any longer. It had run out of steam.

Some years later I sat next to Zaks at the opening night of *The Nance*, which I'd orchestrated. We had a lovely conversation, friendly as can be. I was very pleasant, and he was very pleasant. But I happen to know he had nixed me on a couple of other projects. In fact, I didn't get the orchestrator job on the recent *Hello Dolly with* Bette Midler, *even though* I had been requested by Jerry Herman, because Zaks said no. Jerry Herman was at the end of his life and called to tell me and apologize profusely that he was just too ill to fight for any demands. Larry Hochman was hired and did his usual excellent job. However, they went through some machinations and had to redo some things, because of choices that Jerry Herman wasn't able to oversee.

While I was sad not to be part of Jerry Herman's final Broadway triumph, I was glad for the success of the show. On both of my experiences with *La Cage,* I'd had run-ins with the directors, for totally opposite reasons. But I loved the show and was happy to have been part of both productions. There was a later production imported from the UK with a smaller cast and orchestra, and it was a great success. Jerry Herman was thrilled that he went out with people remembering his successes and not his very few failures. That was his plan!

White Christmas finally started getting some more productions, thanks to producer Kevin McCollum, who had the rights. Walter Bobbie was brought in as director and Randy Skinner replaced Thommie Walsh as choreographer. The show was getting full production values and opened at the Curran in San Francisco with a wonderful orchestra and cast. The show was solid and became a staple, touring everywhere, and in stock, and finally opened on Broadway in 2008. But the production at the Curran was the beginning of the first-class productions that had begun at the Muny, thanks to Paul Blake. I was very proud of the orchestrations and the dance music/vocals that Bruce Pomahac put together. Rob Berman was the very capable music director. I also had some very strong help from Pete Myers, whom I asked to do "Blue Skies" and "I've Got My Love To Keep Me Warm" and some smaller bits. I knew that I needed someone to be the real deal for those charts and Pete came through for me. They are great arrangements, and he did receive some credit in the program. I was always first to include him and acknowledge his contributions to the success of the show.

We ultimately ended up recording the orchestra tracks in London with some of my favorite musicians, including Ralph Salmins on drums and Derek Watkins on lead trumpet. It was a wonderful recording and wonderful show. Kevin McCollum was so pleased with my work that he offered me *Drowsy Chaperone* as orchestrator. Later, I received Tony nominations for my orchestrations on both *White Christmas* and *Drowsy Chaperone.*

Doug Besterman asked me to help out with finishing the orchestrations for *Guys and Dolls* at the Piccadilly in London. This starred Ewan McGregor, Doug Hodge, Jenna Russell, and Jane Krakowski. My old pal Jae Alexander was the MD. I was a ghost for Doug on this one again and wasn't present for rehearsals. My colleague and friend Mark Cumberland was the copyist. I was told that Jae made sure that everyone knew what I had written. It was a formidable amount of material, including "I'll Know," "Guys and Dolls," "Sit Down, You're Rockin' the Boat," Adelaide (added from the film), "Marry the Man Today," and some other bits and pieces. I was happy to help Doug out, but there was no reason not to be getting credit this time, especially since the music/orchestrations were the best part of this production.

One amusing little story. I wrote the chart for "Adelaide's Lament," which Doug told me didn't work just right, so he doctored it a bit. I really didn't care much. He added a tenor saxophone noodling around a bit, which gave it some character, I suppose. I was taught not to add too much comment from the orchestra with comedy numbers that depended on lyrics ... that it was best to leave the jokes on stage. This kind of orchestration, which was becoming more and more popular, really didn't appeal to me. However, each time they do another revival, everyone wants to contribute something new. There have been so many revivals of *Guys and Dolls,* and each one has had a new orchestration. There was a revival with Nathan Lane and Faith

Prince that had new orchestrations by Michael Starobin, and it was excellent. Each time, it's the "definitive" version.

A few years later, I was asked by London music director Gareth Valentine to do another *Guys and Dolls*. We tried another approach, and it was thought to be pretty good. Gareth did some marvelous dance music. On my own, I pulled out my original chart, prior to its being doctored, and submitted it as my new chart for "Adelaide's Lament." Even Mark Cumberland, who had copied both versions, wasn't aware of my subterfuge. My old arrangement of "Adelaide's Lament" was proclaimed a masterpiece. My point being, that it all depends on the whim of the moment and the reaction of the powers that be. There is still another production and a movie being planned, and it will all be done again.

I should point out that when Steven Spielberg did the recent new film version of *West Side Story*, he reverted back to the original Broadway orchestrations. They are pretty hard to beat. He just had them re-recorded with Dudamel conducting. And they added more strings. It sounded pretty great.

I was asked to do the Cy Coleman Tribute at the YMHA in New York. It was a very nice event with Michelle Lee, Elaine Stritch, Robert Goulet, Neil Simon, Sheldon Harnick, Lucie Arnaz, Stephanie Pope, Dana Moore, David Zippel, Judy Kaye, Randy Graff, Dee Hoty, and others tributing Cy. I had never actually worked for Cy Coleman, but we had done some fun stuff, working together on charity galas where I was conductor, and I was honored to be asked to do this memorial tribute after his passing. Sadly, another giant was gone.

At Doug Besterman's suggestion, I ended up doing a few numbers for Stephen Sondheim's seventy-fifth at the Hollywood Bowl in 2005. I wrote a chart for "What More Do I Need?" for Anne Hathaway.

Steve was present and very complimentary. Gemignani conducted, and Streisand showed up to speak. I got to see Len Cariou and Angela Lansbury, who were also performing, and was able to introduce daughter Jamie to them both. Len couldn't believe this was the same girl he'd known as a baby learning to walk backstage at *Teddy and Alice*. Stritch was there, and I was always happy to see her. I don't know why, but I always got along great with her.

It wasn't the best of the Sondheim tributes, but a lot of nice things were said. Now that he is gone, it's difficult to put together a tribute. So many were done while he was still alive, and I think that's a good thing. At least, he got to appreciate them and revel in his own success.

Chapter Thirteen

David Krane and Stephen Cole asked me to work on a project called *Aspire,* that they'd written to open a new sports arena in Qatar. It was being produced by Egyptian investors and the Sheik of Doha. The lead producer was named Ahmed, and he was the person we were dealing with. David and Stephen later wrote a musical about the making of *Aspire,* which was nowhere as good as what *really* happened …

Through Don Oliver, we decided to record in Bratislava, Slovakia, where there was a very good orchestra and a very good contractor, Marian Turner. Marian is a great gent, and his wife plays harp. We were promised a Slovakian chorus that could sing in English, and because of the economy in Slovakia, the price was right. David, a skilled musician and arranger, was quite facile at doing the routines, and would then give them to me to orchestrate. I knew the music would have worth and would shine with the large symphony orchestra.

We met up with the Egyptians in London in the heat of summer. There had recently been a terrorist bombing, and the Egyptians were treated very poorly at the hotel. We were all staying at the very posh Langham on Regent Street!

We were taken to a nearby piano dealership on Cromer Street, which is an Arabic district. It was very, very hot when we went in. They closed the doors, turned on the AC, and closed every window in the shop, so Stephen and David could perform/audition the piece for the Egyptian producers. They sat at a table at the end of the room with their scripts in Arabic, reading from right to left, and chain smoking. Mobile phones were open, so the Sheik in Doha could hear the audition. I was turning pages for David at the piano.

David said to me, "With names like Krane, Cole, and Blank, do you think they know we're Jewish?"

I said, "David, they can smell us. They hired us because we're Jewish. Who else would be insane enough to hire us and put this on?" We're Musical Theatre People!

David and Stephen started singing, "Aspire … go higher … to inspire," etc. etc. etc., and I tried very hard to stifle my laughter. They wrote nice stuff but watching these two little Jewish boys prancing at the piano for the stone-faced Arabs was quite a sight. It felt as if they'd written *Tales of the Talmud* set to music, and we were going to be executed and never seen again, if our producers didn't like it.

When they got to the end, Ahmed proclaimed without much enthusiasm, "Berry, berry gud."

I said to him, "Ahmed, we all read right to left, we don't eat pork, and we're all circumcised. Why don't you like us?"

He said, "If you finish on time, I like you just fine."

He also told me he wanted an oud in the orchestra. An oud is like a lute/guitar, and unless you give it a solo, it's like any other guitar. Since I didn't think he planned to go to the recordings, I decided not to worry about that.

We went to Bratislava. I had written pounds and pounds of arrangements. Mark Cumberland had copied. We carried cases of music to Bratislava and stayed in the Crowne Plaza Hotel, which was very pleasant and a short walk from the recording studios. I conducted. Nobody spoke English, and the personnel changed at every session. But all was good, and the music was being recorded very nicely.

Ahmed's Italian girlfriend, Dona, was our chaperone, taking us to meals and saying she was Muslim and didn't drink, so they wouldn't pay for the alcohol. We ordered wine at every meal, and she always said, "I'll have just a little." She was, after all, Italian. But, true to her word, she wouldn't pay for it. David spoke to her in French, which he spoke fluently. He was using familiar words and calling her the devil in French. I had other words for her, and they weren't cute.

When I started training the choir, they were singing "ASSSSSSspeer…"

"No, Aspire … not ASSSSSSSpeer."

David complained that we were supposed to have an English-speaking choir.

"Vot do you mean? Ve are speaking the English … ASSSSpeer."

We decided we needed to go to London and record with local singers there. They engaged Pippa Alion, a very reputable casting agent, to hire the singers. She didn't know that we needed session singers and she hired actors. So, they could act … and sing out of tune with a lot of character. I was not very happy. At the session, I told Dona that the singers needed a break.

"Break? No Break. They are dogs."

I was considering just walking out the door, heading for Heathrow Airport, and going home. This was awful! And at that point, we had only been paid a portion of our fee. The rest was due on delivery in

Doha. I told David, "We are never going to be paid the remainder of our money."

He said, "Nonsense … it's the Sheik of Doha."

I sensed that these guys were frauds and would rip us off. However, there was another recording session with the singers, and I was the only one who could do it. We also brought in drummer, Ralph Salmins to redo the drum parts. The percussionist in Bratislava was not as on top of it as he might have been, and we needed some drive. Ralph was a pro and fixed everything without us having to change anything. It made all the difference, especially with "ASSSpeer" and the out-of-tune actors.

Next stop was Doha, Qatar, for the rehearsals and the show. I decided to go back to LA, because there was absolutely no need for me to be there. The tracks were recorded, and I had no desire to be around a bunch of people who were normally hostile to both Jews and Americans. I knew we were not going to be paid … and I like wine with my food, which is not so popular in Doha.

David and Stephen went to Doha, rode camels, and made a video about their trip. Despite the show they wrote about the making of this epic, there was nothing funny about Ahmed and his henchmen. And Dona, his girlfriend, was a nightmare.

Aspire had a giant production at the stadium opening, with camels all over the stage and a lot of British actors pretending to be famous Muslim characters. The scam company that Ahmed had formed to finance everything was called Capacity World. It was never to be seen again, and after all this, we discovered his name wasn't even really Ahmed. I could never pronounce it to his satisfaction in any event. "It's Acchh-med." He said my pronunciation was too Jewish. And … we never did get our final payment.

Michael Crawford was doing a concert with the New York Pops in Newport News, Virginia. I invited Mike Berkowitz to play drums. Skitch Henderson was conducting the first half of the concert, and we would do the rest.

Skitch was the original MD for the Tonight Show with Johnny Carson. He had been a band leader and an arranger at MGM along the way and was well-liked and quite an audience-pleaser. He was let go from the Tonight show for some sort of scandal. Then, Skitch was chosen to be MD for the New York Pops. In his dotage, he was a loved and respected figure in New York City. As Irv Kostal once told me, "If you live long enough, everyone loves you." At the time, Irv was referring to George Abbott, the famed director/writer who lived to be 106.

I found Skitch to be a cantankerous old curmudgeon. He resented the young people coming up and ran the Pops in a very protective manner. One day, he was rehearsing the orchestra and being a little grumpy. He clapped his hands for the orchestra to stop and said, "Nein nein nein."

Berkowitz and I were standing off to the side, waiting our turn and wondering why he was shouting at the orchestra in German. The orchestra started playing, and once again Skitch clapped his hands, saying, "Nein nein nein."

Then came the realization that he was rehearsing "Claire De Lune," which has a musical meter of 9/8. He was telling the orchestra that there were nine beats to the measure. "It's in nine!" We had a good laugh, and he was done.

We rehearsed the orchestra in record time and had a wonderful performance. Crawford was in top form. Why we were in Newport News, who knows? The New York Pops is a nice group, and New York is lucky to have a pops orchestra to call their own. Steve Reineke ably leads them now, and they do a lot of worthwhile concerts.

Barry Manilow was doing a recording of greatest hits of the '50s, and Michael Feinstein recommended me to orchestrate. Barry asked me to do "Rags to Riches," a song written by the team of Adler and Ross (*Pajama Game* and *Damn Yankees*). Jerry Ross, the composer, had died very young, but was obviously a big talent, with all the great songs he wrote with Adler for those shows. This song had also been a huge hit for Tony Bennett in the '50's.

Barry and I discussed over the phone the arrangement and various elements of it. He and I were known to each other, but hadn't actually met up since 1968, when he recommended me to Adam and Ira in the Catskills. I showed up at the recording session and Barry recognized me—and I pointed out that I was the sixteen-year-old kid from 1968. It was a nice recording session and a successful recording for Barry.

Next on the agenda was *The Drowsy Chaperone*.

Kevin McCollum had hired me to orchestrate on the basis of my work for *White Christmas*. *The Drowsy Chaperone* had started out as a party-favor musical in Toronto, written by Don McKellar, Lisa Lambert, and Bob Martin, as a bonbon to celebrate Bob's marriage. Kevin had picked it up, and had high hopes for it.

Casey Nicolaw was hired to direct/choreograph and was the perfect choice this piece. It starred Sutton Foster, Beth Leavel, Lenny Wolfe, and a great supporting cast. Sutton could do anything ... a true "triple threat" and a charming tour de force. Glen Kelly, part of the dream team from *The Producers,* was dance arranger/musical guru, and Phil Reno was MD.

I determined that an orchestra of twelve to fourteen players would be sufficient, and deliberately chose not to use any strings, as I didn't want it to sound like another '20s musical like *The Boy Friend* or *Chicago*. I wanted to make it sound like the MGM version of a '20s musical.

Casey was doing a lot of dancing/staging, and I needed a strong brass section. So, I decided to go with five brass and four reeds (a cut-down Big Band), and a rhythm section. A keyboard synth was only used for sound effects, and a spot to put an assistant conductor in the orchestra. For a show that takes place in the '20s, a synth sound would've been a curious inclusion.

Charlotte Wilcox was the GM for the show and an old friend. It was a pleasure to do business with her and make this all happen. I brought Mark Cumberland over from the UK to copy. We tried to make a deal with other copyists, but it wasn't working. Kevin was trying to do it as inexpensively as possible, to give the show a chance to run.

The Drowsy Chaperone was an odd title, and it was an odd musical. I went to rehearsals to pick up the routines, and I didn't really get it at first. I saw the humor, but it was very inside. I did, however, enjoy the numbers I saw and the materials I got from Glen. Back at home, I said to Kaylyn that I didn't know about this one. I did understand the overall character of the show, though, and I knew what to write. Glen did a great job with the routines and arrangements, and I was the right guy to realize these for the orchestra. Casey did fabulous work putting it all together, and the cast was magnificent. The tech and dress rehearsals went relatively smoothly, and everything sounded good, but the show was falling a little flat, so I came home feeling pretty apprehensive.

We had our first audience at the Ahmanson in LA. The house lights dimmed, everyone settled down, and there was a long expectant pause. Out of the darkness came Bob Martin's voice: "I hate theatre." There was a huge laugh from the audience, and voila—before the lights came up, the show was a giant hit. All it had needed was the audience. Who knew?

The preview period went well, and was thankfully uneventful, with only a few minor changes. The band, contracted by trumpeter Stu Blumberg, was excellent. I had written woodwind doubles up and down, and the players were nailing everything.

One night as I was leaving the theatre to go backstage, I heard someone with a very loud voice saying, "These are the best orchestrations I've heard in a very long time." I was, of course, thrilled by the compliment and turned around looking for who had said it. Obviously, I was hoping it was either Steven Spielberg or John Williams, though I was expecting it to be a relative, as it was so effusive and complimentary. But I couldn't find the perp.

Next day, my phone rang and it was Joe Soldo. Joe said that Dick Williams had told him it was the best orchestrations he had heard in the theatre in a very long time. Dick was Andy Williams's brother and one of the Williams Brothers. It meant a lot to me that a great musician like Dick thought enough of my work to mention it to Joe. Dick didn't know me or know that I knew Joe, he was just passing on his good thoughts.

I really felt that I had finally become what I was trying to be—the musician that Irv, Don, and Rudi had hoped for me to be. The cherry on top of the sundae was that I was nominated for a Tony Award for Orchestrations for my work on *Drowsy*.

While I'd been thrilled that *Producers* had won a Tony for Doug with my contributions, I hadn't actually shared that award. I was also proud of myself for having written every note of *Drowsy* on my own. It was a coming-of-age for me, just to have done it and to be nominated by my peers. Win or lose, I was a happy man.

My friend Sam Lutfiya recommended me to orchestrate a new production of *Dr. Dolittle*, with Tommy Tune directing and starring, along with Dee Hoty. Michael Biagi would be conducting with Patti Colombo choreographing … all friends.

I asked Mark Cumberland to copy, and we tried out in Chattanooga, Tennessee. Gordon Harrell, also a good buddy from *Teddy and Alice* and *La Cage*, did the dance music. It was a lot of fun to work on and a very entertaining show, but it didn't do the business they had hoped for. The score was very good, and the show really deserved greater success.

Marc Shaiman asked me to orchestrate his new show with Martin Short, *Fame Becomes Me*. It was a partial fiction/partial truth biography of Martin Short with many funny episodic scenes and a funny/entertaining score by Marc and Scott Witman. We had a little band and it was fun to write. The supporting cast was very funny, as well. One of the funniest performances was Brooks Ashmanskas playing Bob Fosse, doing exaggerated Fosse-style movements with an endless cigarette going. In another scene, he came out on stilts as Tommy Tune, sitting in a chair with his long legs crossed, and endlessly making "jazz hands."

The show tried out in Toronto and Chicago. As funny as it was, it really was an evening of Marty Short. Marty is a charming, very talented guy, but as much as everyone enjoyed the show, it couldn't sustain a run for very long, and it finally closed.

I kept very busy conducting several concerts with Michael Crawford, including another tour of Australia and New Zealand. How lucky was that, not only getting to those fun places, but being paid to go. I was very fortunate.

Through Lee Roy Reams and his friend Deborah Strobin in San Francisco, I was hired to be MD for a fund raiser for stem cell research, with Marvin Hamlisch and Julie Andrews. I was so happy to finally meet Julie, and we talked at length about Irv Kostal. When I mentioned Irv to Julie, she said, "How did you get that old salt to take a liking to you?" She was clearly affectionate in talking about him, and it was nice to hear her experiences with him first-hand. Besides working together on *Mary Poppins* and *The Sound of Music*, Irv had been her arranger and MD for the "Julie Andrews and Carol Burnett Live at Carnegie Hall" TV show concert. Carol Lawrence turned up for our show with one of her sons, too, to say hello to Julie. It was a very pleasant evening, and I spent a bunch of time catching up with Marvin, as well.

Barbra Streisand was planning a big tour. She hadn't been performing live for a very long time, other than one little tour with Marvin Hamlisch conducting. Now she was going out again, to the UK and other venues. Bill Ross was to be her MD, and he asked if I would like to expand and orchestrate the "Funny Girl Overture" for Barbra's tour. It was Ralph Burns's overture, but it needed a little adjusting and tweaking for their bigger orchestra. I was honored to be asked. I also got to do a few other bits, including an arrangement of "Something's Coming" for the four boys who were opening Barbra's show.

Bill suggested that they might need an assistant conductor for the tour, and asked if I would be interested. That meant a very high-paying job, and the only way I'd ever conduct was if Bill was hit by a meteor on his way to work. It sounded like an ideal job—a trip to the UK and elsewhere, lots of money, and no responsibility whatsoever.

They were rehearsing the show at some studios out in Burbank, and Bill asked if I would come over and conduct a few numbers at rehearsal. I thought about it for ten seconds, then said that I'd love to IF that meant I was the assistant conductor. Bill said that this would lock it up, but I said that it was unnecessary for me to audition at this point in my life. I had been conducting and arranging shows for thirty years. He was embarrassed but indicated that it wasn't going to happen unless I did this. While it would've been nice to go ahead and conduct for Barbra for a few minutes, I realized that I might not be the only one "auditioning," for the job, and I passed on the opportunity. I heard that very respected and multiple Emmy Award-winning conductor Ian Fraser was brought in. Ian conducted a few numbers and was not engaged ... proving that my instincts were correct. They decided that Randy Waldman, the pianist, would conduct in an emergency. Too bad! No harm done. I happened to be in the UK when Barbra was performing there, and Bill made sure I was invited as an honored guest. That was fun stuff!

In 2006, I received both a Tony and a Drama Desk nomination for the Orchestrations for *Drowsy Chaperone*. Even though *Drowsy* won Tony Awards for Best Score, Book, Featured Actress, Costumes and Scenic Design, the Orchestration award went to Sarah Travis for the John Doyle production of *Sweeney Todd*, where there was no orchestra in the pit, and the actors played the musical accompaniment on stage. While I was disappointed, it was nice to attend the Tonys, and I was happy for the success of *Drowsy*.

Thanks to Ted Chapin, Bruce Pomahac, and John Mauceri, I was asked to orchestrate a suite of music from Adam Guettel's *The Princess Bride* for the Hollywood Bowl Orchestra. Adam is Mary and Hank Guettel's son, Mary being Mary Rodgers, daughter of Richard Rodgers. It was a nice feather in my cap to do this suite. Unfortunately, Adam didn't have the rights for *The Princess Bride*. Bill Goldman, the author, went ballistic, and that was the end of that. It's too bad because it was very interesting stuff.

Mary said to me after the concert, "Thank you for making it sound like Daddy wrote it."

I found out later, that Adam hated what I had done, and Mary thought it sounded terrible. After hearing it a second time, though, she realized that it actually sounded pretty good. Much later, Adam came back to Ted Chapin and said that he was wrong, and it had sounded pretty great. Ted Chapin, Bruce, and ultimately Mary were my greatest supporters. I was unofficially proclaimed the court arranger at R and H, and it all paid off for me much later.

While we were recording *White Christmas* in London, Ted asked me if there was a reasonably-priced place in Europe to record *Allegro*. There had never been a proper recording of that, except for the truncated original Broadway cast recording in 1947. I suggested recording in Bratislava. With Don Oliver helping to organize, we went to Bratislava and I conducted the recording of *Allegro* cover to cover. Later on, Bruce Pomahac supervised adding the voices, and it turned out to be quite a successful recording. Steve Sondheim even wrote me a note to compliment it, and Mary Rodgers was very happy with the result. While we were in Bratislava, we recorded the score of *Sound of Music*, as well, for possible later release. We also took a pass at recording Adam's *Princess Bride* Suite, not to be released, but just to have it, since it had become a no-go situation.

Allegro was released with Patrick Wilson, Audra McDonald, Marni Nixon, Liz Callaway, Norbert Leo Butz, Lauran Benanti, Judy Kuhn, Danny Burstein, and others performing. It was a wonderful recording all around.

A lot of stuff was happening for me. I was conducting for Michael Crawford now and then, and doing some fundraisers for the Motion Picture and TV fund, where I conducted for Shirley MacLaine, Catherine Zeta Jones, and Chita Rivera.

Through conductor Eric Stern, I was recommended to Betty Buckley. Betty and I hit it off easily, and I conducted quite a few concerts for her. We always got along famously and made really beautiful music at the concerts. Soon, I was conducting for Betty on a regular basis. Once, we were working with the Ft. Worth Symphony, Betty's hometown. At the rehearsal, she was doing "As If We Never Said Goodbye," which is a very intense number with several tempo changes, requiring much musical flexibility. She was facing the auditorium, and I was behind her, facing upstage to the orchestra. I had done this before, but it was very tricky.

At one point, Betty Lynn was very emotional and jumped some bars. I quietly yelled out the bar numbers, the orchestra made the jump, and we continued as if nothing had happened. We finished and Betty Lynn was very happy, but a moment later, she realized what she had done. She is a consummate musician. She opened her arms and said to me and the audience: "Larry Blank, I love you." I turned to her and the orchestra and, never one to miss a punchline said, "I love you, too, Betty Lynn, but it's ok to see other conductors." I loved working with Betty Lynn, and we always had great fun.

I helped John Mauceri put together an arrangement of "Rhapsody in Blue" for Herbie Hancock and Lang Lang for the Grammy Awards, When I showed up at the rehearsal, I had a reunion with Ken Ehrlich, the producer for the Grammys. He asked me if I'd like to conduct for Josh Groban and Andrea Bocelli singing "The

Prayer" with David Foster at the piano. That was a surprise, and a real treat from Ken. Thanks to our earlier connection through Katie Couric, I got to conduct on the Grammy's.

Through Michael Feinstein, I was introduced to Kim Poster. Kim was a New Yorker, who had re-located to London. She was general manager and producer for shows in London, and we bonded. Kim was an only child, and we adopted each other. I became the brother she never had, and she became my second sister and cohort in loving musical theatre. I worked with her on a little musical called *The Black and White Ball* with some Cole Porter songs.

Kim saw a production of *Fiddler on the Roof* in Sheffield and decided to bring it into the West End. The production had some very good values and good performances, especially by actor Henry Goodman. But the music had become a bit distorted in this local production, and Kim wanted to restore its original values. She brought me on board to re-orchestrate for a smaller band for the West End. Sheldon Harnick and Jerry Bock both agreed to having me on board, because of my relationship with Irwin Kostal, who had done *Fiorello* and *Tenderloin* for them. In fact, Irv was supposed to do *Fiddler* originally, but couldn't do it because of his commitment to the film *Mary Poppins*. Don Walker did the splendid orchestrations. My job was to reduce it to its basics, creating more of a Klezmer sound. I basically did a reduction of Don Walker's orchestrations, and it sounded great—almost like Don Walker had done it.

I recommended Jae Alexander as MD. Jae, a Welshman, was as far away from being Jewish as one could be. However, he had fantastic energy and enthusiasm, and could handle the method-styled approach of the very talented Henry Goodman. Jae loved the music, and he kept everything in line.

To fix the musical staging, Kim brought in Sammy Dallas Bayes, who had been Jerome Robbins's associate originally. Lindsay Posner, the director, was not exactly a musical theatre man, but was very good with actors and all the rest.

It was a wonderful production with many outstanding performers, including Alexandra Silber as Hodel. It was recorded sometime later and made for a very good recording. Bock and Harnick were so pleased with my orchestrations, that they are still offered as an alternative to the full orchestration.

Thanks to Kim, there was a huge resurgence of revivals of *Fiddler*. This culminated in my orchestrations being used some years later for the New York production I mentioned earlier, that was entirely in Yiddish and directed by Joel Grey. The record producer did another recording of this *Fiddler,* and we added, as a bonus, all the cut songs (orchestrated by me) from the original show. It's a really good recording, and I'm very proud of it.

Sometime later, Kim did the same with *Carousel,* and asked me to re-orchestrate, with the full approval of the Rodgers and Hammerstein Organization. David Firman was engaged as MD. David, a dear friend, is one of the most skilled pianists and conductors, and did an exquisite job with the show. Kim asked Lindsay Posner to direct and Adam Cooper to choreograph. They both did a wonderful job. It needed a little supervision, and at my suggestion they brought in Larry Fuller to help clean it up. Larry had been a dancer in one of the first revivals in New York City in the mid-fifties. It was a really first-rate production.

David Firman had a conflict with Carousel's extended tryout around the UK, so Kim asked if I would fill in for those weeks. I was so happy to be conducting it with my re-orchestration, which was once again, a reduction of Don Walker's work. Sylvia Addison fixed (contracted) a first-rate orchestra of seventeen musicians to play in the West End pit and for the tryout tour, and it sounded wonderful. We had Skaila Kanga, one of the finest studio harpists in the world, and her husband Harold Fisher was playing drums and percussion. The rest of the band were a bunch of London's best.

Mary Rodgers came to see the show in Milton Keynes (a small city in the UK). Bruce Pomahac thought that Milton Keynes was my assistant. Mary told me that "Daddy would've been very happy," and that it sounded like the original. I was pleased and very flattered to hear that. In fact, my reduced orchestration is offered as the alternative for productions and is used quite regularly.

My legacy of *Fiddler* and *Carousel* means a lot to me, and I'm grateful to be able to preserve the essence of Don Walker's work. When productions are done using these orchestrations, they are getting the real idea of what it sounded like. With today's cut-down orchestras, I'm glad to have been part of these two productions, and I'm grateful to Kim for entrusting them to me.

Through John Barrowman, I had been introduced to Anthony Cherry. Ant was the producer for *Friday Night Is Music Night* for BBC Radio 2. I had written a few arrangements for him, and he started asking me to do arrangements and conduct concerts on a semi-regular basis. One day, Anthony asked me to conduct a "Jerry Herman Tribute Show" for *Friday Night is Music Night*. It was a wonderful opportunity, however, conducting for Jerry Herman was Don Pippin's regular gig. Don was my mentor. I couldn't do this to him, and told Ant straight out. He said that he had done many shows with Don, and it was my turn. He also told me point blank that if I turned it down, it would go to a local in the UK, and not to Don.

I was in a tough spot. Don was eighty-two years old and not doing much, but he really was the energizer bunny, and I didn't want to stand in his way. I called Jerry Herman, while sitting in Anthony's presence, and told him the dilemma. Jerry was very pragmatic and decent and said, "Larry, it's your turn. Don and I should be in the audience." I told him that I couldn't bear to tell Don, and he said, "Don't worry, I'll do it." I accepted the job from Ant and asked if we could include Don as a special guest. He said, "That's really not necessary," and that was that.

I got back to the States and my phone rang. It was Don. He had heard that this was happening from another source. Jerry had never called him. He started screaming at me and asked how I could do this to him and stab him in the back. I tried to tell him the story, but he would have none of it. He said I had messed up all his plans and so on, and he hung up on me. I was quite distraught. I tried through several sources to straighten this out, but Don would still not hear any of it. I also wrote him and told him exactly what happened. Ultimately, I begged Ant to make Don a special guest, and we did that. But Don was very unhappy, and our relationship was not the same. Since we had been through so much together over the years, we were, at least, superficially friendly through the concert.

With time and realization, our relationship eventually returned to almost normal. I say "almost," because Don was aging and he was losing some of his edge, and he realized it too. I continued to support, include, and defer to him whenever possible, and we did restore our friendship. However, as happens with mentor/student relationships, the roles had reversed somewhat, and we both had to adjust.

I was never going to damage our relationship with something so trivial as a one-off concert, or for that matter, with any job at all. I made sure he was there and got his proper acknowledgement. This continued until the very last time he conducted, which he did at my insistence. At Jerry Herman's Memorial in Feb 2020, he conducted the "Mame" number in its entirety.

I had become very busy conducting again, for various performers like Betty Buckley, Michael Crawford, sometimes with Michael Feinstein, and quite regularly with top UK talent through my friend Ant Cherry. What a treat to work with the great BBC orchestra for *Friday Night is Music Night*. Ant would engage Annie Skates and Capital Voices, the best session singers in the UK, and we all had lovely times and made great music on a regular basis. I was also asked to write new overtures for these concerts, celebrating different composers like Frank Loesser, Jerry Herman, Johnny Mercer. The orchestra would read what I wrote and play it beautifully—instant gratification! Ant made me the BBC's "Broadway Maestro."

This connection with Ant and the BBC orchestra also led to my involvement with the Olivier Awards (the UK version of the Tony Awards), and eventually, producer Julian Bird made me the MD for the Oliviers. This was an incredible opportunity, which gave me a chance to get familiar with all the artists in the West End.

Having the BBC Concert Orchestra at my disposal for the Oliviers meant that my friend/colleague Mark Cumberland and I were able to write anything that was needed, and hear it played instantly. What a pleasure! Julian always had great ideas for the memorial sequences each year. While it was sad to see all the people that had passed, we were able to give them a lovely send-off with great music and singers. We often used the Arts-Ed Choir as backup, which was a great plus.

White Christmas opened on Broadway at the Marquis Theatre in 2008, and I was again nominated for a Tony and Drama Desk award for Orchestrations. I was very proud of these orchestrations. It was old-time Broadway in the very best tradition of the Broadway sound.

My friend Steven Suskin wrote a book called *The Sound of Broadway Music,* in which he chronicled the history of Broadway orchestration and how it evolved. Steven went through many scores and discovered who had really written what (ghosting), and for whom. Irv Kostal had told me how much he had done for Don Walker during the '50s. It's amazing to see who was behind all the orchestrations we were listening to on Broadway. Irv Kostal, Red Ginzler, Jim Tyler, Larry Wilcox, and many others were the helpers behind the scenes for all the regulars. It was a large, collegial group that built the sound. Everyone was mentoring everyone else and being supportive. What a great musical legacy they provided.

Steven Suskin formed two symposiums to promote and educate about his book. One was at Lincoln Center, and another was in DC for the Library of Congress. I sat on a panel with John Kander, Hal Prince, Paul Gemignani, Red Press, Don Pippin, Marion Evans, Elliot Lawrence, Sid Ramin, Rob Fisher, and Ted Sperling, and was so flattered to be part of this world.

My great friend Michael Feinstein is a conduit to music of the past, present, and future. His love for the material of Broadway, Hollywood, and the great American/European songbook is contagious, and our collaboration continues to inspire me and bring great joy.

Because of the over-enthusiastic productions of Barry Mishon and David Gest, I conducted for many, many stars and musical giants. These two gents were hellbent on doing galas celebrating the great talents of the past—Barry, out of being a giant fan, and David, out of being a promoter and dealer of memorabilia. Though they had different motives, they achieved the same result, some great and memorable events for the public.

At one of David Gest's celebrations in the early 90's, Gladys Knight was performing. I had worked with Gladys before with Marvin Hamlisch. She was friendly, musical, and easy to work with. She beckoned me over and said very nicely, "Larry, why aren't there any brothers in the band?" She had earlier called David Gest over, and he was steaming with anger. David looked at me accusatively, as if I had stolen Michael Jackson's glove, one of David's prized possessions from his collection of memorabilia. I beckoned over the music contractor, who was tall, very Caucasian, and a very fine trumpet player. He was a bit flummoxed by the question, so I looked at Glady's and said,

"Obviously, he doesn't know any black people." There was stoned, bewildered silence from Gladys, David, and the contractor. She looked at me and started laughing, knowing that I was telling her the ironic truth. "I can't argue that" she said. It was only by the good grace of Gladys that I survived that unfortunate incident. The very real issue of diversity was coming to the fore, long overdue.

Marc Shaiman asked me to be the co-orchestrator (with him) for the musical *Catch Me If You Can*. Marc and Scott Wittman had written a wonderful score, and the script was by Terrence McNally. It was a lot of hard work and, with the help of Russ Bartmus as copyist, we turned out the pages. The show opened at the Fifth Ave Theatre in Seattle, and I had high hopes for it because, though it was flawed, it had a great deal of heart, and a first-rate creative team and cast. Jack O'Brien was the director, and Jerry Mitchell the choreographer. Aaron Tveit and Tom Wopat were really excellent as Frank Abagnale Jr. and Sr., and the amazingly talented Norbert Leo Butz played FBI agent Carl Hanratty.

I would sometimes sit in the back of the theatre and have a chat with producer Margo Lion. When Margo asked me what I thought of the show, I told her that I had the same positive feeling about *Catch* that I'd had with *Playing Our Song* and *The Producers*. I told her to bring the show into Broadway, and it would be a huge success. She felt it needed more work. I told her that it did, but it was manageable. She was thinking of bringing in some help with the book and postponing it until the next season. I told her that, in my opinion, it was a no-brainer, and she should bring it in now.

Of course, I'm not the Sage of Broadway, and I don't claim to know it all, or even to be a great predictor. However, I had been going to the theatre since 1961 as an enthusiastic kid, and it was my life's blood. Despite my advice, Margo, under guidance from others, replaced Terrence McNally and postponed the opening till the next season.

The show went back into rehearsal. Jack O'Brien clearly bequeathed a lot of the new stuff to Jerry Mitchell. Jerry, who is very talented, built up the production numbers as good choreographers do. However, one of the great numbers, a two-hander with Aaron and Tom called "Butter Out Of Cream," was turned into a full-blown production number, brilliantly staged by Jerry. Unfortunately, it took the warmth and charm out of the previously sweet, fun interaction between father and son. The expansion (in my opinion) turned Aaron's character into a slick operator, instead of a kid who'd become a criminal out of bad parenting. It took the heart out of the show, turning it into slick, first class, mostly entertaining musical theatre ... but with no heart.

When we got to Broadway, *Book of Mormon* had just opened a few weeks before us, and became the giant success of that moment in time. While *Catch Me If You Can* was a good show, because of timing, it sadly became an also-ran. The orchestrations were nominated for a Tony.

At the Tonys, when they announced: "And the winner is Larry … Hochman for Book of Mormon," Marc Shaiman turned to me and said, "Man, you really fucked up." (meaning, the wrong Larry). Marc really deserved a Tony for Best Score, and I was very disappointed for him.

Catch will always be a staple in summer stock and regionals, because it has a great story and a great score. The songs are catchy. I was asked to do a twelve-piece orchestral reduction, and it plays really nicely for future productions.

Later, I was involved with a musical based on the iconic film *A Christmas Story*. Remember the famous line, "You'll shoot your eye out"? The show happened at the Kansas City Repertory Theatre. It had all the right ideas, with a score that really didn't work. Since producer, Jerry Goehring, was still very enthusiastic about it, I hooked up Ian Eisendrath as music director. Ian was the music supervisor at the Fifth Avenue and had been very helpful with *Catch*. He told me that he wanted to get to Broadway, so I had recommended him to do new projects. He is a first-class talent, and I was happy to help. He also helped Jerry to get a further production at the Fifth Avenue.

After Kansas City Rep, Jerry Goehring and Fifth Ave producer David Armstrong knew *A Christmas Story* needed new music and lyrics before they brought it to Seattle, and several teams were auditioning. Jerry sent me the various audition recordings. I told him that the team of Justin Paul and Benj Pasek were the best, hands down, and they were hired to do the show.

I had a great time orchestrating the show in Seattle, and ultimately it ended up on Broadway and as a TV movie. Justin Paul and Benj Pasek later moved on to do *The Greatest Showman* and *Dear Evan Hansen*, and Ian Eisendrath's career has zoomed along with theirs, all well deserved. I was happy to be part of that and to help them along, as I had been helped at the start of my career.

During the summer of 2012, Marvin Hamlisch asked if I would conduct his opening number at Pasadena Pops. He was doing a show with Michael Feinstein and thought it would be fun. I showed up at the rehearsal and was shocked to find Marvin looking very gaunt and not well. He went to the piano as I got up in front of the orchestra, and he started playing without us. He was terribly disconnected and playing just horribly, and I stopped him. It was so unlike him.

The concertmaster, Aimee, asked me what we were going to do, and I told her to just stick with me. At the performance, we were supposed to skip the national anthem, but then as we walked onto the stage together, they announced the national anthem.

Marvin said, "You or me?"

I said, "It's your orchestra!"

Marvin made a big fuss with the orchestra and audience and said, "We are going to exit and come back."

We did and it was funny. I then went to the podium and Marvin started playing, and it was quite terrible. He had no rhythm and bad aim, and it was just shocking to all of us. I did the best I could, but I was very saddened by his obvious difficulty, and just felt bad for him. As I exited, he beckoned me back to the piano and interviewed me in front of the audience, talking about how we began our relationship on *Playing Our Song*. I was very uncomfortable and finally got off the stage. When I got to the wings, there were tears in my eyes, because I knew something was so wrong. This was like the last meal I'd had with Irv Kostal, where he told me I didn't need him anymore.

Marvin did the rest of the show, and when Michael appeared, they were very funny together and it was the old Marvin. At the interval I asked Michael Feinstein why I was there. He said, "Don't you know? Marvin didn't think he would make it through the show, and he knew you could finish it, because you knew his material and my show, as well."

I had heard that Marvin had some health issues and had to leave the stage on a previous engagement. What we didn't know at the time was that Marvin had a kidney transplant some six months before.

The next day, Artie and JoAnn Kane, who went back to Marvin's beginnings (and mine), phoned. They had been there and were commiserating with me about the sad evening. They agreed that he was a mess and, because of our old friendship, wanted to talk about it.

Two weeks later, I opened my computer in the middle of the morning and saw that Marvin had died in San Diego. He had been in a hotel room with his friend Richard Kagan and had choked on a sandwich. Richard was unable to revive him. While most people were quite surprised, I was not. He was just sixty-eight years old. There is so much to say about this, but it was shocking to me emotionally, then and now.

I was asked to finish Marvin's season at the Pasadena Pops. Michael Feinstein was asked to be the Pops Conductor for the next season, and I was given a position as Resident Pops Conductor for the orchestra. I was asked to conduct many tributes to Marvin across the country, which I was happy to do to show my respect for the man who had made my career on Broadway come to fruition. It was a sad time for all and a tremendous loss for everyone.

Shortly thereafter, *A Christmas Story* was brought to Broadway. It was a glorious production directed by John Rando. Warren Carlyle did the choreography and Glen Kelly did some new dance music.

Opening night at the Lunt-Fontanne Theatre in New York was a thrill for me. I thought that the score sounded absolutely fantastic in the theatre, and it was a reminder to me of what Broadway shows could sound like in the theatre. I was disappointed that there was no Tony nomination for the orchestrations on *A Christmas Story*. It wasn't that I cared so much about winning a Tony, as I appreciated that a nomination was industry recognition for the contribution.

As I point out at my concerts, being nominated for three Tony Awards means that I didn't win three times. It always gets a good laugh from the audience, but I mean it. Still, it was really great to be acknowledged three times for my work as an orchestrator.

For a very long time, Anthony Cherry would keep me busy with concerts in London with the BBC Concert Orchestra, making me the "Broadway Maestro" for Friday Night is Music Night. We did many notable shows with many wonderful performers, celebrating the great American and British song books.

Since the passing of Marvin Hamlisch in 2012, I have been working regularly with the Pasadena Pops, CEO Lora Unger, my dear friend Michael Feinstein, and his partner Terrence Flannery on many shows and concerts, doing the music we all love.

Both of these jobs, the BBC Concert Orchestra, and the Pops, have large orchestras. So while Broadway has reduced orchestras, I'm still getting to work with traditional sized orchestras and the music I love. It gives me great pleasure to continue the work that I was trained to do.

The Pasadena Pops holds a special place in my life and work. I'm working with the best musicians in the world on a regular basis. Louise Di Tullio is one of the most respected flute players in the world. She is well-known for her work on many Hollywood films, especially for John Williams. When I joined Pasadena Pops, she was first flute. I knew her from the recording studios, and it was always a pleasure to see her. Her husband, Burnett Dillon, was lead trumpet in the pit of Phantom, as well. Her flute playing in the studios is legendary.

One time I conducted a concert with the Pops at the Arboretum in Arcadia. The orchestra was soaring, and I was so pleased to see and hear Louise in front of me. I had heard that she was retiring shortly, and when I saw her in the parking lot after the concert, I ran up to her to say thanks.

When I got to her, she said, "Larry, it's so nice to see you!" She gave me a little hug and then said, "What are you doing here?

I said, "Louise, I was conducting."

"Was that you?" she said, and she added that her eyesight was failing and she just looked up to see the downbeats.

That has kept me from thinking too much of myself. Every time I get too big for my shoes, I think of Louise in the parking lot.

In 2014, my sweet and funny mother Dorothy died, just past her ninety-eighth birthday. She was totally there until the end. The last time I saw her, she told me it was the last time. She said she'd had enough and had been suffering from terrible arthritis in her hands. She told me her hands hurt all the time and she was tired of the constant pain. She added that there was room in the family plot for me, and I told her I'd be cremated. She slapped the table and said, "Not while I'm alive." So, we left each other in good humor. She passed a short while later.

At her funeral I said that I was upset that she'd made me an orphan. I don't know if she appreciated my getting laughs at her gravesite.

During this difficult period, a very wealthy doctor asked me to work with him on a musical for which he had written the book, music, and lyrics. He was a rather eccentric character with seemingly unlimited funds. We approached many talented performers around the country and in the UK, as well as many of the crème de la crème orchestrators.

The doctor was so fussy, that I decided not to be one of them. Every time I submitted something, he had more "improvements" of his own. We decided that I would be just the MD/conductor.

We did many recording sessions in Seattle with an orchestra mostly made up of the Seattle Symphony. This was my doing, as I had done a lot of work with them and had a very warm and positive relationship. They knew me and I knew them, and a lot of work was created for them. I was being paid very well for this job, although the doctor/composer was somewhat abusive in his demands and relationships. I couldn't have agreed with him less about his musical decisions, and I really was ashamed of myself for taking part in it just for the money. After a particularly contentious session, where I applied my conducting skills to make a symphony orchestra match up with a synth rendition of the orchestration (which he seemingly preferred), I was given a dressing down.

He said that I should be speaking Italian to this venerable symphony orchestra, that it was offensive to them for me to say "louder," as opposed to "forte," or "softer," rather than "pianissimo," and similar comparisons. He accused me of being insensitive to the sensibilities of such a formidable group. He referred to my conducting as summer-stock conducting. Fortunately, I already had the check he'd given me for the session in my pocket. I got up in front of the orchestra and told the musicians that the composer had requested I speak to them more respectfully in Italian. I grabbed my baton and proudly announced, "Con formaggio!" and conducted my very last session on this project with the redoubtable members of the Seattle Symphony.

The recording was released with my name nowhere to be found. The name of a colleague of mine was listed as the conductor/music director. The truth is, I'm very glad my name wasn't on it. It was an embarrassing project and another lesson to never stick with something just for the money. You really need to believe in what you are doing.

In the spring of 2014, my dear friend Anthony Cherry suggested we write a musical together. The title was *A Life More Wonderful*. It was to be a sequel to the famous film *It's a Wonderful Life*, but we didn't have the rights to that. Anthony came to Los Angeles with book and lyrics, and we wrote a song a day. After calculations, we realized we had written one new song for every two bottles of red wine. Whether it was the wine or hubris, we thought we had written a pretty good musical.

This was followed by a workshop with actors in the UK, including Anne Reid, Kevin Whately Anna Jane Casey, Scarlett Strallen, Michael Xavier, Stephen Ashfield, Jamie Muscato, Jim Graeme, Mark Hadfield, and Caroline Sheen. Sometime later, we re-wrote some songs and created some new ones, then did a demo in 2015 at London's Dean Street Studios with Katie Bernstein, Jamie Muscato, Stephen Ashfield, Emma Williams, and Graham Bickley. These are big names in the UK musical theatre.

In the end, we were "snookered" by a lack of rights. It deserves to be produced.

In 2016, another dear friend and mentor, Jack Lee, passed. Jack was another of my friends who was always there and always supportive, no matter what. From the day I first met him in the pit of *Irene* in 1973, he was a trusted and loyal friend. At Jack's memorial, I got re-acquainted with Laurence Guittard, whom I had first met when he was understudy to the principal men on *Lolita, My Love*. We had also worked together on *Most Happy Fella*, where he played Joe. He was now retired as an actor/singer and focusing on his first love, music composition. He was working on an opera and, apparently, Jack had suggested that I could be helpful. In time, we followed up and have become great lunch buddies. I suggested that Larry orchestrate his opera himself because he has all the necessary skills. I was just looking over his shoulder to help, if needed, with an able assist from Adam Jones to get it all notated in Finale. This is an ongoing project and we amuse ourselves talking of our travels through show business over the same time period. His opera will eventually get produced, and Larry will get recognition as a talented composer.

In 2016, I was asked by Cameron Mackintosh to hang around his new production of *Half a Sixpence,* in case orchestrator Bill Brohn, who was aging and not in good health, became unable to finish. I did. Bill did his usual wonderful job and passed shortly thereafter.

I have been kept busy in France, as well as the UK. Friend and Colleague, David Charles Abell, recommended me to the Opera de Toulon, and they have hired me over and over to do concerts for them in the South of France. I have conducted full productions of both *Wonderful Town* and *South Pacific* in their glorious opera house.

The very talented Alex Lacamoire asked me to collaborate with him in the preparation of the music for *Fosse/Verdon* for television. It was such a treat to work with "Lac" and recreate much of the music from Bob Fosse's shows, and the orchestrations of Don Walker, Red Ginzler, and Ralph Burns. I had such fun going to the music I know and love and having great musicians to record it.

Producer Sam Haskell called and asked me to score/orchestrate/conduct Dolly Parton's music for the Netflix movie, *Christmas on The Square*. Michael Feinstein had recommended me to Sam. He wanted

Dolly's music to be "Broadway-fied," and I was the one to do it. I engaged young Adam Jones to be my associate. He is now well on his way to having a big career, and I am so happy to pay it forward, the way others paid it forward to me.

The film won an Emmy for Outstanding Television Movie and for Outstanding Choreography. While in production, I asked Dolly if she wanted me to change anything. She said, "Well darlin,' you already changed all my chords." She is a delight.

Photo Section

*Angela Lansbury, Kaylyn Blank, LB
and Bob Callely at Tony Nominee Party 2011*

Larry Hochman, Doug Besterman, and LB Tony Nominees 2011

Don Pippin and LB
At Jerry Herman Memorial Concert

LB and Don Pippin
In Tampa 1987

Larry at Age 4

Larry in 1978

Larry in 2011

Christine Baranski and LB at Closing party for Sweeney Todd in Los Angeles 1999

LB, Kelsey Grammer and Ken Howard from closing party for Sweeney Todd 1999

Ken Howard, Kelsey Grammer, LB and Jerry Sternbach rehearsals for Sweeney 1999

Larry in the pit 1982

Larry rehearsing BBC Concert Orchestra in London   *Larry conducting BBC Concert Orchestra in London*

Dorothy Blank and LB (Mom at age 95)

My beautiful wife Kaylyn and me somewhere in Europe.

*The "kids" Michael, Dani, Jamie Blank
with LB at a BIG birthday party*

Kaylyn and LB in Italy

*Irwin Kostal and
LB in 1987*

*LB and Marvin Hamlisch
before Marvin's last concert
in Pasadena 2012*

*Dani Blank, Don Pippin,
LB and Ed Shea in NYC*

Michael Crawford and LB in Australia during rehearsals.

*Elaine Stritch and LB at the Hollywood Bowl
for Sondheim's 75h*

*Christina Saffran, Debbie
Gravitte, LB and Meredith
Patterson before concert in
Pasadena*

*LB entering the stage to conduct the
Pasadena Symphony*

LB and Shari Lewis with road manager Tod

*LB and Alex Lacamoire while
working on FOSSE/VERDON
recording sessions*

*Richard Lewine, LB, Dorothy Loudon and
Tony Tanner rehearsing in 1975*

*LB, Van Alexander, Dolores Hope, Billy May
and Bob Hope in 1995*

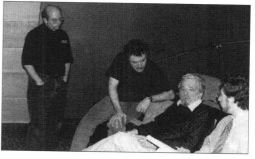

*Jerry Sternbach, LB and Steve
Sondheim in Los Angeles 1999*

*Steve Sondheim, Eric Shaeffer,
LB and Chris Ashley
at the Kennedy Center 2002*

*LB and Jerry Herman at
recordings sessions for Miss
Spectacular 1999*

*Jason Robert Brown, LB, Michael
Isaacson, Doug Besterman and Steve
Sidwell at a Luncheon*

Robert Klein, Debbie, Gravitte, Lucie Arnaz, LB at 40th Reunion for Playing our Song.

Paul Blake, LB, Lee Roy Reams, Charley Repole, Karen Morrow, Howard Keel, Lara Teeter, and Thommie Walsh at the MUNY for White Christmas 2000

Michael Feinstein, Paige Cavenaugh, and LB backstage at Carnegie Hall
Photo by Roddy McDowall

Jodi Benson, LB, Donna McKechnie, Don Pippin and Doug LaBrecque backstage with the Philly Pops 2014

LB conducting the Pasadena Pops

LB and Michael Feinstein backstage in London

Cy Coleman, Sally Kellerman, LB and Yuriko Byers 1995

LB, Marc Shaiman and John Mauceri recording That's Entertainment III in Los Angeles

Larry Fuller, Susan Edwards Martin, Carol Lawrence and LB. Backstage in Pasadena

Jenna Russell, LB and David Curry backstage in Toulon, France

LB with Comanche 8355P circa 1985

*Kaylyn and Larry
Blank in Malibu*

*LB and Martine
McCutcheon backstage at
the Palladium in London*

*Georgia Engel and LB
Backstage in Pasadena
after a concert*

TWO CONCERTS in the UK
for producer Barry J. Mishon

339

Afterword

My wife Kaylyn and my children, Jamie, Michael, and Danielle (Dani) are always in support, and despite busy schedules of their own, always manage to be there for me.

On June 9, 2022, my mentor, supporter, and life-long friend and colleague Don Pippin passed at age ninety-five. It seems that at this point in my life, it is my mission to pass on what he and so many passed on to me. I think that is the point of writing this history of my life. You need to have mentors and people to show you the way. I've been very fortunate to have so many, who gave life to my ambitions and dreams, and helped me to achieve them.

I will continue to work until I choose not to, hopefully before someone chooses for me. I will continue to pass on good advice and, hopefully, some employment to others and keep them from the poorhouse, as so many did for me.

And so it goes. I remain positive. No matter how much everything changes, it remains the same.

One of the last things dear Georgia Brown said to me was, "You don't know your career is happening, till it's over."

Today, July 15, 2022, is my seventieth birthday. Happily, there's still more to come!

Thank You

To my agents at Curtis Brown in London:

Alastair Lindsey-Renton & Helen Clarkson, and especially
Adam Maskell aka SAM (Super Agent Man)

Rhonda Hayter for her patient editing

Ghislain Viau for his creativity and design in making this happen

And to my beautiful wife, Kaylyn Dillehay Blank for her patience
with correcting my grammar, syntax, and spelling that made this
book possible.

Printed in Great Britain
by Amazon

54149392R00196